I0461444

Living the Irish Wheel of the Year

of the Year

A Guide for Practicing Pagans

Donald Quill

Copyright & Publication Information

Living the Irish Wheel of the Year: A Guide for Practicing Pagans

© 2025 Forgotten Rites Publishing. All rights reserved.

Published by Forgotten Rites Publishing

First Edition, 2025

ISBN: 979-8-9989881-3-4

No part of this book may be reproduced, stored in a retrieval system, or transmitted in any form or by any means - electronic, mechanical, photocopying, recording, or otherwise - without the written permission of the author.

This book is for educational and inspirational purposes. The practices, rituals, and traditions described herein are intended to support spiritual exploration and should not replace professional medical, psychological, or spiritual counsel.

The author and publisher make no representations or warranties regarding the efficacy of any practices described.

For The Mórrígan

Great Queen of the ravens' flight,
Sovereign of shadow and foresight,
Washer at the ford, keeper of fate,
Who stands where life and death meet—

You taught me to see with crow's eyes,
To walk the mist between worlds,
To honor the turning of the year
Not as spectacle, but as sacred truth.

This work is an offering laid at your threshold,
Born of devotion, written in service,
That others might hear your call
And answer with courage and reverence.

You who demand honesty, transformation, and fierce love—
May this book honor your name,
And guide those who seek your wisdom
Back to the old paths you guard.

In gratitude and awe,
Your priest and servant.

Author's Note

This book emerged from a question I have carried for many years: how do we honor the old ways while living in the new world? How do we step onto a path that was walked thousands of years ago, in a landscape across the ocean, and make it real and alive in our own time and place?

I wrote this guide because much of what is readily available about the Wheel of the Year tends toward the general, the broad, the pan-European. And while that has its value, something essential was being lost - the particular flavor of Irish tradition, the specific stories that shaped the Celtic understanding of time and season, the deep relationship between the Irish people and their land.

For years, I studied the fragments that remain - the medieval manuscripts, the folk practices, the archaeological evidence, the place names that still whisper their old meanings. I walked the land where these traditions originated. I listened to what the spirits and ancestors seemed to be saying through the mist and stone. And slowly, a clearer picture emerged: an Irish Wheel, distinct in its rhythms and meanings, waiting to be remembered and revived.

What you hold in your hands is not scholarly doctrine, though it draws from scholarly sources. It is not a strict "how-to" manual, though it offers practical rituals. It is an invitation - an invitation to step into a conversation between past and present, between the land beneath your feet and the spirits that move through it, between who you are now and who your ancestors were.

This book is for seekers who feel the pull of something old. For those who have wondered why the autumn equinox stirs something in their chest, or why they feel most alive by a bonfire on Samhain eve. For solitary practitioners building a personal practice, and for community leaders crafting group rituals. For people with

Irish heritage seeking reconnection, and for others across the world who simply feel called to this path.

You need not have Irish ancestry to walk this Wheel. Spirit knows no borders, and the gods travel well. What matters is sincerity - showing up to the fire, to the rain, to the turning seasons, with an open heart and willing hands.

Read this book as you need to. Some may follow it chapter by chapter. Others may be drawn to specific festivals or practices. Some may use it as daily devotional reading. There is no wrong way. The Wheel invites participation, not perfection. Trust your own knowing. Honor what resonates and set aside what does not.

My deepest hope is that these pages serve as a bridge - helping you find your footing on the path of the Irish Wheel, rooted in tradition yet alive in your own time. May you find in these words a homecoming to something ancient and true

Table of Contents

Introduction - Why the Irish Wheel Still Matters

The Wheel of the Year is more than a circle of seasonal festivals. It is a living, breathing current, a spiritual rhythm that pulses through the land, the air, and the blood of those who remember. To live by the Wheel is to step outside of linear time and into a sacred spiral, one that folds in upon itself like mist over an ancient hill. Each turn brings us closer to the heart of the Earth and the spirit of our ancestors.

It is not just a ritual calendar or an agricultural chart, it is a cosmology of belonging. The eight points of the Wheel serve as doors through which we enter the deeper mysteries of life, death, rebirth, and transformation. In ancient Ireland, these were more than seasonal shifts; they were mythic thresholds where gods walked among mortals and the land itself became sentient. The turning of the Wheel was mirrored in the hearth, in the field, in the sacred grove, and in the beating of the human heart.

In this guide, we explore the Wheel through an Irish lens, rooted in native traditions, seasonal markers, and the mythic consciousness that shaped the Celtic worldview. We will walk the paths of Brigid and the Morrígan, plant seeds at Imbolc and reap grain at Lughnasadh, light fires on hilltops and leave offerings at wells. We will listen to the voices in the wind and remember that we are not separate from the land, but of it.

Getting Started: A Guide for Complete Beginners

If you're new to Irish Paganism or Pagan practice in general, welcome. This section is designed to help you start from zero, with practical guidance on setting up your first altar, choosing initial practices, and building a sustainable foundation for your spiritual journey through the Wheel of the Year.

You Don't Need to Know Everything First

One of the biggest barriers for beginners is the feeling that you need extensive knowledge before you can begin practicing. This is not true. Irish Paganism is a practice, not a test. You learn by doing, by observing, by building relationship over time. Start with questions, uncertainty, and willingness to learn as you go.

Your First Altar: A Practical Shopping List

- Essential (Under $20): A small table or shelf, one white candle with matches, a small bowl for water, a plate for offerings, and a cloth to cover the surface.
- Helpful Additions (Under $30): A second candle, incense or herbs for cleansing (juniper, rosemary, mugwort—not white sage), seasonal items from nature, and a journal.
- What You Don't Need: You do not need athame, chalice, pentacle, or wand. These are Wiccan tools, not Irish requirements. Irish practice is simpler: fire, water, earth, and honest words.

Your First 30 Days: Building Daily Practice

- Days 1-7: Morning and evening, light a candle, take three breaths, speak gratitude or release. Spend 5-10 minutes outdoors daily noticing seasonal signs.
- Days 8-14: Add three things you're grateful for each time you light the candle. Begin journaling one paragraph daily about nature observations.
- Days 15-21: Choose one deity from Chapter 7. After gratitude, say: '[Deity name], I honor you. I invite your presence if you wish to know me.' Research this deity daily.

- Days 22-30: Make one simple offering this week. Try one longer practice (15-30 minutes) weekly. By Day 30, you should have a comfortable rhythm established.

Common Beginner Questions

Q: Do I have to be Irish to practice? A: No. Sincere respect and genuine relationship matter more than bloodline.

Q: Can I practice alone? A: Yes. Solo practice is completely valid. Irish Paganism has no requirement for groups.

Q: What if I make mistakes? A: You will. The deities aren't punitive. With sincerity and respect, mistakes are learning opportunities.

Q: Do I need all eight festivals? A: No. Start with one or two that call to you. Better to celebrate fewer festivals deeply than all eight superficially.

Red Flags to Avoid

Avoid teachers or groups that: claim you need expensive tools or their specific training, mix Irish and Indigenous practices without distinction, use racist rhetoric, demand money for 'secret knowledge', discourage questions, promise magical wealth or power, appropriate from closed traditions, or treat deities as servants to command.

Moving Forward

You now have practical starting tools: an altar setup, a 30-day practice plan, and answers to common questions. The chapters that follow give you historical context, theological depth, and seasonal practices. But you don't need to read them all before beginning. Start your daily practice now, today. The Wheel is turning. Step onto it. Welcome home.

You will encounter the sidhe, the spirits of place, and the whisper of old gods who never truly left. The land of Ireland is rich with sacred time, thin places, holy wells, standing stones, and burial mounds aligned with the sun. These are not relics but living participants in a conversation between past and present. By tuning ourselves to the Wheel, we enter that conversation.

This book is not a scholarly tome, though it draws from history. Nor is it a strict ritual manual, though it provides rites and practices. Instead, it is a companion. A whisper at your hearth fire. A crow's call across the moor. A guide for those who seek to live in rhythm with the old ways while rooted in the modern world. It is a pathfinder for souls who long to live not just seasonally, but sacredly.

Why an Irish-centric approach? Because much of the modern pagan Wheel draws from a mix of British and pan-European influences, often distilling eight festivals into a generalized framework. Yet Ireland held, and holds, its own unique cycle of story and practice. The timing of the seasons was shaped by her weather, her crops, and her gods. The festivals were not evenly spaced but emerged organically from the needs and observations of the people. In returning to the Irish perspective, we rewild the Wheel. We plant it again in native soil.

To understand this Wheel is to remember the spirits of land and lineage. It is to reclaim ancestral memories, not through fantasy but through relationship, by watching the hawthorn bloom, hearing the wind shift at Samhain, and kneeling at the roots of a tree to listen. These practices need not be grand. Lighting a candle with intention or placing a stone on your altar with reverence is enough. Spirit listens to sincerity more than spectacle.

You will find in these pages both tradition and innovation. Where historical sources are available, they are honored. Where gaps exist, we fill them with respectful reconstruction, poetic vision, and grounded intuition. This is the work of any modern practitioner: to stand with one foot in the old world and one in the now, singing the same songs in a new tongue.

For readers far from Ireland, this book offers practical adaptations. You will find native herb substitutes, suggestions for altar items sourced locally, and ways to mark the seasons even in cities of steel and glass. Spirit knows no border. The gods travel well. The rhythms of the Earth remain accessible to all who seek them, even in unfamiliar landscapes. We are all inheritors of this Wheel, if we choose to step onto it.

This work is for solitary seekers and community leaders, for those new to the path and those who have walked it many years. It is for anyone who has felt the ache at Samhain, the surge at Beltaine, the stillness of the winter solstice and the rush of the spring. It is for those who have wondered why they cry at the sight of frost or feel peace in the fog. The Wheel helps us name those feelings and sanctify them.

The Wheel of the Year is not a doctrine. It is a dance. It calls not for memorization, but participation. You need not get it "right." You need only show up (to the fire, to the rain, to the moment) and let the land teach you. Let the ancestors remember through you. Let your breath align with the breath of the seasons.

And so we begin, at the still point, with open hands and an open heart. Let the Wheel turn and let us turn with it.

Chapter 1: Root and Flame – The Origins of the Irish Year

The Irish understanding of time and season did not emerge from abstraction. It developed from direct and continuous relationships with the land. People tracked the movement of the sun, observed the changing behavior of animals, noted the blooming and withering of plants, and responded to the needs of crops and herds. From this attention to the land and sky, a cyclical understanding of the year emerged. It was not a linear progression, but a spiral marked by points of change; transitions marked by both necessity and meaning.

In pre-Christian Ireland, the year was primarily divided into two halves: the dark half and the light half. This division was practical. The dark half, beginning with Samhain in late October, was a time of reduced agricultural activity, increased attention to domestic and spiritual life, and preparations for winter survival. The light half, beginning with Bealtaine in early May, was the period of planting, tending, herding, travel, and social gatherings. This binary division was supported by cross-quarter festivals that further marked seasonal transitions.

Archaeological evidence supports the importance of seasonal observance, revealing that the people of ancient Ireland were not only deeply connected to the rhythms of the earth but also remarkably sophisticated in their understanding of celestial cycles. Megalithic monuments such as Brú na Bóinne (Newgrange), Loughcrew, and Carrowkeel bear witness to this relationship. These sacred structures were not built at random; they were aligned with precision to significant solar events, especially the solstices and equinoxes, revealing a cosmology that saw time itself as sacred.

Newgrange is the most iconic of these sites. Over five thousand years old, this passage tomb is constructed with a roof box designed to admit the first rays of the rising sun on the winter solstice. For just a few moments, a shaft of golden light pierces the darkness, illuminating the inner chamber with a brilliance that feels more mystical than mechanical. This event only occurs for a few days at the turning of the year, marking a profound moment of cosmic renewal. The feat is not just architectural; it is spiritual uniting the cycles of death and rebirth, darkness and light, stone and star.

At Loughcrew, similar alignments are found with the spring and autumn equinoxes, when sunlight touches engraved stones inside the cairns. These were not simple calendars. They were ceremonial spaces of communion between the seen and unseen worlds. Light entering a sacred tomb was not merely illumination, it was presence. It was a blessing. It was a way of saying: the gods still see us, the ancestors still walk with us, and the land remembers.

Such constructions show that marking time was not only about agricultural planning but also about cosmology, sovereignty, and the enduring relationship between people, deities, and landscape. In these stone temples of light, we glimpse how seriously the Irish ancients took the rhythm of the year, not as superstition or metaphor, but as sacred reality made manifest in earth and sky. Such constructions show that marking time was not only about agriculture, but also about cosmology, community, and continuity.

Modern neo-pagans recognize the Wheel of the Year as a contemporary framework that integrates four ancient Irish festivals. Samhain, Imbolc, Bealtaine, and Lughnasadh, with the solstices and equinoxes. This integration has created a symbolic map of time, now widely embraced by diverse Pagan traditions around the world.

While these eight festivals are often presented as evenly spaced spokes on a symbolic wheel, their original observance in Ireland was more fluid, deeply embedded in agricultural rhythms, weather patterns, and the needs of local communities.

The fire festivals of Samhain, Imbolc, Bealtaine, and Lughnasadh stand out for their strong roots in Irish myth and folk practice. They are bound to the pulse of rural life and to sacred lore. Oral tradition, mythic cycles, and early medieval manuscripts associate these celebrations with deities and spirits, with landscape features, and with specific types of communal rites. These were the moments when people gathered to light fires, perform blessings, make offerings, and tell stories that kept the spiritual world interwoven with the daily one. Samhain opens the veil to the ancestors. Imbolc ushers in healing and inspiration. Bealtaine kindles desire and vitality. Lughnasadh honors toil, triumph, and the fruits of labor.

The solstices and equinoxes, though less prominent in Irish mythic texts, were still observed through architecture and seasonal markers. Their modern inclusion brings a solar dimension that complements the earth-based wisdom of fire festivals. They add symmetrical rhythm and celestial rhythm to the Wheel, creating a space to honor balance, peak, and return. This marriage of solar and agrarian observances enriches the spiritual cycle, encouraging reflection on both inner transformation and outer seasonal change.

Each festival marks a shift: from death to rebirth, stillness to motion, sowing to harvest, light to darkness. Together, they form not a rigid doctrine but a living rhythmal way to move in harmony with the sacred tides of the land and the spirit. Each festival marks a shift: from death to rebirth, stillness to motion, sowing to harvest, light to darkness.

The importance of these turning points was not only agricultural. They served as spiritual hinges in the Irish calendar; moments when the veil between worlds thinned, and the everyday was punctuated by the mythic. At Samhain, the year descended into darkness, the last of the harvest was gathered, and people gathered to share food, light fires, and honor the ancestors. It was understood to be a liminal space in time, when the barrier between the living and the dead was porous, and when omens, dreams, and divinations held unusual weight. Samhain was more than an ending; it was a descent into the deep soil of remembrance.

Bealtaine, by contrast, was the season's joyful exhale. Twin fires were lit and passed through not only for purification but also for blessing. It marked the beginning of the season when the world was in full bloom, and human life echoed that flourishing. Young couples would court, cattle were moved to higher pastures, and charms of protection were sung or spoken into the air. It was a festival of fecundity, of new unions and new ventures, steeped in both merriment and magic.

Each of these sacred thresholds was marked not merely by celebration but by actions that sustained the health of the land, the safety of the people, and the balance between seen and unseen forces. These were times when people did not merely observe nature; they engaged it, answered it, and danced with it. The festivals themselves acted as conversational points between the human and the divine.

These festivals reflected the cultural rhythms of the people. They functioned as seasonal anchors, reminders of when to plant, when to pray, when to release, and when to rejoice. But more than this, they created a shared sense of sacred time. In an oral culture where myth was the heartbeat of understanding, seasonal rituals were not just community events but reenactments of the mythic cycles themselves. To light a fire at Bealtaine was to echo the light kindled in the Otherworld; to sing at Lughnasadh was to honor the sorrow and strength of Tailtiu, Lugh's foster-mother, whose death gave rise to the festival.

The Wheel, as practiced ritually, became a storytelling device. Each turn reinforced ancestral memory and spiritual identity. It reminded each generation that they were not isolated in time, but part of an ongoing dance of dark and light, life and loss, action and stillness. Through the Wheel, people not only remembered the gods, they kept them alive in breath, soil, and song. Stories of the gods and ancestors were tied to these seasons, creating a rich tapestry of ritual, meaning, and belonging.

The idea of the Wheel as a unified cycle with eight evenly spaced festivals is largely a modern synthesis, shaped by British Druidry, Wicca, and contemporary Pagan reconstructionism. While ancient Irish practice did not likely follow this precise structure, the core intent; attunement to the land's cycles and honoring the sacred in time, remains deeply intact. The solstices and equinoxes, with their cosmic symmetry, enhance the visceral, earthbound wisdom of the fire festivals. They provide a celestial counterpoint, bridging solar knowledge with soil-based knowing. yet the underlying structure honors a universal truth: that light and darkness dance in constant rhythm, and that human life flourishes when it moves in harmony with the turning of the earth.

As we explore the Wheel of the Year through an Irish lens in the chapters ahead, we do so not to replicate the past but to root our present more deeply in ancestral soil. We do not seek to live as our ancestors did, but to live in relationship with the same sacred patterns they honored. The land still speaks. The seasons still shift. And the sacred rhythm continues to call those who listen with open hearts, steady hands, and the will to remember.

Chapter 2: Threads Through Stone – Time, Land, and the Otherworld

To understand the Irish Wheel of the Year as a spiritual system, it is necessary to explore the land-based cosmology that shaped its origin. This worldview was not merely a backdrop to daily life; it was the breath and rhythm of the world itself. In pre-Christian Ireland, the physical and spiritual realms coexisted not as distant domains but as interwoven threads in the same tapestry. The land was more than terrain; it was a living memory, a sacred partner in the unfolding of time.

The natural world was infused with consciousness. Trees whispered ancestral truths, rivers remembered ancient migrations, and stones stood sentinel at places where story and spirit converged. The people lived not beside nature, but within it, attuned to its patterns and presences. To pass through a wooded glen or approach a standing stone was not just a physical act, it was a crossing into layered meaning.

Hills, rivers, trees, and stones held agency and memory. Certain sites were revered as thresholds; thin places where the veil between the seen and unseen wore thin. These were not metaphors; they were spatial truths within the Irish soulscape. Here, the sacred was not sought in distant heavens but found beneath one's feet, among bog and branch and breeze.

Ireland's sacred geography played a central role in how time was measured and experienced. Passage tombs such as those at Brú na Bóinne, Loughcrew, Knowth, and Carrowkeel were aligned with solar events like the solstices and equinoxes. These alignments were not coincidental. They represent a cosmic choreography: light and shadow interacting with stone, marking time not with numbers but with presence. These monuments were ceremonial calendars, yes, but they were also spiritual thresholds, echo chambers for ritual, and wombs of rebirth.

To step inside Brú na Bóinne during the winter solstice, when a single beam of sunlight threads the passage to strike the chamber wall, is to witness a moment of ancestral brilliance. It is not simply architecture, it is cosmology rendered in stone. Such structures reveal a belief that time was cyclical, regenerative, and inseparable from the land itself. They remind us that ancient Irish spirituality did not observe nature from afar, it lived within it, listened to it, and shaped story and season accordingly.

The Irish concept of the Otherworld further shaped perceptions of time and season. Unlike in many modern cosmologies that place the spiritual realm above or below, the Irish saw the Otherworld as intertwined with this one; neither distant nor removed but layered and near. It was not a place to ascend to or descend into, but one to cross into, often through the natural landscape: the hollow hills, sacred springs, caves that breathed mist, and still lakes reflecting more than just the sky.

This Otherworld was not a land of exile or punishment. It was a place of beauty, mystery, danger, and profound wisdom. In myth, its inhabitants; the sidhe or aes sídhe; were the divine remnants of the Tuatha Dé Danann, transformed after retreating from the visible world. These were not diminutive fairies of Victorian imagination, but potent, shape-shifting beings associated with prophecy, war, poetry, and sovereignty. They were not always benevolent, nor always cruel, they were forces of nature, wild and revered.

Entry into the Otherworld could be sudden and disorienting. A mist might rise over a bog, a door might open in a hill, a song might lure someone across the veil. Such moments were more likely during liminal times of the year (especially at Samhain and Bealtaine) when thresholds became permeable. These festivals were not just seasonal turnings but cosmic invitations. The living could commune with the dead, the gods might whisper in dreams, and fate could be altered by ritual and intention.

To the ancient Irish, these encounters were not hallucinations but revelations. The Otherworld informed the seen world, and those who walked between them (poets, druids, seers) held great responsibility. They carried messages across realms, often at great personal cost. Understanding this cosmology shifts how we view the Wheel of the Year: not merely as an agricultural observance, but as spiritual navigation through realms seen and unseen. Each point on the Wheel becomes a crossing, a sacred opportunity to listen, to remember, and to awaken.

The Four Treasures of the Tuatha Dé Danann; the Stone of Fál, the Sword of Nuada, the Spear of Lugh, and the Cauldron of the Dagda; illustrate a symbolic structure tied not only to sovereignty and seasonal progression, but also to elemental balance and spiritual ethics. These mythic tools, described in the Lebor Gabála Érenn and echoed in bardic tales, embody the sacred foundations upon which both rulership and ritual were formed.

According to Irish mythology, the Tuatha Dé Danann were divine beings who arrived in Ireland bearing these four magical treasures from four great cities of the Otherworld: Falias, Gorias, Findias, and Murias. Each city was known not only for the item it held, but for the wisdom, skill, or spiritual mystery it taught. These were not just centers of power; they were schools of sovereignty, discipline, and the arts. The treasures they carried were imbued with those teachings, each one representing a vital dimension of the Irish spiritual path.

These items were not simply magical artifacts within the tales, they were embodiments of values. They form a mythopoetic structure for the inner work of the spiritual seeker: the grounded presence of the Stone, the discernment of the Sword, the passionate drive of the Spear, and the nurturing depth of the Cauldron. Each one maps onto both seasonal transitions and personal transformation. They serve as inner guides as much as outer legends, tools to meditate with, invoke in ritual, and use as touchstones throughout the sacred year.

The Stone of Fál, also known as the Lia Fáil or "Stone of Destiny," was said to roar when the rightful king of Ireland stood upon it. It was not merely an artifact of legend, but a living witness to the contract between land and ruler. This sacred stone, once located on the Hill of Tara (the ancient seat of Irish kingship) was a touchstone of sovereignty, both literal and symbolic. It bound the fate of kings to the spirit of the land itself.

As a symbol, the Stone is associated with the element of earth, representing grounding, endurance, and the immovable truth of one's path. It is the soil beneath one's feet, the ancient bones of the land, and the weight of lineage. It asks: Are you steady enough to hold what the land requires of you? In a seasonal context, the Stone aligns with those moments when decisions must be made from a place of inner stillness and strength, particularly around the equinoxes, when balance must be held amid change.

Spiritually, the Stone of Fál reminds the practitioner that true power is not taken but conferred by right relationship. It speaks to consent, not domination. It teaches that sovereignty begins with integrity, and that leadership, whether of a community or one's own life, is only as strong as the roots from which it grows. To meditate with this symbol is to ask: Am I in right relation with my land, my lineage, and my purpose?

The Sword of Nuada, forged in the city of Findias, was said to cut through any enemy and always strike true. This was no ordinary blade; it was the weapon of Nuada Airgetlám, the silver-handed king of the Tuatha Dé Danann, and a symbol of unyielding clarity. In stories, it never missed its mark, and it was said that no foe could escape its edge once it had been drawn. But its power was not merely in combat, it was in the certainty of truth.

As a spiritual symbol, the sword embodies discernment, justice, and the courage to act with integrity. It is linked with the element of air, which governs thought, logic, communication, and the breath of inspiration. To wield the Sword of Nuada is to cut away illusion and face reality without flinching. It invites us to be precise in our intentions, to speak truth even when it is uncomfortable, and to weigh our choices with conscience rather than convenience.

Seasonally, the sword aligns with times of tension or decision, moments where the future pivots on a single choice. This might arise near Imbolc, a festival of beginnings, or during Lughnasadh, when reaping what has been sown forces honest assessment. It is also a tool of spiritual defense, cutting through fear and delusion to uphold what is just.

To meditate with the Sword of Nuada is to ask: Where am I called to take a stand? What must I sever to walk in truth? Its edge reminds us that while clarity may divide, it also frees. Justice, like the sword, must be tempered with wisdom, or it risks becoming cruelty. But when wielded with a steady hand and a clear heart, it becomes the sharp edge of transformation.

The Spear of Lugh, from the city of Gorias, was so powerful it had to be kept in a vat of water to keep it from igniting everything around it. It was said to blaze with divine energy, impossible to resist in battle, a weapon of pure will honed to a radiant point. Lugh himself. God of light, mastery, and many skills; was known for wielding it not just with force, but with focused brilliance. The spear was not a symbol of reckless violence, but of a decisive, radiant purpose.

This treasure embodies the element of fire: passion, courage, momentum, and transformation. It burns away hesitation. It sets into motion what is stagnant. It is the strike of inspiration, the spark that ignites action, the flame that forges resolve. Where the Stone roots and the Sword judges, the Spear moves. It is the breath held before a leap, the raised torch before a declaration.

Seasonally, the Spear of Lugh aligns with the height of the sun's power, particularly during midsummer and Lughnasadh, the festival named for him. These are times when action must be taken, crops must be cut, and strength must meet labor. The spear marks these moments as ones not of rest, but of assertion; when we give shape to what we've envisioned, and leap toward harvest with fearless momentum.

To meditate with Spear is to ask: Where is my energy being called? What fear must I transmute into motion? What idea, long held, must finally be brought to life? In rituals, it may be invoked when direction falters, when drive wanes, or when courage must rise. The Spear does not wait, it flies. And when cast in alignment with one's truth, it lands precisely where it must.

The Cauldron of the Dagda, from Murias, never ran empty and was said to nourish all who gathered around it. More than a symbol of plenty, it was the embodiment of sacred hospitality, a virtue central to Irish culture. The Dagda, known as the Good God, was not called so because he was morally perfect, but because he was good at all things. His cauldron never failed in its purpose: to feed, to heal, to sustain. In myth, it restored strength to the weary, revived warriors, and symbolized the regenerative power of community and care.

The cauldron is a transformation vessel echoing the womb, the well, and the sea. It is a feminine symbol of receptivity and flow, but also of mystery and depth. Spiritually, it speaks to nourishment beyond the physical: the replenishment of spirit, the holding of grief, the incubation of insight. Its element is water, emotional, intuitive, cleansing. To sit at the Cauldron is to be held by something greater than oneself.

Seasonally, the cauldron aligns with the dark half of the year, particularly Samhain and the deep winter months. These are the times of storytelling around hearths, of ancestors at our shoulders, of silence as a form of reverence. In these months, the cauldron does not demand action, it invites reflection, dreaming, and healing. It teaches that rest is not idleness, and that care is a radical act.

To meditate with the Cauldron of the Dagda is to ask: What am I truly hungry for? Where can I offer nourishment, to myself, to others, to the world? It is a call to generosity, not from obligation, but from fullness. In ritual, the cauldron may be placed at the center, filled with water or wine or symbols of life. It reminds us that to gather is sacred, to feed one another is holy, and to receive without shame is its own kind of strength.

Together, these treasures reflect a balanced system of elemental and ethical principles: earth (sovereignty), air (judgment), fire (will), and water (sustenance). They mirror not only the cycles of nature, but the interior landscape of the human soul. Each treasure carries a lesson; a call to alignment, to transformation, and to sacred responsibility. Seen through this lens, the Wheel of the Year becomes more than eight seasonal festivals; it becomes a full-spectrum map of living in right relationship with self, spirit, and land.

In modern neo-pagan practice, understanding this framework invites practitioners into deeper engagement. Recognizing sacred time as both environmental and mythic allows for a layered experience of the year. One may track the sun and moon while also attending dreams and omens. One may light a fire not just to mark a solstice, but to call upon the spear's momentum or the sword's discernment. Practice becomes ritual when it is informed by meaning.

We need not return to a distant past to walk this path. We need to learn to see with mythic eyes. A city park may contain a sacred tree. A kitchen hearth may become an altar. What matters is not the exact replication of ancient rites, but the restoration of reverence. The land still speaks, even in unfamiliar tongues. The ancestors still listen, even in lands they never walked. And the gods (those who still linger) respond to those who call with sincerity.

In the chapters that follow, each of the eight festivals will be examined with this worldview in mind. These celebrations are more than seasonal observances; they are spiritual thresholds, invitations to participate in the ongoing story of the land. The rituals and reflections offered here are grounded in tradition but shaped for modern lives. By approaching the Irish Wheel of the Year not just as a calendar, but as a living relationship with time and place, neo-pagans can co-create a path that is both historically rooted and spiritually resonant.

Chapter 3: Practicing Across Oceans – American Ground, Irish Roots

For many modern neo-pagans, the desire to engage with the Irish Wheel of the Year emerges from a deep yearning to live in harmony with natural cycles and to reclaim ancestral or spiritual connections to pre-Christian traditions. This longing often arises not only from a place of spiritual exploration, but from a sense of disconnection in a world increasingly defined by artificial rhythms. Amid the hum of machines and the glow of screens, many feel called to reattune themselves to the deeper, older pulse of the earth.

The Irish Wheel of the Year offers a sacred pattern; a spiraled rhythm that honors light and shadow, life and death, sowing and harvest. But for most readers of this book, especially those outside of Ireland, engaging this pattern raises an essential question: how do we practice something so deeply tied to a specific land and culture while rooted in a different geography? This chapter offers practical guidance for adapting Irish-based seasonal practice to other landscapes, especially within the United States, where the terrain, seasons, and cultural context are distinct.

Rather than being a barrier, this difference can become an invitation to deepen one's practice. To walk the Irish Wheel on American ground is to engage in a form of spiritual translation, one that asks not for imitation, but for respectful adaptation. It requires looking to the land beneath your feet and asking, not "How can I recreate Ireland here?" but "How can I honor the sacred cycle in this place, with these winds, these rains, these changes?"

One of the most immediate challenges is seasonal difference. Ireland's temperate oceanic climate is characterized by gentle transitions, misty weather, and consistent rainfall throughout the year. Winters are rarely harsh, and summers are cool and lush. By contrast, many regions of the United States experience dramatic seasonal swings, from deep freezes in the north to subtropical blooms in the south. These differences shape how the seasons feel in the body and the land.

For instance, the signs of spring observed at Imbolc in Ireland, the emergence of snowdrops, lambing season, and the first gentle thaw; might still be buried under snow in New England or fully underway weeks earlier in southern states like Georgia or Texas. What signals Imbolc in Ireland might more closely resemble Ostara or even Beltane in some parts of North America. This discrepancy may seem disorienting at first, but it is not a flaw. It is a sacred invitation to attune to the unique cadence of the land you inhabit.

Rather than clinging rigidly to dates on a calendar, practitioners can begin to see the festivals of the Wheel not as fixed points, but as thresholds, living, breathing markers of transition in the natural world. The first frost, the blooming of wildflowers, the ripening of berries, or the departure of migratory birds may each signal the turning of the Wheel. Honoring these cues allows the practitioner to step into a more intimate and reciprocal relationship with their ecosystem.

Flexibility is not a compromise of tradition, it is its fulfillment. The ancient Irish themselves observed seasonal change not by calendars, but by the signs offered by sky, soil, and seed. We do not dishonor their legacy by doing the same where we are. In fact, by watching our own land with reverence, we continue their tradition in a way that is alive, rooted, and true.

The festivals of the Wheel should not be understood as rigidly tied to calendar dates, but as markers of natural thresholds: the first frost, the full bloom, the last harvest. Practitioners are encouraged to observe their own local landscapes and align their celebrations accordingly. If the land is still deep in winter on February 1st, then Imbolc may need to be observed when the first true signs of spring appear. This principle applies across the Wheel and is a vital part of rooting spiritual practice in real experience.

Another concern is cultural sensitivity and respect. Practicing an Irish spiritual framework on non-Irish land requires awareness, humility, and intentional engagement. The land in North America, like much of the world, is layered with its own Indigenous histories, peoples, and sacred geographies. These histories are not passive backdrops; they are living, enduring presences. Honoring the Irish Wheel of the Year in such a space must never come at the expense of erasing or overshadowing the spiritual lineages already embedded in that place.

This means practitioners must cultivate practice of listening. Before planting Irish symbols in foreign soil, one must first ask: who walked here before? Whose stories rise from this ground? What treaties, struggles, and wisdom live in the wind and water here? Answering these questions doesn't require co-opting Indigenous practices; it requires acknowledging that we are not the first to call this land sacred.

One way to navigate this responsibly is by establishing a relationship with the land as it is; not by trying to make it "feel Irish," but by learning its rhythms, honoring its character, and approaching it as a partner. The Irish Wheel can be walked in many places, but it must be walked with reverence. Offering gratitude, caring for native plants, learning local history, and practicing humility are small but powerful acts of spiritual respect. When Irish practice meets Indigenous awareness, something deeper is possible: a form of seasonal spirituality that is rooted, responsible, and relational.

Creating household rituals, altars, and seasonal observances grounded in the Irish Wheel can be done anywhere, regardless of living situation or environment. What matters most is not the scale, but the intention and consistency behind the practice. In cities, where green space may be limited, even a windowsill altar or a single candle lit at the right moment can open the heart to the sacred. A jar of gathered rainwater, a stone from a beloved path, or a sprig of rosemary can carry as much power as a great stone circle when chosen with reverence.

Urban practitioners might mark the festivals with simple but potent acts: cooking seasonal meals that reflect the spirit of the time, lighting a candle at dawn or dusk, or placing offerings of bread and berries beneath a favored tree in the park. These rituals, though quiet, weave spirit into daily life. In suburban or rural settings, the options expand, small outdoor shrines, herb gardens planted in tune with the seasons, bonfires shared with friends. Each act becomes a verse in a song sung to the land.

The key is observation and engagement. Walking the same trail once a week and noting the subtle shifts in season. Honoring a household altar by refreshing its elements with the changing festivals. Gathering with others in small circles (even virtually) to share stories and reflect on the Wheel's turning. These practices anchor the sacred in the rhythms of life and remind us that spiritual power is not confined to ancient groves. It lives in kitchens, bedrooms, sidewalks, and fields. It is called forth by attention and devotion. What matters most is consistency, reflection, and engagement with the turning of time.

Another helpful practice is the creation of a personal seasonal journal or devotional calendar. More than just a record of dates or weather patterns, this journal becomes a sacred mirror, reflecting your relationship with the land, the seasons, and yourself over time. Beginning by noting small, observable changes: the first frost on the morning grass, the return of a particular bird, the flowering of a local tree. These markers serve as anchors, helping you build a relationship with the rhythms of the place you inhabit.

Devotional entries can also include reflections on rituals performed, dreams received during liminal times, poems inspired by seasonal shifts, or meditations on the elements. Over time, the journal becomes a personal Wheel, a spiraled testament to your own path. You notice patterns not only in nature, but within your spirit. What festivals bring clarity? Which ones stir grief or joy? What themes revisit you each year like tides returning to shore?

Calendars may also be adapted to mark these shifts. Perhaps you highlight when local trees begin to bud, or the full moons that align with key festivals. These tools transform the abstract into the lived, and they encourage consistency, creativity, and rootedness.

Through these practices, the Wheel of the Year becomes not only a cultural inheritance but a lived relationship, rooted where you stand, yet reaching across oceans to honor where your spirit feels called.

Adapting across oceans does not dilute the tradition. Rather, it strengthens it. When Irish seasonal spirituality is practiced with intention, knowledge, and respect, it becomes a living system; one that breathes in new soil while keeping its roots intact.

The next chapter will begin our exploration of the festivals themselves, starting with Samhain, the gateway to the dark half of the year.

But before we cross that threshold, let us return to the body, the body that walks the land, feels the wind, and gathers the signs. Stand outside at twilight. Listen. Breathe in the air where you are. What season stirs in your lungs? What memory rises from the soil beneath your feet? This is your practice beginning, not in Ireland, not in myth, but in this breath, this place, this moment.

As we prepare to enter the sacred cycle of the festivals, carry this with you: you are not disconnected. You are not too late. The Wheel turns where you are. And it waits, always, for your first step.

Navigating Two Worlds: Irish Deities and Local Land Spirits

One of the most challenging aspects of diaspora practice is learning to honor both Irish deities and the spirits of the land where you actually live. This is not a problem with a single solution, and different practitioners will find different approaches that work for them. What matters is approaching the question with humility, respect, and genuine commitment to relationship rather than extraction.

First, recognize that this is a both/and situation, not an either/or. You are not choosing between Irish deities and local land spirits. You are learning to maintain relationships with both, understanding that each serves a different function in your spiritual life. The Irish deities connect you to ancestral wisdom, cultural heritage, and the mythological framework that gives meaning to your practice. Local land spirits connect you to the physical place where you live, the ecology that sustains you, and the ground beneath your feet.

Begin by making clear offerings to the land itself, not through an Irish lens but on the land's own terms. Learn what grows there naturally. Discover what indigenous peoples called that land and, if possible, which nations stewarded it. This is not academic research but relationship-building. Visit the same natural place repeatedly—a park, a waterway, a patch of woods—and simply be present. Notice what changes seasonally. Listen more than you speak.

When you call on Irish deities, be explicit about where you are. "Brigid, I call to you here on Lenape land, on the traditional territory of the Lenni-Lenape people, by this river that feeds into the Atlantic." This acknowledgment reminds both you and the deity that you are practicing in diaspora, that the land has its own history and spirits, and that you come as a guest rather than a conqueror.

Addressing Indigenous Land Rights and Sovereignty

The uncomfortable truth that many diaspora Irish Pagans must face is that we practice on stolen land. In the United States, Canada, Australia, and other settler-colonial nations, the ground we call sacred was taken through genocide, forced removal, and broken treaties from Indigenous peoples who stewarded it for thousands of years before European arrival. Acknowledging this is not performative guilt; it is historical accuracy and ethical necessity.

Land acknowledgments have become common in Pagan circles, but acknowledgment without action is hollow. If you genuinely honor the land, you must also honor the people whose land it is. This means:

Learning whose traditional territory you occupy. Use resources like native-land.ca to identify Indigenous nations in your area. Learn their history, their current struggles, and their ongoing presence. Indigenous peoples are not historical footnotes; they are living communities with contemporary concerns.

Supporting Indigenous sovereignty concretely. Donate to Indigenous-led organizations. Support land back movements. Attend Indigenous-led events when invited (as a respectful guest, not a spiritual tourist). Vote for policies that protect Indigenous rights, water, and land. Buy from Indigenous artists and businesses rather than appropriating their symbols.

Never appropriating Indigenous spiritual practices. Smudging with white sage, sweat lodges, vision quests, medicine wheels—these belong to specific Indigenous traditions and are not yours to take. Irish Paganism has its own smoke cleansing traditions (with herbs like juniper and mugwort), its own purification practices, its own wisdom traditions. Use those.

Understanding that your right to practice freely on this land is built on Indigenous dispossession. Hold that tension honestly. It should inform how you practice, making you more humble, more grateful, and more committed to justice.

Practical Framework: Working with Both Irish and Local Spirits

Here is one framework that many diaspora practitioners find useful, though you should adapt it to your circumstances and conscience:

Create two altars or altar spaces: One dedicated to Irish deities and ancestors, focused on your spiritual and cultural lineage. Another dedicated to local land spirits, focused on the place where you live. These need not be elaborate—a shelf or a corner of a table suffices. The separation acknowledges that these are different relationships with different responsibilities.

Begin rituals with land acknowledgment: Before calling Irish deities, acknowledge the land and its spirits. A simple formula: "I stand on [Indigenous nation] land, traditional territory of the [people], land that was never ceded, never sold, never given up. I acknowledge the spirits of this place, the waters that flow here, the plants and animals that make this home. I come as a guest, and I ask permission to practice here."

Make regular offerings to the land: Separate from your Irish deity work, make offerings to local land spirits. Water for the earth. Biodegradable items that belong to that ecosystem. Your time spent in cleanup and stewardship. Your voice speaking against environmental destruction. These offerings should have no "Irish" quality—this is not about Irish practice but about honoring where you are.

Learn the Irish concept of dúthchas: This word encompasses a complex relationship between people, land, and belonging that developed over generations. In Ireland, families had dúthchas—a deep, inherited connection to specific places. As diaspora practitioners, we do not have dúthchas to American (or Canadian, or Australian) land.   Indigenous peoples do.   Recognizing this distinction keeps us humble and reminds us that our relationship to this land is necessarily different from our ancestors' relationship to Irish land.

Build relationships slowly and with consent: Both with Irish deities (who may or may not wish to travel to diaspora lands) and with local land spirits (who may or may not welcome you).   Pay attention to how you feel when practicing.   Notice synchronicities, dreams, and intuitions.   If something feels wrong or unwelcome, pause and reassess.   Not all relationships are meant to be, and forcing them serves no one.

Stories from Diaspora Practitioners

Many Irish American Pagans report that Irish deities adapt well to diaspora practice, particularly deities like Brigid (whose worship spread widely even in ancient times), Manannán (as a traveler and psychopomp), and the Mórrígan (whose concerns with sovereignty translate across contexts).   Some practitioners experience deities requesting specific acknowledgments of place or particular offerings that reflect the local ecosystem.

Others find that certain deities seem less present in diaspora, or that their relationship shifts.   One practitioner describes feeling Lugh's energy primarily during Lughnasadh celebrations with their Irish-American community, but not in daily practice—as if Lugh's connection to the harvest is so tied to Irish land that it does not fully translate.   This practitioner honors Lugh culturally and ancestrally but works primarily with local land spirits for agricultural magic.

Still others develop hybrid practices, where Irish seasonal frameworks organize the year, but ritual content draws heavily on local ecology.   An Imbolc ritual might honor Brigid's flame but use plants native to the practitioner's bioregion, offer local water from a nearby spring, and include acknowledgment of local Indigenous spring traditions as distinct from but parallel to Irish practice.

There is no single right way to navigate this complexity. What matters is that you remain thoughtful, ethical, and committed to genuine relationship with both Irish deities and the land where you live. This requires ongoing work, regular self-examination, and willingness to change your practice as you learn more. The tension is not a problem to solve but a reality to hold with integrity.

The Reciprocity Principle

In Irish tradition, reciprocity is sacred. When you take from the land, you give it back. When deities grant you blessings, you make offerings. In diaspora practice, this principle becomes even more important. If you are benefiting from living on stolen Indigenous land, you have an obligation to give back—not just to the spirits but to the people whose land it remains.

Reciprocity might mean: Land stewardship work that benefits local ecosystems. Financial support to Indigenous communities and causes. Using your voice and vote to support Indigenous sovereignty and environmental protection. Learning and teaching accurate history. Making space for Indigenous voices in Pagan communities when they choose to speak (and not tokenizing them or demanding their labor).

The Irish deities understand reciprocity intimately. They will not be offended by your commitment to justice and right relationship with Indigenous peoples. In fact, many practitioners report that their relationships with Irish deities deepened once they began taking diaspora ethics seriously, as if the gods respected the integrity of practicing with honesty rather than convenient fantasy.

Moving Forward

Diaspora Irish Paganism is necessarily complicated. You are reaching backward to ancestors and forward to descendants, honoring deities whose homeland you may never see, practicing on land with its own gods and its own tragic history. There are no easy answers, and anyone who tells you otherwise is selling something.

What you can do is practice with integrity. Acknowledge complexity rather than papering over it. Build real relationships rather than extracting spiritual experiences. Give back more than you take. Honor both Irish tradition and local land. Support Indigenous sovereignty in concrete ways. And trust that the deities and spirits recognize sincere effort even when you stumble, which you will, because this work is hard.

The Irish have a long history of diaspora, of being scattered by famine and colonization, of maintaining cultural identity in foreign lands. Your practice is part of that story. But it is also part of a story about settlers on stolen land, and you must hold both truths at once. This is the real work of diaspora spirituality—not just maintaining connection to your roots, but doing so ethically in the place where you've been planted.

Chapter 4: The Irish Wheel Is Not the Wiccan Wheel

For many readers, the Wheel of the Year first comes into view through modern Pagan paths, most commonly Wicca or eclectic traditions. It is often encountered through books, online communities, or seasonal rituals that present it as a neatly defined framework: eight sabbats, four solar points, four agricultural festivals, a balance of light and shadow. For those newly awakening to a Pagan path, this system can feel like a breath of order in a chaotic world, a sacred symmetry of Earth and sky.

On paper, it appears universal, precise, and balanced. But the Irish Wheel was never so tidy. It was born from land, livestock, fire, and myth, not mathematics. It is not a calendar you can simply overlay upon any landscape. It grew from Ireland's weather, its hills, its kinship bonds and sacred stories. Where Wicca often begins in structure, the Irish tradition begins in relationship, between people and their places, ancestors and their descendants, the rhythms of animals and the cycles of rain.

To understand the Irish spiritual calendar is to step into a world where time was lived, not counted. The old rites marked thresholds, the rising of milk in the ewe, the ripening of grain, the moment between sun and snow. These were not fixed dates on the wall. They were sacred convergences of nature and necessity, tuned not to planetary perfection but to survival and story. The first sign of spring might be the cry of a newborn lamb, not a square on the calendar. The coming of winter might be marked by the return of ancestral dreams, not a calculated solstice.

The difference is not simply one of cultural emphasis. It is about the way time itself is perceived. To the ancient Irish, time was not linear but cyclical, spiraling in patterns shaped by the land's needs, the moon's pull, and the memory of the tribe. While modern Paganism often favors precision and cosmic order, traditional Irish time is better understood as a series of thresholds, initiations, and mythic doorways; each one guiding the soul and the community through the year.

Irish Time Is Organic Time

In Wiccan practice, solstices and equinoxes often carry the greatest ritual weight. These solar points divide the year into quarters and emphasize cosmic balance: light and dark, above and below, goddess and god. They offer a cosmological harmony tied to the sun's journey, a map of light's waxing and waning.

But in early Irish tradition, the cross-quarter days. Samhain, Imbolc, Bealtaine, and Lughnasadh; were the pillars of spiritual and social life. These were not symbolic placeholders; they were deeply rooted in community survival and ancestral memories. They governed the agricultural calendar, the tribal laws, the festivals of kingship, and the movements of livestock. These four hinge points marked when people gathered, stories were retold, animals were moved, fields were blessed, and rites were performed to keep life balanced between seen and unseen worlds.

• Samhain opened the dark half of the year and the gates to the ancestors. It was the end of the harvest, the start of winter, and the liminal space where the living and the dead might speak. Oaths were renewed, debts forgiven, and fires extinguished and relit from a central flame. It was a time to turn inward, to remember, and to release.

• Imbolc marked the lactation of sheep, the first stirrings of life beneath the frost. It was a time of blessing the tools, visiting sacred wells, and invoking Brigid's healing and fire. The return of fertility was not symbolic; it was vital to survival. The hearth was relit with new intention, and households asked for the goddess's favor to see them through the final edge of winter.

• Bealtaine brought the great fire, the pairing of cattle and lovers, and the opening of the summer pastures. Twin bonfires were lit to drive cattle between them, a rite of purification and protection. Households celebrated fertility, creative passion, and the renewal of bonds. It was a festival of wildness, of green bursting into bloom, of sacred unions both physical and spiritual.

• Lughnasadh gathered the first fruits, honored the dead, and pledged loyalty to land and law. Games were held, contests of poetry and skill tested the community's strength, and offerings were made for a successful harvest. It was a time to gather, to witness feats of strength, to share bread, and to ensure justice was upheld before the waning days returned.

The solar days were known, but not as fixed public festivals. The winter solstice was observed at Newgrange through the chamber's light alignment, a stunning architectural achievement that still stirs wonder today. But for the ancient Irish, it was not the communal festival that modern Yule has become. It was a moment of deep interiority, mystery, and alignment with the unseen. It was a private offering from stone to sun, a ritual of memory carved into the bones of the land.

These moments did not gather crowds but rather whispered to a few, the guardians, the priests, the ones who listened. Light cutting through stone was not a public spectacle but a sacred conversation between ancestors and eternity. The tombs themselves, such as those at Newgrange and Loughcrew, were aligned with pinpoint precision to capture the light only on very specific mornings. That sliver of illumination became a breath of the gods, a symbol of rebirth, a signal that the darkness would not last forever.

The equinoxes, while significant in other cultures, were rarely emphasized in Irish myth or law. They may have held importance agriculturally, marking balance points in the year, but they were not central to the ritual life of the people. Their presence is felt more in the turning of the fields than in the lore of the fires.

This is not to say Irish tradition ignored the sun. Far from it. The builders of Newgrange, Loughcrew, and other passage tombs clearly understood solar movement. But their sacred architecture spoke in symbols, not schedules. The moment of illumination in a chamber was more than an astronomical event, it was an act of mythic alignment, a whisper between stone and sky, a revelation intended for the dead and the gods.

The Calendar of Fire and Field

The Wiccan Wheel draws equally from Celtic, Anglo-Saxon, and even Mediterranean influences. It is a modern synthesis, elegant in its symbolic symmetry, designed to reflect harmony and duality. It provides a structured spiritual year, often tied to solar and elemental polarity: light and dark, god and goddess, summer and winter. In contrast, the Irish Wheel did not seek balance in abstraction; it responded to the lived experience of its people. It is a calendar of survival and sovereignty, rooted in land-tending and kinship, in soil and in song.

The Irish Wheel speaks in the language of cattle herding, tribal kingship, mythic geographies, and generational memory. It begins not in Yule or at the Spring Equinox, but in Samhain, when the veil thins and the cycle of rebirth begins in the womb of death. This is not poetic metaphor, it is cosmological truth. For the ancient Irish, death was not the end of the cycle but the place of beginning, a return to source.

Even timekeeping itself bore different assumptions. The Irish day began at dusk, not dawn, echoing the spiritual priority of darkness as a generative force. Months followed the shifting moon, not the Roman calendar. Festivals did not fall on rigid dates but flowed with local climate and need. A festival might begin when the sheep began to lamb, when the first ripe berry was found, when a certain wind rose in the valley. Imbolc began when the ewes gave milk. Lughnasadh arrived when the grain bent gold. Such timing was relational, not imposed.

The Irish year was layered with nuance. Public festivals, household observances, tribal gatherings, and sacred rituals all wove together in overlapping cycles. Kinship, story, obligation, and place all formed the matrix of sacred time. The bones of the year were communal, but the flesh was regional and even personal. No two tuatha followed the same rhythm, and that variability was accepted as part of the Wheel's life.

Time was not counted in minutes or degrees but in moments that mattered: the first frost, the rising river, the return of swallows, the crack in the earth where green first showed. The living world, not an abstract schedule, dictated when the people gathered, when they prayed, and when they rested.

This fluidity often confuses modern practitioners looking for precise dates. But it also offers great freedom and resilience. It invites us to observe, to wait, to attune ourselves to the rhythms of the land wherever we are. The Irish Wheel becomes not a fixed diagram but a living relationship, a breathing bond between body and earth, memory and motion, threshold and return.

Why It Matters

If you are walking an Irish Pagan path (even from across an ocean) it matters that your rituals are rooted in the worldview they come from. Traditions carry the memory of a people, and when those traditions are transplanted without context, they can become hollow or misaligned. This doesn't mean rejecting Wiccan practice if that's part of your background. But it does mean honoring the difference, and choosing consciously, with reverence.

Calling on Brigid is not the same as invoking a generic fire goddess. She is not just a symbol of warmth or healing, she is a cultural force, a sovereignty figure, a goddess of the hearth and the forge whose presence is entwined with the Irish imagination. To celebrate Imbolc is not simply to light a candle in February; it is to listen for the hooves in the dark, to feel the thaw beneath your threshold, to offer cloth to the well, and to ask what in your life must be rekindled. To mark Samhain is not to cosplay Halloween, it is to remember your dead, name them, feed them, and keep their place warm at your table and your altar.

Understanding that Irish time is not Wiccan time allows you to return to the land; not just Ireland's, but your own, with deeper respect. It teaches you to follow signs, not schedules. It asks you to slow down, to observe, and to reconnect with a way of being that centers place over plan, presence over prescription. And it invites you to hear the year not as a wheel ticking through segments, but as a heartbeat, uneven, alive, and sacred.

Walking Forward in Practice

So what does this mean for your own ritual year?

It means that when planning your sabbats, you might look first to the weather, the land, and the signs around you. Let the earth be your guide. Has the frost settled? Have the first flowers broken through? Has the sun begun to return in earnest, or is it still hiding behind cold gray skies? Let your celebrations respond to the truth of the season, not just the calendar. You do not need to recreate ancient Ireland, but you do need to be in dialogue with your place.

It means that your altars, symbols, songs, and prayers can begin to reflect the Irish roots of these festivals more deeply. Sing the songs that name the land. Use words that remember your ancestors. Offer milk when it flows. Bake bread when the wheat is ready. Work with plants native to your region while understanding their analogs in Irish lore. Honor Brigid not only with candles but with acts of healing and inspiration.

And it means that your own local environment becomes part of the sacred rhythm. Whether you dwell in urban rooftops or deep forest, the land where you live will begin to teach you its version of the cycle; one that harmonizes with the old Irish ways, not because it copies them, but because it listens. When you listen too, the Wheel turns not on paper, but in your bones.

In the chapters ahead, we will explore each festival in full, returning always to the principle that the Wheel is not fixed. It turns with land. And the land turns with us.

In the chapters ahead, we will explore each festival in full, returning always to the principle that the Wheel is not fixed. It turns with land. And the land turns with us.

Chapter 5 – Cross-Quarters and Quarter Days Explained

To walk the Wheel of the Year is to walk a circle divided not simply by days or months, but by energies, rites, and natural thresholds. The circle is not a calendar in the modern sense, it is a cycle of transformation, tied to the pulse of the land and the stories carried by wind and stone. Yet for many beginning practitioners, the terms "cross-quarter" and "quarter day" are often sources of confusion. Are they solstices? Are they moon phases? Why does Samhain matter more than the equinox?

This chapter offers a clear, culturally grounded explanation of how these sacred days function in the Irish calendar, both ancient and modern. When understood properly, these markers do more than divide the year. They shaped it. They offer both rhythm and revelation. The Wheel is not a wheel of precision, it is a wheel of feeling, of kinship, and of timing drawn from breath and soil.

Let us begin by reorienting ourselves not to abstract celestial mechanics, but to the feet on the earth and the fires in the hearth. The Irish Wheel of the Year does not demand uniformity; it asks for participation. It invites you to stand where you are, to feel what the land feels, and to enter the turning with reverence. It is a sacred choreography between time, place, and presence. And it begins with understanding the difference between the high, bright silence of the sky, and the warm, pulsing memory of the earth.

The Four Quarter Days: Solar Anchors

Quarter Days refer to the four solar points that anchor the turning of the year:

Winter Solstice (around December 21)

Spring Equinox (around March 21)

Summer Solstice (around June 21)

Autumn Equinox (around September 21)

These are the moments when the sun stands still (solstice) or balances day and night (equinox). In many Indo-European traditions, they are celebrated as solar events. In Irish culture, however, their role is more subtle, more sacred than celebratory, and less prominent than what many modern practitioners might expect.

Of these, the Winter Solstice held special reverence. At Newgrange (Brú na Bóinne), the rising sun on solstice morning enters a narrow roofbox above the entrance and travels down the stone passage to illuminate the burial chamber deep within. This stunning precision reveals that the ancient Irish did not simply observe solar cycles; they embedded them into the bones of their sacred architecture. The sun's light was not just a phenomenon. It was a messenger.

But this solar reverence did not translate into widespread public celebrations. The solstices and equinoxes may have been moments of private observance, used by druids and wise ones to mark seasonal shifts, conduct divinations, or realign with cosmic patterns. They held cosmic significance, yes, but for the elite few, not the gathered many.

Folk life moved differently. The common people who tilled the soil and kept the herds felt no great compulsion to mark equinoxes with ceremony. These days passed mostly in silence. They may have served as pivot points for those attuned to the sun's zeniths and crossings, but they left little mark in myth or custom. The folk calendar turned not by light alone, but by lambs and berries, by fire and frost.

The sun spoke in mystery and stone, but it was the land that called the people to gather. Thus, the quarter days stood in the background, powerful, precise, but secondary to the tides of lived ritual. The people waited for the true markers of communal time: the cross-quarter days.

The Four Cross-Quarter Days: Festivals of the People

These were the high days. The turning posts. The hinges on which the whole year turned:

Samhain – Beginning of winter

Imbolc – First signs of spring

Bealtaine – Opening of summer

Lughnasadh – First fruits of the harvest

These festivals did not merely fall halfway between solstice and equinox; they opened tides of transformation. Samhain did not mark the midpoint between autumn and winter when winter began. Bealtaine did not balance spring and summer; it ignited the fire of summer's rise. These cross-quarters were not points between, they were thresholds unto themselves.

They divided the Irish year into its mythic halves:

Samhain and Imbolc – Belonged to the dark time, the inward spiral

Bealtaine and Lughnasadh – Belonged to the bright time, the outward flow

In these seasons, the fabric of the world thinned. Sacred time surged. Law was set aside, marriages made or broken, herds were driven, fires were lit. Kingship was tested, prophecy awakened, and the veil between this world and the next shimmered and gave way.

The cross-quarter festivals arose not from astronomy, but from agriculture, animal life, and the stories of gods and spirits. They were earthly, tribal, and embodied. The signs of their arrival were not written in stars but in hooves and roots and wind. Lambs at Imbolc. Green flame at Bealtaine. Ripe barley at Lughnasadh. Cold wind and bare trees at Samhain.

And they were Otherworldly. The sidhe stirred on these days. Ancestors drew near. Deities walked and spoke. Sacred fires were kindled not as ornament, but as shield and beacon. It was said the world turned inside out, and if you stood still long enough, you might hear your name whispered from beyond.

A Calendar of Action

The Irish year was not symmetrical. It was practical. Cross-quarter days are closer to thresholds than to mathematical divisions. The people of Ireland did not consult planetary charts, they watched their sheep, their soil, and their skies. They were not seeking perfection in angles; they were seeking readiness in the world around them.

• Imbolc – Began when ewes gave milk and the frost began to loosen its grip
• Lughnasadh – Began when grain turned gold and the first harvest could be reaped
• Samhain – Began when the final fruits were stored and the cold returned
• Bealtaine – Began when the world flushed green and cattle were driven to summer pastures

These were not dates. They were signs. And those signs were read with eyes honed by memory and muscle, by hunger and hope. The Irish Wheel is a calendar of action, not abstraction.

Modern seekers often ask, "What day is Samhain this year?" But the older wisdom asks instead, "What do you see? What do you feel in the wind?" In this way, ritual becomes responsive, fluid, and alive.

To walk the Irish Wheel is to listen with the skin. To smell the change of season in the soil. To feel the shift not only in temperature, but in tone. What does the land ask of you today? That question was more important than whether the sun stood still or the moon waxed full.

In this way, time itself becomes sacred, not in how it is measured, but in how it is noticed. Every threshold is both an invitation and a challenge. Will you cross it, or sleep through its turning?

The Folk Mindset: Time as Threshold

To the pre-Christian Irish, time did not tick forward in uniform segments, it spilled, swirled, surged, and retreated like mist on the moor or tide along the shore. Days began not at dawn, but at dusk. Months bent themselves to the rhythms of the moon. Time flowed in curves, not lines.

Festivals did not arise because the calendar told you so. They arrived like birds returning north, or the river breaking its ice. One sensed them. One prepared. One responded. Sacred time emerged, like a pattern seen only when one stepped far enough back to recognize the dance.

Cross-quarter days, then, were less about mathematical exactness and more about mythic invitation. Each one opened a door; and behind that door was a different aspect of being. Samhain, a door into death and ancestry. Bealtaine, a door into union and wild desire. Lughnasadh, a door into labor and offering. Imbolc, a door into healing and awakening.

This was not a metaphor alone. In Irish myth, thresholds were liminal spaces where fate stirred: at fords, on hilltops, in doorways. The cross-quarters mirrored these places in time. They were not pauses. They were crossings.

When we begin to think in thresholds, rather than quarters, we start to align not just our rituals, but our perception. Time becomes felt. The Wheel becomes not a symbol, but a spiral beneath the skin. And walking it with awareness, we walk into mystery, not to tame it, but to honor it.

Today's Practice

So how do we live this in a modern world filled with deadlines, clocks, and digital calendars?

Begin by rooting your practice in observation. Let the signs of your local environment shape your rituals:

Are the buds opening?

Are the animals stirring differently?

Has the scent of the wind changed?

Is there more light on your doorstep in the morning?

Trust your senses. Let them lead you into presence.

You can also return to the Irish rhythm by letting your major observances fall on the cross-quarters. Make Samhain your sacred new year. Make Imbolc your time of inward healing and blessing. Make Bealtaine your season of risk and connection. Make Lughnasadh your call to offer your strength.

Let your altar reflect this living rhythm:

Imbolc – Set white cloth and small bowls of water or milk as offerings to Brigid. Light a single white candle and place it in the window to welcome renewal and healing.

Bealtaine – Adorn your altar with fresh flowers, woven greenery, and symbols of fire. Include two red candles to represent the twin flames of purification.

Lughnasadh – Decorate with bread, grain, berries, and simple tokens of the first harvest. Lay down tools or tokens of work to honor labor and skill.

Samhain – Use black and red cloths, candles for each ancestor you wish to honor, and a plate of food set aside to feed the spirits who walk again.

Chapter 6 – Neolithic Sites and the Solar Calendar

Long before Ireland was divided into kingdoms, and long before the first myths of the Tuatha Dé Danann were whispered into sacred air, the people of this land watched the sky.

They were not astronomers in the modern sense. They had no telescopes or equations. What they had was stone, shadow, and time. From these, they carved an architecture of meaning that still stands today: Newgrange, Knowth, Loughcrew, and Carrowkeel, silent, moss-draped chambers that capture the light of solstice dawns and equinox noons with startling precision.

This chapter explores how these Neolithic structures formed the oldest expression of what would become the Irish spiritual calendar, and how we, as modern practitioners, might listen again to their ancient song.

Newgrange and the Winter Solstice

At the heart of Ireland's solar mystery is Newgrange (Brú na Bóinne), a massive passage tomb built over 5,000 years ago. Long before the pyramids, its architects aligned a narrow passageway to catch the first light of the Winter Solstice sunrise. For a few minutes each year, a shaft of sunlight pierces the roof-box, travels down the long interior corridor, and illuminates the central chamber.

This moment is more than spectacle. It is cosmic resurrection. In the cold dark of the year, light is reborn in the womb of the earth. The land itself becomes a cauldron of renewal. To witness this alignment is to stand in a temple where earth, sun, and spirit speak in light.

The structure itself was built with astonishing precision. The mound rises in an almost perfect circle, encased in quartz and granite, many of which were carried from distant regions of Ireland. The inner chamber features a corbelled roof that has remained dry for millennia. The very stones of Newgrange are carved with swirling spirals, triple curves, and sunbursts, an unspoken language, perhaps, that held cosmological meaning for those who built it.

For our ancestors, this was not symbolic. It was essential. The return of the sun marked the turning of death into life. The dead were buried here to await that return. And perhaps, in some way, to rise with it.

Newgrange was not a tomb in the modern sense, it was a portal. A place where the veil between the living and the dead, the earthly and the divine, grew thin. The solstice beam was a promise that darkness would not reign forever.

Other Sacred Alignments

Newgrange is not alone. Across the Boyne Valley and beyond, Neolithic monuments echo this astronomical intimacy:

Loughcrew cairns align with the Spring and Autumn Equinoxes, bathing their interiors in balanced light. Visitors to Cairn T during the spring equinox can see sunlight glide across carved symbols deep within the passage.

Knowth and Dowth contain multiple solar and lunar alignments, their passageways tuned to different celestial events. Knowth's art features over a third of all known megalithic carvings in Europe.

Carrowkeel, in the west, is believed to align with the setting sun at Samhain. Its chambers sit atop ridges that peer across a broad and windswept valley, sacred to both sun and spirit.

These sites suggest a people who did not merely observe the heavens, they built with it, embedding cosmology into architecture.

Their calendars were not etched on paper but carved into stone and shadow.

Unlike many modern structures, these sites were not meant to be seen from the outside alone. They were meant to be entered, to draw one into the womb of the land. The journey inward mirrored the passage through time itself, from light to darkness and back again.

The Meaning of Solar Time

In ancient Ireland, time was not abstract. It was experienced through place. The return of the sun was not a date, it was a moment felt within the land. These sacred places served as living calendars, marking the year not just in solar terms but in spiritual rhythm.

The solstices and equinoxes offered moments of cosmic stillness. The longest night. The balanced day. The sun's zenith. The Earth's inhale and exhale. These were thresholds through which one might cross into deeper understanding.

We often forget, in the world of clocks and screens, that time once meant light and shadow. It meant watching for the moment the sun slipped between two peaks, or the day the trees began to bud. The builders of these stone temples lived by these rhythms. They trusted them.

And yet, as we saw in the previous chapter, these solar points were not the high holidays in later Irish folk tradition. They remained vital undercurrents (observed in stone and spirit) but it was the cross-quarter days that shaped tribal life.

This distinction matters. It reminds us that the Irish calendar is both celestial and seasonal, both mythic and practical. One can honor the solstices without mistaking them for the heartbeat of the people's year. The stones spoke to the sun, but the people danced with the soil.

Practicing in the Modern World

What might these ancient alignments teach us today?

First, they teach patience. The builders of Newgrange waited all year for a single beam of light. This was a spirituality of long attention, of stillness and alignment. Can we, too, learn to slow down? To watch? To wait for the light, not summon it?

Second, they teach us embodied time. The solstice is not a moment on a clock, it is a felt event. We can mark it by sitting in silence before dawn. Lighting a single flame. Standing beneath a cold sky with our feet in the frost.

Third, they teach us humility. We do not control the sun. We do not direct the wheel. But we can participate in it, build our shrines to it, and open our hearts as the light returns.

Create personal observances that reflect this reverence:

Build a solar shrine that faces east. Choose a location in your home, garden, or sacred space where the rising sun can be seen or symbolically welcomed. Incorporate traditional Irish symbols such as spirals, triskele designs, or sun motifs etched in stone, wood, or cloth. Allow the changing light to interact with these elements as a way of marking the turning seasons.

Light a candle at dawn. On the solstice, offer a prayer of renewal as the day begins. Use a handmade or beeswax candle if possible, and consider facing east while speaking your intention.

Observe light in nature. Spend time in a quiet place outdoors. Watch how light falls on trees, stones, and water throughout the day, and reflect on how this rhythm shapes your own spirit. Journal or sketch what you see to deepen awareness.

Over time, these practices become sacraments of rhythm. Not reenactments, but revelations.

Sacred Sites in the Diaspora

Not everyone can visit Newgrange. But we can build mirrors of intention. Create small altars that face the rising or setting sun. Align our home shrines with the cardinal points. Mark the solstices and equinoxes with fire and stillness.

We can also seek virtual pilgrimages: high-quality documentaries, drone footage of Irish tombs, or sunrise livestreams from the Office of Public Works. We can bring Ireland into our homes with reverence.

Here are some accessible tools:

The OPW's annual livestream – Watch the Winter Solstice sunrise at Newgrange as it happens, streamed live by the Irish Office of Public Works.

Documentaries – Secrets of the Stones and Ireland's Ancient East are both available on YouTube and RTÉ's digital archives. The former delves into archaeological interpretations of sacred Irish sites, while the latter offers a broader cultural and mythological context. These are excellent visual primers for spiritual deepening.

Virtual museum exhibits – Explore online collections of megalithic art and Neolithic artifacts through institutions like the National Museum of Ireland or international platforms such as Google Arts & Culture.

And if you live near megalithic sites in the U.S. or elsewhere (stone circles, medicine wheels, earthworks) learn their story. Honor the land beneath your feet. Practice your Irish calendar, but honor your current soil.

Include in your ritual journal a section for Seasonal Light Observations. Sketch how the sun rises in different months. Note how your body responds to changing daylight. Mark when birds return, when shadows lengthen, when your soul quiets.

Closing Reflection

The Neolithic sites of Ireland whisper an ancient truth: that time is sacred when lived in alignment with light and land. The solar calendar was not just about dates. It was about presence. Awareness. Gratitude.

To sit at Newgrange in the cold wind of December and watch the rising sun reach into stone is to remember what we are made of: earth, bone, breath, and light. It is to remember that long before gods had names, the land itself was holy.

By remembering this, we bring our practice into deeper resonance. We step into the rhythm of ancestors who built with stone, who waited for the sun, and who understood that every threshold begins in shadow, but ends in light.

We need not live in ancient times to be ancient in spirit. Every dawn is a solstice waiting to be honored. Every room can become a chamber of renewal. And every step into the light can be made sacred, if we choose to walk it with care.

Chapter 7a: The Major Deities of the Irish Wheel

The Wheel of the Year in Irish paganism is not merely a calendar of solar and seasonal observances; it is also a sacred choreography of deities whose presences rise and shift with the rhythms of the land. While many modern practitioners associate gods and goddesses with particular festivals or times of year, Irish cosmology is complex, poetic, and interwoven. Rather than assigning a single god to a single day, it is often more accurate to explore how each deity's influence emerges, recedes, or transforms across the turning of the seasons.

This chapter is a guide to the major deities most often invoked in Irish Pagan practice today, especially within the context of the eightfold Wheel. Each section explores a deity's mythic role, seasonal resonance, spiritual function, and guidance for honoring them in a modern context.

We begin not at a particular point on the Wheel, but at its center, with Danu, the mother of waters and origin of the Tuatha Dé Danann, from whom all flows. Around her orbit the fierce and shadowed Mórrígan, the healing and light-bearing Brigid, the kingly Dagda, the solar Lugh, the liminal Manannán mac Lir, the craftsman Goibniu, the guardian Ogma, and others who keep the balance of dark and light.

These are not distant mythological figures. They are presences that still speak, in wind, crow, flame, song, mist, memory, and bone. As you turn the wheel, their voices may change, but they are always there.

Danu – The Great Mother

Danu is the wellspring from which all divine essence flows in Irish tradition. Though she is one of the most ancient and least descriptively documented deities in the surviving texts, her presence is foundational. The Tuatha Dé Danann (the People of the Goddess Danu) carry her name as a birthright. She is not only the mother of gods but the animating force of the land, the rivers, and the unseen wisdom woven through all things.

Often associated with water, rivers, and fertile earth, Danu is a sovereign force without spectacle. She does not roar or rage. Instead, she endures. In her presence, we find the deep-rooted stillness of the earth before planting, the quiet womb of winter, the source that gives without seeking praise.

Seasonal Resonance: Danu can be honored at any point on the Wheel, but she is especially potent during the quiet times. Winter Solstice, Imbolc, and early morning rituals in spring. She represents origin, patience, gestation, and ancestral memory. She is the space before the seed, the soil that remembers the last harvest, the waters that run beneath frozen land.

Spiritual Role: Danu embodies sovereignty, not in rule, but in presence. She reminds us to return to what is essential, to sit with what is unsaid, and to trust what is growing out of sight. She is the voice in the stillness, the source beneath the surface, and the breath before the first word. Those who work closely with her often describe a sense of quiet clarity, a pulling back from distraction to stand in grounded power.

Honoring Danu Today:

Mythological Depth:

Danu's name echoes through the mists of Irish tradition as the ancestral mother from whom the Tuatha Dé Danann take their name. Though her stories are fragmentary, her presence is undeniable. She is the river and the rain, the well and the womb. In some traditions, she is linked to the Danube River, suggesting migrations and ancient memory carried through water and blood. She is not a goddess who demands center stage in myth, but rather one whose presence underlies all the others. Without Danu, there would be no divine family, no gods at all.

In the earliest layers of Irish tradition, Danu may be connected to Anu, another primordial mother figure whose name survives in the landscape itself: the Paps of Anu (Dá Chích Anann) in County Kerry, two breast-shaped hills that speak to the nourishing, life-giving aspect of the divine feminine. Whether Danu and Anu are the same goddess or sister aspects of one force is a question each practitioner must answer for themselves through study and experience.

Seasonal Associations:

Danu's energy flows through the entire Wheel but manifests most powerfully during Imbolc and the Spring Equinox, when the earth's creative potential begins to stir. She is present in the first snowmelt that feeds the streams, in the greening of fields, in the quiet fertility of seeds still underground. At Beltane, her presence is felt in the union of land and sky, the marriage that brings forth life. During the harvest festivals, she is the sustaining abundance, the fullness of what was planted returning to nourish her children.

Winter is not Danu's absence but her rest, her retreat into the deep waters beneath the earth, where she renews herself for the coming spring. Work with Danu in winter through stillness and dreaming, through honoring the hidden sources of life that sustain us when the surface world seems barren.

Offerings and Altar Practices:

Create a Danu altar with a central bowl of water, preferably from a natural source: a stream, river, spring, or collected rainwater. Surround it with river stones, shells, or crystals associated with water (aquamarine, moonstone, pearl). Offerings to Danu include milk or cream poured onto the earth, wildflowers floated in water, poems or songs offered aloud, and acts of nurturing toward others or yourself.

On the first day of each month, refresh the water in your Danu bowl and speak a prayer of gratitude for the sources that sustain you. This simple practice deepens your relationship with her over time. If you have access to a sacred well or spring, visit it seasonally and leave offerings of silver coins, white stones, or ribbons tied to nearby branches.

Devotional Prayer to Danu:

"Danu, mother of waters, mother of gods, You who flow through all things, From the depths of the earth to the rain that falls, I honor your presence in my life. Teach me the way of the source, The patience of the well, The generosity of the river. May I offer as you offer, May I sustain as you sustain, May I remember that all things return to the mother. Danu, I honor you."

Personal Gnosis and Relationship Building:

Developing a relationship with Danu requires patience and receptivity. She is not a goddess who appears in dramatic visions or speaks with thunder. Her voice is the whisper of water over stone, the gentle insistence of growth, the knowing that comes from deep within. Begin by simply sitting with water—a bowl, a stream, the ocean if you can reach it. Watch it. Listen to it. Let your mind soften and your heart open.

Keep a journal dedicated to your work with Danu. Record dreams, synchronicities, and moments when you feel her presence. Notice patterns in how she appears to you. Some practitioners experience her as a grandmother figure, wise and warm. Others feel her as pure elemental force, vast and impersonal yet deeply nourishing. There is no wrong way to know her, only your way.

Acts of service to water are acts of devotion to Danu. Clean a local stream. Conserve water in your daily life. Support organizations that protect watersheds and aquifers. Danu teaches that devotion is not separate from action, and that caring for the physical world is a form of prayer.

Water offerings: Pour fresh or spring water onto the earth with a whispered thanks.

River walks: Leave small, biodegradable gifts at a stream or riverbank.

Ancestor candles: Light a single candle in a darkened room while meditating on the lineage you carry and the land you live on.

Gardening or composting: Engage in acts of nurturing the land; especially those that involve restoration and replenishment rather than immediate reward.

Danu asks little and offers much. In her presence, you are not asked to prove, only to be. In honoring her, you step into rhythm with something older than stories, something living in root, tide, and stone.

The Mórrígan – Sovereignty, Shadow, and Prophecy

The Mórrígan is one of the most enigmatic and multifaceted figures in Irish mythology. She is not a single, easily defined goddess, but a force composed of aspects: sometimes appearing as a trio, sometimes alone, always bearing the mantle of prophecy, transformation, and the sovereignty of land and spirit. She is the

crow on the battlefield, the washer at the ford, the veiled woman at
the edge of knowing.

She is a goddess of war, yes; but not in the simplistic sense
of violence. The Mórrígan governs the cycles of death and rebirth,
the sacred right to rule, and the revelation of uncomfortable truths.
Her presence is unsettling because it is honest. She sees the rot
beneath the bloom, the cost beneath the crown.

Seasonal Resonance: The Mórrígan walks closest at Samhain
and during the waning times of the year, late autumn into winter.
Yet she also rises in times of decision, thresholds, and
transformation. She is not bound to one season but is strongest
when change is near.

Spiritual Role: She is the challenger, the prophetess, the
sovereign queen who asks if you are truly prepared for what you seek.
Working with the Mórrígan is not about comfort, it is about
awakening. She reveals what is hidden, demands authenticity, and
offers protection through fierce clarity. Her crows are not merely
omens, they are guides.

Honoring the Mórrígan Today:

Mythological Depth:

The Mórrígan's presence in Irish mythology is both
formidable and complex. She is often described as a triple
goddess—Badb, Macha, and Nemain—though whether these are
separate entities or aspects of one being remains a matter of
interpretation. She appears throughout the Ulster Cycle and the
Mythological Cycle, most famously in her encounters with Cú
Chulainn, where she offers him her favor and, when spurned,
becomes his adversary.

Her most iconic appearance comes before the Second Battle
of Mag Tuired, where she mates with the Dagda on the feast of
Samhain, straddling the River Unius. This union is not romantic but

ritualistic, a sacred marriage that ensures victory for the Tuatha Dé Danann. After the battle, it is the Mórrígan who proclaims the victory and, in some versions, prophesies the end of the world in a dark and haunting poem that speaks of chaos, betrayal, and the unraveling of order.

The Mórrígan is deeply connected to the land itself, to sovereignty, and to the rightful kingship. She appears as a washer at the ford, cleaning the armor and weapons of those destined to die in battle. She is the crow or raven on the battlefield, circling above the fallen. She is prophecy and doom, but also transformation and terrible freedom. To work with the Mórrígan is to accept that some things must die for others to live, that darkness is not evil but necessary, and that sovereignty—over land, over self—is earned, not given.

Seasonal Associations:

The Mórrígan's power peaks at Samhain, the threshold when the veil between worlds thins and the dead walk close to the living. This is her time, when prophecy and shadow work are strongest. She is also present at the Autumn Equinox, when the balance tips toward darkness, and at Imbolc, when transformation begins beneath the surface. Work with her during liminal times: dusk and dawn, crossroads, thresholds, and moments of personal or collective transition.

In battle or conflict—whether physical, emotional, or spiritual—the Mórrígan walks with those who face hard truths. She does not promise comfort, but she promises honesty. She is the goddess of sovereignty, and sovereignty requires clear seeing, even when what you see is difficult.

Offerings and Altar Practices:

The Mórrígan's altar should reflect her fierce and liminal nature. Use black, red, and deep purple cloths. Include crow or raven feathers (ethically sourced), bones, dark stones like obsidian or black tourmaline, and representations of weapons (a knife, an athame, or even a symbolic blade drawn on paper). Offerings to the Mórrígan include red wine or dark beer, raw meat left for wild animals, blood from your own moon cycle (if appropriate for you), and poems or songs that honor death, transformation, and sovereignty.

One traditional offering is to visit a river or stream at twilight and wash something symbolic of what you need to release—a stone representing old fears, a piece of fabric from a difficult chapter of your life. Speak to her as you wash it, asking her to witness your release and your transformation.

Devotional Prayer to the Mórrígan:

"Mórrígan, great queen, phantom queen, You who know the price of sovereignty, You who stand at the ford and see what comes, I call to you with respect and with clarity. Teach me to face what I must face, To release what I must release, To claim what is rightfully mine. You who are crow and prophecy, Battle and transformation, I honor your fierce and necessary work. Mórrígan, I see you."

Personal Gnosis and Relationship Building:

The Mórrígan is not a goddess for the faint of heart, but neither is she cruel or capricious. She demands honesty, courage, and a willingness to do your own inner work. Many practitioners report that working with the Mórrígan feels like having a fierce and demanding teacher who will not accept excuses but who also will not abandon you when the work gets hard.

Begin by studying her myths carefully. Read the source material, not just modern interpretations. Notice how she operates in the stories: what she values, what she punishes, what she rewards. Approach her with respect but not with fear. She responds well to those who meet her eye and speak plainly.

Shadow work is central to relationship with the Mórrígan. Journal on your own darkness, your rage, your fears, the parts of yourself you've been taught to hide or suppress. She will not judge these parts; she will help you understand and integrate them. Divination, particularly with ogham or tarot, can be a powerful tool for receiving her guidance. Pay attention to crows and ravens in your life; their appearance is often meaningful when you're working with her.

Offerings of blackberries, red wine, or iron: Left at crossroads or thresholds.

Divination and truth-seeking: Especially through dreams, scrying, or omen reading.

Shadow work: Journaling or meditations that face internal fears, truths, and unresolved conflicts.

Acts of courage: Standing up for justice, speaking difficult truths, or protecting others in need.

To honor the Mórrígan is to relinquish illusions. She grants clarity, not ease. But those who walk with her often find their path straightened by fire and sharpened by flight. She does not merely watch the Wheel turn, she ensures it turns with purpose.

Brigid – Flame of Healing and Inspiration

Brigid, daughter of the Dagda, is among the most beloved and widely venerated of the Irish deities. She is the bright flame of poetry, healing, and smithcraft, and her legacy echoes from ancient pagan Ireland through her transformation into Saint Brigid in Christian tradition. Where Danu is the deep well, Brigid is the rising fire, the spark that illuminates, warms, and transforms.

She is a goddess of thresholds, associated with both birth and renewal, and her sacred fires were kept by nineteen priestesses at Kildare. Brigid bridges worlds: between the dark of winter and the first stirrings of spring, between inspiration and action, and between tradition and new creation.

Seasonal Resonance: Brigid's presence is most deeply felt at Imbolc, the festival that marks the first stirrings of spring. Yet her flame is also kept through long winters, offering hope and vision. In any time of healing, learning, or creative birth, she is near.

Spiritual Role: Brigid embodies three sacred functions: the poet, the healer, and the smith. As poet, she brings vision and articulation. As healer, she mends not only body but spirit. As smith, she tempers raw material into form. She guides the process of becoming, gently, powerfully, and always toward growth.

Honoring Brigid Today:

Tending a flame: Light a candle each morning at your hearth or altar with a prayer for inspiration, healing, or strength.

Sacred wells and waters: Visit springs or holy wells, or keep a blessed bowl of water on your altar. Whisper prayers into it.

Creative work: Dedicate time to writing, crafting, or making something new in her name.

Healing rituals: Offer herbs, salves, or even kind words to those in need. Brigid honors both intention and action.

Mythological Depth:

Brigid's mythology is unique among Irish deities in that her worship continued relatively unbroken through the Christianization of Ireland, transforming her from pagan goddess to beloved saint. This continuity speaks to the depth of devotion she inspired and continues to inspire. As daughter of the Dagda, she stands among the Tuatha Dé Danann as a figure of illumination and transformation.

In the ancient world, Brigid's sacred fire at Kildare was tended by nineteen priestesses, never allowed to extinguish. This practice continued under the Christian Saint Brigid, whose monastery at Kildare maintained the eternal flame for centuries. The fire represents not just physical warmth but the spark of inspiration, the heat that tempers metal, and the light that drives back ignorance and illness.

Brigid is associated with holy wells throughout Ireland, particularly those that heal eye ailments and bring fertility. Water and fire, seemingly opposite elements, unite in her. She is the forge's flame that shapes the blade, but also the cool water that tempers it. She is the poet's sudden insight, but also the patient craft that gives it form. She is the midwife's steady hand and the mother's fierce protection of new life.

Seasonal Associations:

Brigid's primary festival is Imbolc (February 1-2), marking the first stirrings of spring and the lactation of ewes. This is when her presence is most powerfully felt, when we celebrate the light's return and the promise of growth to come. But Brigid's flame burns year-round. Work with her at Beltane for fertility and creative projects, at Lughnasadh for the harvest of artistic work, and throughout winter as the maintained flame that keeps hope alive in darkness.

The spring months are ideal for invoking Brigid's healing aspect. The summer months call on her smith and craftsperson energy for manifesting projects. Autumn is the time to honor her as the poet who helps us name what we've learned. Winter reminds us that Brigid's flame endures even in the darkest nights, and that tending it is holy work.

Offerings and Altar Practices:

Brigid's altar thrives with living flame. Keep a candle burning as often as practical—a tea light, a seven-day candle, or a dedicated oil lamp. Surround it with symbols of her three aspects: a pen or quill for poetry and inspiration, healing herbs (especially dandelion, blackberry, and mugwort) for her healer aspect, and a small hammer, nail, or piece of iron for her smith nature.

Traditional offerings include milk, butter, fresh bread, poetry read aloud, and creative work made in her honor. Many practitioners create Brigid's crosses from rushes or wheat at Imbolc, hanging them above doors for protection and blessing. Fresh flowers, especially white or yellow blooms, please her throughout the year.

Consider keeping a Brigid jar or box where you place requests for healing, inspiration, or creative breakthrough. Write them on paper and place them near her flame. When the situation resolves or the inspiration comes, burn the paper in thanksgiving.

Devotional Prayer to Brigid:

"Brigid of the sacred flame, Brigid of the healing well, Brigid of the poet's tongue and the smith's sure hand, I call to you across the threshold. Light my way when darkness gathers, Heal what hurts within and without, Temper me as you temper metal— Through fire and water, make me whole. Brigid, keeper of the flame, I honor you and tend your light. May inspiration find me, May healing flow through me, May my work be true and strong. Brigid, I honor you."

Personal Gnosis and Relationship Building:

Brigid is one of the most accessible and responsive of the Irish deities. Many practitioners report feeling her presence as warm, encouraging, and patient. She is a goddess who meets you where you are and helps you grow from there. Begin working with Brigid by lighting a candle each day and speaking to her honestly about your struggles, your hopes, your creative blocks, or your need for healing.

Keep a Brigid journal dedicated to creative work, healing processes, or inspirational insights. Date each entry and review it seasonally to see how her influence manifests in your life over time. If you write, paint, craft, or work with your hands in any way, dedicate that work to Brigid. She honors all forms of making and creating.

Visit holy wells if you can, or create your own sacred water practice. Collect water from a meaningful source and bless it in Brigid's name, using it for healing, inspiration, or house blessings. Pay attention to fire in your environment—candle flames, hearth fires, even the pilot light on your stove. Brigid lives in these flames, and tending them mindfully is a form of devotion.

The Dagda – Keeper of the Cauldron

The Dagda is the great chieftain of the Tuatha Dé Danann, a god of strength, abundance, fertility, and deep, earthy wisdom. Known as the "Good God" (not because of morality, but because he is good at all things), the Dagda carries a great club that kills with one end and revives with the other, a cauldron that never runs empty, and a harp that can change the seasons with its music.

He is a god of paradox: fierce in battle, jovial in feast, lusty and wise, profound yet playful. The Dagda represents the deep knowledge of the land and the balance between discipline and joy. He is the nourishing father, the working druid, the laughing sage. Through him, the sacredness of food, sex, labor, music, and sovereignty is revealed.

Seasonal Resonance: The Dagda's presence is especially strong at Lughnasadh, the first harvest, and at the Winter Solstice, when abundance is remembered in the heart of scarcity. His cauldron and harp are symbols of both nourishment and magical transformation, perfect for liminal moments.

Spiritual Role: The Dagda teaches the sacredness of fullness, of enough. He reminds us that delight, nourishment, and laughter are not distractions from the path but essential rites of being alive. He is both worker and king, god and farmer. He asks you not to fast in his name, but to feast in gratitude.

Honoring the Dagda Today:

Prepare a sacred meal: Particularly one shared in community or enjoyed in silence with reverence.

Mythological Depth:

The Dagda, "the Good God" (good at everything, not morally good), is the great father figure of the Tuatha Dé Danann, a deity of immense power, abundance, and earthy wisdom. His name literally means "the good hand," suggesting his role as provider and protector. He carries two primary symbols: the great club that can kill with one end and revive with the other, and the cauldron of plenty (Coire Ansic) from which no one ever leaves unsatisfied.

The Dagda's mythology presents him as both mighty and approachable, powerful yet sometimes comical. Before the Second Battle of Mag Tuired, he is forced by the Fomorians to eat an enormous meal of porridge from a pit, eating until his belly is grotesquely distended. Yet even in this humiliation, he maintains his humor and his dignity. Later, he mates with the Mórrígan at Samhain, a sacred union that secures victory for his people.

The Dagda also possesses a magical harp, Uaithne, which can play three strains: the grief-strain that makes all who hear it weep, the joy-strain that brings laughter, and the sleep-strain that brings peace. When stolen by the Fomorians, the Dagda calls it back to his hand, and it kills nine men as it flies to him. This harp represents the Dagda's mastery over emotion, music, and the power of sound to shape reality.

Seasonal Associations:

The Dagda's presence is felt most strongly at Samhain, when he mates with the Mórrígan, and at the Winter Solstice, when his cauldron represents the promise that abundance will return even in the darkest time. His energy is also powerful at Lughnasadh, the harvest festival, when the fruits of the year's labor fill the cauldron of community. Work with the Dagda when you need grounding, abundance, protection, or the wisdom to nourish yourself and others.

The Dagda's aspect as father and provider makes him particularly accessible during times of scarcity or fear. He reminds us that the cauldron is never truly empty if we maintain faith in the cycle, care for our community, and share what we have. His club teaches that protection and nurturing are not opposites—sometimes the fiercest love is the willingness to defend what matters.

Offerings and Altar Practices:

The Dagda's altar should reflect abundance and earthiness. Use a large bowl or pot to represent his cauldron, filled with seasonal offerings: grains, fruits, nuts, or coins. Include a staff or walking stick to represent his club, and any musical instrument to honor his harp. Earth-toned cloths in brown, green, or gold suit him well.

Traditional offerings to the Dagda include generous portions of food and drink—he appreciates abundance and sharing. Porridge or oatmeal is particularly appropriate given his mythological feast. Beer, mead, or whiskey are welcome libations. Music played in his honor, especially harp or drum, pleases him greatly. Acts of generosity toward others, especially feeding the hungry or sharing resources, are among the highest offerings you can make to the Dagda.

Create a Dagda practice of filling a bowl on your altar at each new moon with coins, dried goods, or other symbols of abundance, then at the full moon, donate or share these items with your community. This practice embodies his principle that the cauldron fills by being emptied, that generosity creates abundance rather than depleting it.

Devotional Prayer to the Dagda:

"Dagda, good hand, generous father, Keeper of the cauldron that never empties, Wielder of the club that protects and renews,

Master of the harp that shapes emotion, I call to you with gratitude and respect. Teach me your wisdom of abundance, Your knowing that there is always enough, Your courage to protect what matters, Your joy in sharing what you have. Dagda, fill my cauldron as you fill your own— Not with hoarded wealth but with generosity, Not with fear but with faith in the cycle. Dagda, good god, I honor you."

Personal Gnosis and Relationship Building:

The Dagda is often experienced as a warm, paternal presence—not stern or distant but grounded, protective, and good-humored. Working with him can feel like having a wise grandfather who teaches through stories, laughter, and practical demonstrations rather than lectures. Begin by offering him food and drink regularly, speaking to him as you would a beloved elder.

Practice generosity as a form of devotion to the Dagda. Share meals with friends and strangers. Donate to food banks. Cook for others with love and care. The Dagda teaches that the spiritual and the practical are one, that feeding bodies is sacred work, and that community is built around the shared table.

Study music and sound as magical practice. Learn an instrument if you can, or simply spend time listening deeply to music that moves you emotionally. Notice how different melodies shift your inner state—this is the magic of the Dagda's harp. Use sound in your rituals and daily practice, whether singing, chanting, drumming, or playing recorded music that calls to the divine.

Offer porridge, ale, or bread: Left outside with gratitude and a whispered blessing.

Play music: Especially harp, drum, or voice, music that stirs emotion or moves the air.

Physical work as devotion: Gardening, carpentry, brewing, or any skilled labor done with joy and presence.

To walk with the Dagda is to embrace wholeness. He does not ask for perfection, but for sincerity. He is the god of the feast who blesses the field, the father who laughs and labors, and the guardian who feeds the soul as much as the body.

Lugh – Master of Skills and Light

Lugh, often called Lugh Lámfada (Lugh of the Long Arm), is the many-skilled god of light, craft, justice, and leadership. His arrival among the Tuatha Dé Danann marked a turning point in Irish mythology, not just because of his talents, but because of his character, focused, bright, strategic, and honorable. No single domain defines him, because Lugh excels in all of them: arts, battle, craftsmanship, law, and diplomacy. He represents the excellence that comes from dedication, adaptability, and integrity.

Lugh is associated with Lughnasadh, the first harvest festival, which he founded to honor his foster-mother Tailtiu. This connection marks him as a god who respects both tradition and transition. While his solar imagery is obvious, Lugh's light is not merely that of the sun; it is the brilliance of the mind and the clarity of righteous action.

Seasonal Resonance: Most strongly honored at Lughnasadh (August 1st), Lugh also appears at any time when wisdom, skill, and decisive leadership are needed. His light carries forward from summer and becomes a guidepost for the darker seasons.

Spiritual Role: Lugh embodies mastery through humility. He does not boast without purpose. His presence in one's spiritual life often heralds a time of stepping into one's full potential, especially after a period of preparation or doubt. He blesses action backed by intention and honors those who sharpen their gifts for the benefit of others.

Honoring Lugh Today:

Practice a skill: Dedicate time to honing a craft, whether physical, artistic, or intellectual.

Mythological Depth:

Lugh Lámhfada ("Lugh of the Long Arm") is the shining master of all skills, the polytechnic god whose arrival at Tara changed everything. In the tale of his entry to the court of the Tuatha Dé Danann, Lugh approaches the gates and is asked what skill he offers. "I am a carpenter," he says. "We have one," comes the reply. "I am a smith." "We have one." "I am a champion, a poet, a harper, a hero, a sorcerer, a physician, a cupbearer, a brazier." To each, the same response. Finally, Lugh asks: "Do you have one who is all of these?" Silence. The gates open.

Lugh is the solar deity, associated with light, skill, and sovereignty. He is both the brilliant youth and the accomplished master, embodying potential fulfilled through dedicated practice. His most famous achievement is slaying his grandfather Balor of the Evil Eye at the Second Battle of Mag Tuired, casting a stone that drives Balor's poisonous eye back through his head to destroy the Fomorian army behind him. This act represents the triumph of skill and precision over brute force and tyranny.

Lugh's foster mother Tailtiu died clearing the plains of Ireland for agriculture, and Lughnasadh (the festival of Lugh) honors both her sacrifice and the harvest her work made possible. This connection reminds us that skill and mastery are not abstract; they serve community, they honor those who came before, and they ensure survival and abundance for all.

Seasonal Associations:

Lugh's primary festival is Lughnasadh (August 1), the first harvest and the games held in Tailtiu's honor. But Lugh's energy is present throughout summer, from Beltane through the Autumn

Equinox, when light dominates and growth reaches its peak. Work with Lugh when learning new skills, competing or performing, seeking excellence in your craft, or needing the focused energy of sunlight to illuminate your path.

The summer months are ideal for Lugh-work: taking classes, practicing intensively, preparing for competitions or presentations. His energy supports both athletic and intellectual pursuits, artistic expression, and the mastery of tools and techniques. As the light begins to wane after Lughnasadh, Lugh reminds us to harvest what we've learned and share those skills with our communities.

Offerings and Altar Practices:

Lugh's altar should reflect mastery and excellence. Include tools of your trade or craft—musical instruments, writing implements, athletic equipment, art supplies, culinary tools. Use gold, yellow, and orange colors to represent his solar aspect. Symbols of competition and achievement (medals, ribbons, certificates) honor his drive for excellence. Fresh grain, especially wheat or barley, connects to Lughnasadh.

Traditional offerings to Lugh include the first fruits of harvest, particularly bread made from new grain. Athletic competitions, games, and demonstrations of skill performed in his honor are among the highest offerings. Creating or improving something—writing a song, crafting an object, perfecting a technique—and dedicating that work to Lugh is deeply appropriate. He appreciates dedication, practice, and the willingness to challenge yourself.

Consider creating a Lugh skill journal where you track your progress in whatever you're mastering. Review it at Lughnasadh each year to see how far you've come. This practice embodies Lugh's principle that excellence is built through sustained, conscious effort over time.

Devotional Prayer to Lugh:

"Lugh of the Long Arm, master of all skills, Shining one, polytechnic god, You who proved that excellence has no limits, You who showed that mastery serves community, I call to you with respect and aspiration. Teach me the discipline of practice, The humility of the student, The confidence of the master, The generosity of sharing what I know. Lugh, samildánach, skilled in all arts, Guide my hand and sharpen my mind. May my work be worthy of your example, May my skills serve those I love, May excellence and service walk hand in hand. Lugh, I honor you."

Personal Gnosis and Relationship Building:

Lugh is often experienced as bright, energizing, and demanding in the best sense—he will push you to be better, to not settle, to recognize your potential and pursue it. Working with Lugh requires commitment to growth and a willingness to put in the hours of practice that mastery requires. Begin by choosing one skill or art form to dedicate to Lugh and practice it regularly, consciously improving over time.

Study Lugh's myths carefully, particularly his entry to Tara and his role in the Battle of Mag Tuired. Notice how he combines many skills rather than specializing in one. This is Lugh's gift: the understanding that true mastery often comes from integrating different disciplines rather than narrowing focus. A musician who understands poetry becomes a better songwriter. A writer who learns craft becomes a more skilled storyteller.

Pay attention to moments of clarity, focused attention, and the flow state where time disappears and your work flows effortlessly. This is Lugh's presence. Offer him your best efforts, your willingness to fail and try again, your dedication to improvement. He honors the journey toward mastery as much as the achievement itself.

Share knowledge: Teach what you know, or mentor someone. Wisdom grows when shared.

Offer corn, honey, or woven grain art: These symbolize the harvest of skill and effort.

Hold a ritual competition or showcase: Celebrating communal creativity and strength.

Lugh's light does not demand perfection, it asks for pursuit. To honor him is to rise to the challenge of your own excellence, and to do so in a way that uplifts your community as well as yourself.

Chapter 7b: Land Spirits and Tutelary Deities

Manannán mac Lir – Guardian of the Mists and Thresholds

Manannán mac Lir is the sea-god of the Tuatha Dé Danann, a liminal deity of mystery, protection, and deep magic. He is a psychopomp and a guardian of the borders between worlds, land and sea, life and death, mortal and Otherworld. Cloaked in mists and traveling by wave or horse, Manannán appears when the veil is thinnest or when great transitions are underway.

He is a keeper of sacred knowledge, a trickster, and a generous guide. His gifts are hidden until earned, and his aid is subtle but transformative. In many myths, Manannán offers tools of great power (such as the Crane Bag, filled with sacred treasures) or tests mortals on the edges of their fate.

Seasonal Resonance: Manannán is invoked during Samhain and Summer Solstice, the two great thresholds of descent and ascent. He is also honored during foggy mornings, stormy crossings, and any time of spiritual passage.

Spiritual Role: As a liminal god, Manannán governs journeys of soul, identity, and trust. He appears in dreams, in questions, and in the places where certainty dissolves. He asks for courage not through strength, but through surrender. His presence often precedes a major shift in consciousness.

Honoring Manannán Today:

Visit shorelines, lakes, or rivers: Speak prayers into the wind or the waves.

Mythological Depth:

Manannán mac Lir, son of the sea (Lir), is the psychopomp and guardian of thresholds, the god who rides the waves between worlds. He is lord of the blessed isles in the west where the Tuatha Dé Danann retreated after the coming of the Milesians. He wears a cloak of mists that makes him invisible, rides a horse named Enbarr that can travel over land or sea, and wields the sword Fragarach ("The Answerer") that cuts through any shield and compels truthful answers.

In mythology, Manannán is both guide and trickster, helper and challenger. He appears to mortals at crucial transitions, offering passage to the Otherworld or testing their worthiness. He is associated with magic, illusion, and the art of transformation. His cauldron of regeneration was among the treasures of the Tuatha Dé Danann, and his pigs provided an endless feast that could be eaten one day and restored the next.

Manannán's realm is Tír Tairngire (the Land of Promise) and Mag Mell (the Pleasant Plain), paradisiacal realms beyond the western sea. He is both the journey and the destination, the fog that obscures the path and the light that occasionally breaks through. To work with Manannán is to accept uncertainty, to trust in the process of becoming, and to surrender to the mystery of transformation.

Seasonal Associations:

Manannán's presence is strongest during times of transition: the equinoxes, dawn and dusk, the turning of tides. Work with him at Samhain when the veil thins, at Imbolc when transformation stirs beneath the surface, and during any personal threshold or major life change. He is the deity of voyages, emigration, spiritual journeys, and the space between one state of being and another.

The autumn months, when mists rise from the land and the veil between worlds grows thin, are particularly sacred to Manannán. So too are stormy times, both literal and metaphorical, when the sea reminds us of its power and mystery. Work with Manannán when you need to navigate uncertainty, when you're crossing thresholds, or when you're ready to surrender to transformation even when you can't see where it leads.

Offerings and Altar Practices:

Manannán's altar thrives on liminal imagery. Use fabrics in sea colors: blues, greens, silver, and gray. Include shells, driftwood, sea glass, and vessels of salt water or ocean water if you can collect it. Representations of horses, ships, or waves honor his connection to travel and the sea. Symbols of fog, mist, or clouds acknowledge his cloak of invisibility.

Traditional offerings include coins cast into water (rivers, lakes, or the ocean), libations of mead or whiskey poured into waves or moving water, and objects given to the sea—biodegradable items that will dissolve and return to the water. Music played by the shore, particularly harp or flute, pleases him. Stories told of journeys and transformations honor his role as guide.

Create a practice of visiting water regularly when working with Manannán—weekly if possible. Stand at the shore, beside a river, or even by a flowing fountain. Speak to him honestly about where you are, where you're going, and what you need to navigate the journey. Leave an offering of coins or flowers, and pay attention to any insights or feelings that arise.

Devotional Prayer to Manannán:

"Manannán mac Lir, lord of the western sea, Guardian of thresholds, keeper of the veil, You who guide souls between the worlds, You who ride the waves and walk in mist, I call to you from the shore of the unknown. Teach me to trust the journey, To navigate by stars I cannot always see, To find solid ground even when the fog is thick, To transform as water transforms, endlessly. Manannán, guide and guardian, I stand at the threshold and ask for your blessing. May my journey be true though the path be hidden, May I reach the shore I'm meant to find, May I trust the tides that carry me. Manannán, I honor you."

Personal Gnosis and Relationship Building:

Manannán is experienced by many practitioners as mysterious, playful, and sometimes challenging. He does not always answer directly, and his guidance may come through synchronicity, dreams, or unexpected encounters. Working with Manannán requires comfort with ambiguity and a willingness to trust the process even when you can't see the outcome.

Begin by spending time near water in a contemplative state. Watch how it moves, how it reflects light, how it changes yet remains itself. This is Manannán's nature: constant transformation that is also constant essence. Keep a dream journal when working with him, as he often speaks through the dreamworld where the veil is naturally thin.

Study tales of the Otherworld voyages (immrama) in Irish mythology—these are Manannán's domain. Notice how journeys in these stories transform the travelers, how they return changed even when they return home. Practice divination, particularly methods connected to water like hydromancy (scrying in water) or reading patterns in waves and tides. Trust your intuition deeply when working with Manannán; he teaches that not all knowing comes through the rational mind.

Craft offerings of seaweed, shells, or water: Return them to the tide or place them on your altar.

Engage with divination or dreamwork: Seek symbolic guidance and record what arises.

Mark personal thresholds: New roles, initiations, farewells; invite Manannán's guidance.

To walk with Manannán is to walk into mist, not blind, but trusting. He teaches that transformation is never linear, that wisdom hides in uncertainty, and that the Otherworld is never far. When you honor him, you honor the path between them, and the courage it takes to cross it.

Goibniu – Smith of Immortality and Craft

Goibniu is the divine smith of the Tuatha Dé Danann, renowned not only for his skill in metalwork but for his role in crafting the magical tools of the gods and brewing the ale of immortality. He is one of a trio of artisan gods, along with Credne and Luchta, responsible for forging the sacred weapons used in the battle against the Fomorians. Goibniu's presence represents sacred craft, durability, and transformation through fire and precision.

Unlike modern images of the blacksmith as purely brute force, Goibniu embodies discipline, elegance, and mastery of both form and function. His work is not only physical, but also magical. What he shapes is not merely used, but revered. Through him, labor becomes blessing.

Seasonal Resonance: Goibniu is honored particularly at Lughnasadh and Imbolc, when tools are prepared for sowing or harvest, and when the fires of creation begin to stir again. His forge is the hearth of sacred intent, always ready when you choose to build.

Spiritual Role: Goibniu is a guardian of craft, resilience, and sacred repetition. He teaches that skill is a devotional act. Every hammer strike is a prayer, every well-forged edge a spell. In spiritual practice, he reminds us that mastery arises not just from talent, but from discipline, attention, and heart.

Honoring Goibniu Today:

Work with your hands: Blacksmithing, carpentry, pottery, or any physical creation done with mindfulness.

Mythological Depth:

Goibniu the Smith is one of the triad of craft gods (along with Luchta the Carpenter and Creidhne the Metalworker), but his role extends far beyond mere smithwork. In the Second Battle of Mag Tuired, Goibniu performs a miracle: he forges weapons for the Tuatha Dé Danann with only three blows of his hammer, and these weapons never miss their mark. More remarkably, he brews the Feast of Age (Fled Goibnenn), an ale that grants immortality to those who drink it.

Goibniu represents the transformative power of craft and the sacred nature of work done well. His forge is a place of both destruction and creation—metal is melted down, its old form destroyed, only to be reborn as something new and purposeful. This process mirrors spiritual transformation and the refining of the soul through experience and effort.

In some traditions, Goibniu is associated with healing as well as smithwork, suggesting that the skills of mending and making are interconnected. To repair what is broken, whether metal or spirit, requires the same patience, skill, and understanding of fundamental structures. Goibniu teaches that there is no shame in being broken—only opportunity for skilled mending.

Seasonal Associations:

Goibniu's energy is present year-round, as craft and making are not seasonal activities but constant human needs. However, his presence is particularly strong at Lughnasadh, when the first fruits of labor are harvested, and during autumn and winter, when much craftwork was traditionally done indoors while the land rested. Work with Goibniu when learning new crafts, repairing what is broken, or transforming raw materials into finished work.

The darker half of the year, from Samhain to Beltane, is ideal for sustained craft projects that require focus and patience. Goibniu's forge burns hottest when the outer world is quiet, reminding us that winter is not idle time but a season for transforming our skills and ourselves.

Offerings and Altar Practices:

Goibniu's altar should honor craft and transformation. Include tools of making: hammers, nails, wire, metal objects, or tools specific to your craft. Red and orange cloths evoke the forge fire. Pieces of metal, especially iron, are sacred to him. Small anvils or horseshoes make appropriate symbols.

Traditional offerings include handmade objects crafted with care, ale or beer (especially craft-brewed varieties), and acts of repair—fixing something broken rather than discarding it. Time spent in focused craftwork is itself an offering to Goibniu. He values process over perfection, the learning journey over the polished result.

Create a Goibniu practice of learning one new craft skill each year. Document your progress, including mistakes and failures, which Goibniu understands as essential to mastery. Dedicate your craft time to him, speaking a brief invocation before beginning work.

Devotional Prayer to Goibniu:

"Goibniu, master of the forge, You who shape metal with three blows, You who brew the ale of immortality, You who understand that breaking precedes making, I honor your skill and your patience. Teach me to work with my hands, To transform raw materials into purpose, To see potential in what others discard, To value process as much as product. Goibniu, smith and healer, May my work be worthy of your example, May my craft serve those who need it, May I learn to remake myself as you remake metal—

Through fire, through hammer, into something stronger. Goibniu, I honor you."

Personal Gnosis and Relationship Building:

Goibniu is often experienced as patient, methodical, and deeply focused. He is not flashy or dramatic but steady and reliable, like the rhythm of hammer on anvil. Working with Goibniu requires committing to a craft practice and showing up consistently, even when progress feels slow. Begin by choosing something to make with your hands—woodworking, metalworking, fiber arts, cooking, any craft that interests you.

Keep a craft journal documenting your work with Goibniu. Photograph or sketch your projects at different stages. Note what worked and what didn't, what you learned from each attempt. Review this journal seasonally to see your skill development over time. Goibniu honors the long view, understanding that mastery is built through years of practice, not overnight success.

Practice repair as a spiritual discipline. Before discarding broken items, ask yourself if they can be mended. Learn basic repair skills: sewing, soldering, woodworking, gluing. Each act of repair is an offering to Goibniu and a reminder that transformation often means working with what exists rather than always starting fresh.

Dedicate your tools: Bless the items you use regularly (kitchen knives, pens, hammers) as sacred extensions of your intention.

Light a forge candle: A single flame representing the eternal hearth of divine craft.

Speak blessings over your work: Whisper gratitude or purpose into what you shape, mend, or build.

To walk with Goibniu is to return to the sacredness of making. He reminds us that what we create shapes the world, and that through deliberate, loving work, even the ordinary becomes divine.

Ogma – Champion of Strength and Language

Ogma, sometimes called Ogmios, is the god of eloquence, strength, and the sacred power of speech. He is credited in Irish tradition as the creator of Ogham; the ancient script used for marking trees and stones. As both a warrior and a poet, Ogma bridges the strength of body and the sharpness of tongue. He represents the word as weapon, as binding force, and as bearer of truth.

In myth, Ogma is described as valiant and eloquent, capable of inspiring both awe and allegiance through his words. He embodies the truth-telling champion, the one who carves law into bark and binds oaths in spoken breath. His influence is seen wherever sacred speech occurs, prayers, invocations, songs, and spells.

Seasonal Resonance: Ogma is honored at Imbolc and Lughnasadh, when communication and expression guide new beginnings and communal gatherings. He also walks near during oath-swearing rites, public declarations, and rites of passage.

Spiritual Role: Ogma teaches that words matter. That every name, promise, and invocation carries weight. In him, strength and speech are not separate paths; they are one and the same. He challenges us to be precise, to speak with intent, and to wield our language as a sacred act.

Honoring Ogma Today:

Write with purpose: Journal, compose poetry, or craft charms that speak your truth.

Mythological Depth:

Ogma Grianainech ("Ogma of the Sunlike Face") is the champion of the Tuatha Dé Danann and the credited inventor of the Ogham alphabet, the ancient Irish script carved on standing stones throughout Ireland.   He is both warrior and scholar, embodying the union of physical strength and intellectual power that Irish culture deeply valued. His epithet connects him to the sun, suggesting radiance, clarity, and illuminating wisdom.

In the Second Battle of Mag Tuired, Ogma is described as performing great feats of strength, killing numerous enemies including the Fomorian king Indech. After the battle, he recovers the sword Orna and delivers it to Lugh, demonstrating that even the strongest champion serves the greater good and recognizes rightful leadership. This balance of power with service is central to Ogma's teaching.

The Ogham alphabet itself is a profound magical system, with each letter corresponding to a tree, carrying both linguistic and mystical significance. That Ogma invented this system suggests he understood that language is not merely communication but power— the ability to name, to bind, to reveal, and to preserve knowledge across generations. Ogham carved on stone endures, just as Ogma teaches that words carefully chosen have lasting impact.

Seasonal Associations:

Ogma's presence is felt throughout the year, as both physical strength and linguistic skill are always relevant. However, his energy is particularly strong at Lughnasadh, when games and competitions honor skill and prowess, and at Imbolc, sacred to Brigid who also governs poetry and language. Work with Ogma when you need physical strength, eloquence in speech, protection, or the power of the written word.

Study of Ogham is best undertaken during the darker half of the year when indoor work is favored, though practicing Ogham carving or tree identification can be done year-round. Ogma reminds us that strength serves wisdom, and wisdom requires strength to manifest in the world.

Offerings and Altar Practices:

Ogma's altar should reflect both warrior and scholar aspects. Include representations of weapons (a ritual blade, a staff, or images of swords), books or scrolls representing knowledge, and Ogham staves or stones if you work with this alphabet. Use strong colors: gold for his solar aspect, green for the trees of Ogham, and red for warrior energy.

Traditional offerings include poetry or prose read aloud, physical exercise or martial practice dedicated to him, carved Ogham symbols on wood or stone, and acts of protection for others, especially the vulnerable. Learning and teaching Ogham are among the highest offerings you can make to Ogma. He also appreciates athletic competitions and demonstrations of skill performed in his honor.

Create an Ogma practice of learning one new Ogham symbol each month, studying the associated tree, its folklore, and its divinatory meaning. Carve or draw the symbol while speaking its name and contemplating its essence. This year-long practice deepens your connection to both Ogma and the Irish landscape.

Devotional Prayer to Ogma:

"Ogma of the Sunlike Face, Champion and scholar, warrior-sage, You who gifted us with Ogham's wisdom, You who showed that strength serves knowledge, I call to you with respect and determination. Teach me to be strong in body and mind, To speak with clarity and power, To write words that endure, To protect what matters with fierceness and wisdom. Ogma, inventor of letters, May my words carry weight, May my strength serve justice, May I honor the trees that bear your alphabet, May I remember that language is sacred power. Ogma, I honor you."

Personal Gnosis and Relationship Building:

Ogma is often experienced as both powerful and scholarly, combining physical presence with intellectual depth. Working with Ogma requires balancing body and mind, recognizing that both need development and that each supports the other. Begin by establishing both a physical practice (martial arts, strength training, yoga, dance) and a study practice (learning Ogham, studying Irish literature, writing poetry).

Study the Ogham alphabet seriously if you feel called to Ogma. Learn not just the symbols but the trees, their characteristics, their uses, and their places in Irish folklore and landscape. Visit these trees if possible, touching them, sitting with them, learning from them directly. This embodied study connects you to Ogma's teaching that knowledge is not abstract but rooted in the living world.

Practice eloquence and precision in speech as a devotional discipline. Before speaking on important matters, pause to choose your words carefully. Study rhetoric, poetry, and the art of clear communication. Ogma teaches that words have power to harm or heal, to bind or free, and that we are responsible for how we wield that power.

Speak blessings aloud: Use your voice to affirm, to honor, and to empower.

Study Ogham: Learn the script as a devotional practice and divinatory tool.

Hold your word sacred: Make only promises you intend to keep, and keep them.

To walk with Ogma is to speak and write with soul. He reminds us that language is magic, that truth is strength, and that every word we utter leaves a mark, on the land, on others, and on ourselves.

Chapter 7c: Relating to the Divine: Devotion, Prayer, and Offerings

Ériu – Spirit of the Land

Ériu is one of the three sovereignty goddesses of Ireland, alongside her sisters Banba and Fódla. From her name, the very name of Ireland; Éire, is derived. She is not a goddess of abstract dominion, but one who embodies the land itself: its rolling hills, mists, stones, and sovereignty. When the Milesians came to take Ireland, it was Ériu who met them and offered her name to the land, provided they honor and protect it in turn.

She represents sacred contract between people and place. To invoke Ériu is to root one's magic in the land one walks, especially in the call to protect it, listen to it, and live in harmony with it. Her presence calls for stewardship, reverence, and humility.

Seasonal Resonance: Ériu is timeless, but she speaks loudest at times of oath, planting, and political change. She is often invoked during Samhain or Lughnasadh, when cycles of rule, justice, and harvest meet.

Spiritual Role: Ériu teaches that sovereignty is not given, it is honored. She binds land to spirit and asks, always, whether you walk your path with integrity. In her, one finds the soul of place, and the ethical call to belong through service, not dominion.

Honoring Ériu Today:

Walk the land: Learn its names, its stories, its wounds.

Mythological Depth:

Ériu, one of the three sisters (with Banba and Fódla) who gave their names to Ireland, represents the land itself in its most essential form. When the Milesians arrived in Ireland, each sister requested that the island bear her name, and it was Ériu whose name endured: Éire in Irish, Ireland in English. This naming was not mere vanity but a deep magical binding—to name the land was to claim sovereignty over it, to recognize that land and spirit are one.

Ériu's story reminds us that the land has consciousness, that it chooses its inhabitants as much as they choose it. The bargain between the Milesians and the Tuatha Dé Danann, mediated by the three sisters, established the relationship between newcomers and the ancient powers of place. Ériu teaches that we do not own the land; we belong to it, and our role is stewardship, not dominion.

In some traditions, Ériu is connected to sovereignty itself, the principle that rightful rule comes from the land's acceptance, not from force alone. Kings in ancient Ireland underwent ceremonies marrying them symbolically to the land, represented by a goddess figure. Ériu embodies this sacred relationship between people and place, reminding us that every action we take affects the land, and the land's health affects us.

Seasonal Associations:

Ériu's presence is felt throughout the year, as the land is always with us, but her energy is particularly strong at Beltane, when the land awakens fully, and at harvest times (Lughnasadh and Autumn Equinox), when the land's gifts are most visible. Work with Ériu when you need to deepen your connection to place, when making decisions about land use or environmental concerns, or when seeking to understand your local landscape more fully.

Spring and summer are ideal for direct engagement with Ériu through time spent outdoors, learning the land's contours, and participating in its seasonal rhythms. Autumn and winter are times for reflecting on what the land has taught you and planning how to serve it better in the coming cycle.

Offerings and Altar Practices:

Ériu's altar should reflect your specific place and landscape. Include soil from your land, native plants, stones from local areas, and representations of local wildlife. Use green and brown colors, the earth tones of the living land. Maps or images of your local area can remind you of the broader landscape you're part of.

Traditional offerings to Ériu include returning food to the earth (compost, biodegradable offerings left outside), planting native species, removing invasive plants or trash from wild areas, and acts of environmental stewardship. Time spent learning about local ecology, watersheds, and land history is a profound offering. Speaking prayers or blessings to the land, especially at dawn or dusk, honors Ériu's presence.

Create an Ériu practice of seasonal land offerings. At each festival, spend time consciously connecting with your local landscape. Walk the same path throughout the year, noticing how it changes. Learn which plants emerge when, which birds arrive and depart, how water moves through the land. This embodied, ongoing relationship is how Ériu is truly honored.

Devotional Prayer to Ériu:

"Ériu, spirit of this land, You who gave your name to Ireland, You who know every stone and stream, You who remember all who walked here before me, I honor your presence in this place. Teach me to listen to the land, To walk gently and observe closely, To understand that I am not separate from nature, To serve as caretaker, not master. Ériu, mother of place, May I learn the language of the land, May I honor its gifts with gratitude, May I leave it better than I found it, May I remember I am soil and will return to soil. Ériu, I honor you."

Personal Gnosis and Relationship Building:

Ériu is experienced as deeply present but not necessarily personal—she is the land itself, vast and enduring beyond individual human experience. Working with Ériu requires humility, patience, and a willingness to subordinate human agendas to the land's own rhythms and needs. Begin by simply spending time outdoors regularly, without agenda or expectation, just being present to place.

Study your local ecology seriously. Learn the names of native plants, trees, birds, and animals. Understand your watershed— where your water comes from and where it goes. Research land history: what indigenous peoples lived there, how the land was used historically, what natural features have been altered or preserved. This knowledge deepens your relationship with Ériu in her local manifestation.

Practice environmental ethics as devotion to Ériu. Reduce consumption, support land conservation, vote for environmental protection, and teach others about ecological stewardship. Ériu's honor is not just in ritual but in how we treat the physical land every single day. Every act of environmental care, no matter how small, is a prayer to the spirit of place.

Offer native seeds, clean water, or soil: Gifts of healing for the living earth.

Stand for the land: Participate in conservation, rewilding, or resistance to ecological harm.

Speak her name: In prayer, in ritual, in blessing the ground you live on.

To honor Ériu is to root one's spirituality in reciprocity. She is not a relic, she is the earth underfoot, waiting to know if you remember the promise.

Tailtiu – Sacrifice and Sovereignty

Tailtiu is a queen and foster-mother, remembered most for her death and for the harvest games; Áenach Tailten; that were founded in her honor by her foster-son Lugh. In one of the most ancient mythic echoes of sacrifice for land, Tailtiu cleared the forests of Ireland so the people might grow food. She died from her labors, and it is in her memory that the great games of Lughnasadh were held.

Though not always listed among the Tuatha Dé Danann, Tailtiu's presence is felt in every act of loving service, especially when that service costs something. She is the breath before collapse, the smile before surrender, the spirit of mothers who give until they are spent.

Seasonal Resonance: Tailtiu's story is honored most directly at Lughnasadh. Yet her presence endures in any moment when love and labor are given for the good of the land and community.

Spiritual Role: Tailtiu is the heart of sacrificial love, not in martyrdom, but in meaningful legacy. She asks what you are willing to give, not because you must, but because it will plant something better in your wake.

Honoring Tailtiu Today:

Mythological Depth:

Tailtiu stands as one of the most poignant figures in Irish mythology—a Fir Bolg queen who became foster mother to Lugh of the Long Arm, and who died clearing the plains of Ireland for agriculture. Her name is preserved in Teltown (Tailten) in County Meath, where the great Áenach Tailteann (Assembly of Tailtu) was held each Lughnasadh, featuring games, contests, marriages, and legal proceedings. This gathering honored her memory and sacrifice, making her central to one of the most important festivals of the Irish year.

Unlike many deities whose power lies in battle or magic, Tailtiu's strength is in labor, endurance, and the willingness to give everything for future generations. Her clearing of the forests—a task so monumental it killed her—transformed the landscape into farmland that would sustain countless lives. She represents the hard truth that civilization is built on sacrifice, that progress requires someone to do the backbreaking work, and that we owe a debt to those who labored before us.

Her role as foster mother to Lugh adds another dimension: she is not only the sacrificing laborer but also the nurturer who raises a champion. She represents maternal love extended beyond blood, the choice to care for another's child, and the investment in a future you may not live to see. In honoring Tailtiu, we honor all who have worked to make our lives possible—ancestors, laborers, caregivers, and those whose names we will never know.

Seasonal Associations:

Tailtiu's energy peaks at Lughnasadh (August 1), the festival named in her honor by her foster son Lugh. This is the time of first harvest, when the labor of spring and summer finally bears fruit. Lughnasadh was traditionally celebrated with funeral games at Teltown, athletic competitions, and handfasting ceremonies—all honoring Tailtiu's memory while celebrating the abundance her sacrifice made possible.

Work with Tailtiu during the full harvest season, from Lughnasadh through the Autumn Equinox, when the results of the year's labor become visible. This is when we reap what was sown, gather what was tended, and give thanks for the work that brought forth food. Tailtiu reminds us to honor not just the harvest itself but the exhausting labor that preceded it.

Spring and summer are also Tailtiu's seasons, though in different ways. At Imbolc and the Spring Equinox, invoke her when beginning new projects that will require sustained effort. At Beltane and Summer Solstice, honor her in the midst of labor, when the work is hardest and the outcome still uncertain.

Winter is Tailtiu's rest, earned after a year of work. During Samhain and the Winter Solstice, remember her in stillness, acknowledging that even the strongest workers need time to recover. Honor her by resting without guilt, by allowing yourself the winter fallow that makes spring productivity possible.

Offerings and Altar Practices:

Create a Tailtiu altar centered on the fruits of labor. Include grains (wheat, oats, barley), fresh bread you've baked yourself, tools of your trade or craft, and representations of work completed. A small hoe, sheaf of wheat, or bundle of harvested herbs speaks to her agricultural nature. Include stones from cleared land or soil from your garden if you tend one.

Traditional offerings to Tailtiu include:

Fresh bread, particularly if you've made it with your own hands

Harvest grains or seeds from plants you've grown

Water poured on earth you've tended or worked

Sweat-stained work clothes offered symbolically (then washed with gratitude)

Acts of physical labor dedicated to her: clearing land, gardening, building, crafting

At Lughnasadh, create a special Tailtiu feast featuring foods made from scratch, especially those requiring significant labor: bread kneaded by hand, vegetables you've grown and harvested, meals that take hours to prepare. Invite others to share this feast and tell Tailtiu's story before eating, honoring the work that feeds us.

Establish a daily or weekly practice of offering your labor to Tailtiu. Before beginning work—whether physical labor, creative projects, or professional tasks—speak a brief prayer dedicating your efforts to her. At day's end, report back to your altar: "Tailtiu, I have worked. I offer you my effort. May it bear fruit."

Maintain a harvest journal throughout the growing season, documenting not just what you've grown or accomplished but how much effort it required. At Lughnasadh, burn pages from this journal as an offering, releasing the record of your labor while keeping its fruits.

Devotional Prayer to Tailtiu:

"Tailtiu, Queen of the Fir Bolg,

Mother who cleared the plains,

Foster mother of Lugh Bright-Handed,

You who labored until your strength was spent,

You who died that others might live from the land,

I honor your sacrifice,

I remember your work,

I acknowledge the debt I owe to all who labored before me.

Teach me the difference between service and self-destruction,

Between giving from fullness and giving from depletion,

Between sustainable work and martyrdom.

Help me to labor with love but also with boundaries,

To work hard but also to rest deeply,

To give generously but also to receive gracefully.

May my work honor you,

May my harvest feed others,

May my effort bear fruit for those who come after,

And may I know when enough is enough.

Tailtiu, I honor you."

Personal Gnosis and Relationship Building:

Tailtiu is often experienced as a maternal but demanding presence—she expects you to work, to give, to serve, but also to recognize when sacrifice crosses into self-destruction. Working with Tailtiu requires honest assessment of how you give your energy and whether that giving is sustainable or exploitative. Begin by examining your relationship to work, service, and self-sacrifice.

Keep a Tailtiu journal documenting your acts of service, but also your exhaustion, your resentment, your needs. Review it regularly to see patterns. Are you giving from fullness or from depletion? Is your service honored and reciprocated, or taken for granted? Tailtiu teaches that martyrdom is not virtue, that sustainable service requires boundaries and reciprocity.

Practice saying no as a devotional discipline. When requests for your time or energy come, pause to assess whether you can truly give without depleting yourself. Honor Tailtiu by refusing to replicate the pattern of endless self-sacrifice that killed her. Modern devotion to Tailtiu means learning from her story, not repeating it.

Develop a physical practice in Tailtiu's honor—something that requires sustained effort and builds strength over time. This might be gardening, crafting, strength training, or any work that demands regular, disciplined effort. As you work, meditate on Tailtiu's clearing of the plains, the repetitive labor that transformed landscape into livelihood.

If you have access to land, dedicate a portion of it to Tailtiu. Clear it, tend it, make it productive, but do so at a sustainable pace.

Rest when tired. Ask for help when needed. Let this plot become a living relationship with her, a place where you practice sustainable labor rather than heroic self-destruction.

Visit Teltown (Tailten) if you can, or find a local cleared field, farm, or community garden. Stand at the edge and acknowledge the labor that made this space productive. Pour water on the ground and speak Tailtiu's name. If you cannot visit such a place physically, visualize standing in cleared land, feeling the earth beneath your feet that someone worked to prepare.

For those in helping professions, caregiving roles, or positions of service to others, Tailtiu can be a powerful ally and teacher. Work with her to establish healthy boundaries, sustainable giving practices, and reciprocity in relationships. She understands the burden of endless demands and can help you navigate how to serve without destroying yourself in the process.

Some practitioners experience Tailtiu as stern and uncompromising, demanding evidence of work rather than empty words. She respects action over promises, results over intentions. If you commit to a project in her name, see it through. If you cannot complete something, acknowledge this honestly rather than making excuses. She values truth and effort over perfection.

Practical Practices for Honoring Tailtiu:

Tend the land with care: Garden, gather, or compost with her in mind. Even a single potted plant tended consistently honors her.

Share your harvest: Feed others with what you've grown, made, or learned. Tailtiu's labor fed generations; let yours nourish your community.

Create an offering of effort: Undertake a ritual project, physical labor, or act of devotion completed with love and sustained work.

Remember her in story: Speak her name at Lughnasadh feasts. Share her tale with others. Ensure she is not forgotten.

Participate in or create harvest games: Athletic competitions at Lughnasadh honor her memory. Even friendly contests among friends carry forward the tradition of funeral games at Teltown.

Bake bread by hand: The physical work of kneading honors Tailtiu. Share this bread with others, continuing her legacy of labor that feeds.

Clear something: Whether physical clutter, digital disorder, or metaphorical obstacles, dedicate acts of clearing to Tailtiu.

Rest in her name: Honor her not just through work but through recovery. Take breaks without guilt, acknowledging that sustainable service requires restoration.

Teach a skill: Pass on knowledge of how to make, grow, or create something. Tailtiu raised Lugh; honor her by raising up others' capabilities.

Acknowledge invisible labor: Recognize and thank those whose work makes your life possible—farmworkers, custodians, caregivers, maintenance workers. See Tailtiu in their efforts.

To walk with Tailtiu is to live with love that labors. She reminds us that what we leave behind—if given with heart and wisdom rather than self-destruction—can become the feast of those who come after. In honoring her, we honor all who have worked that we might live, and we commit to working sustainably so that others may thrive when we are gone.

Closing Reflection

To know the deities of the Irish Wheel is not simply to learn their names or their stories. It is to step into an ancient rhythm that still beats beneath the soil and in the breath of every season. These gods and goddesses are not frozen in myth, they are living, evolving forces that rise with the fog, settle in the hearth, and speak through dream and omen.

Each deity offers more than a symbol; they offer a relationship. Whether you walk with Danu in silence, call the Mórrígan in truth, forge under Goibniu's fire, or write in Ogma's name, your path becomes part of a living stream that stretches across generations and across thresholds of belief. In honoring them, we honor the land, our ancestors, our inner voice, and the sacred cycles that sustain all life.

The Wheel turns. And with each turn, the divine calls to us again, not as distant rulers, but as companions in the journey of becoming. Listen for them, in the stillness, the storm, the song, and the soil. They are here. They have always been here. And when you remember them, you remember yourself. She lifts, warms, and weaves. To walk with Brigid is to walk a path of inspiration lit from within; a path that burns away despair and rekindles the will to create, to care, and to continue.

Chapter 8: The Land and the Sidhe

The Irish landscape is not only sacred, it is alive with presence. Ancient hills, river bends, windswept plains, and moss-covered stones have long been recognized as dwellings of spirit, not just scenery. To the pre-Christian Irish, the land was not owned, but respected; not inert, but inhabited. This chapter explores the beings who dwell just beyond the veil (the Sidhe, the ancestors, and other worldly spirits) and the ancient and modern ways we can live in right relationship with them.

From the burial mounds of Brú na Bóinne to the winds that sweep the Hill of Tara, certain places pulse with power. These are the thin places, where the boundary between our world and the Otherworld wears thin. These locations, and the beings who guard or inhabit them, are still active today for those with eyes and hearts open to perceive them.

The Sidhe (pronounced "shee") are not quaint fairies, but potent beings descended from the Tuatha Dé Danann, who chose to dwell in the hollow hills and hidden spaces after their defeat in the mythic cycles. They are powerful, proud, and bound by their own ethics and customs. To call upon them lightly is to court imbalance. To honor them properly is to step into the ancient pact between land and spirit.

In this chapter, we'll explore:

The identity and nature of the Sidhe

The role of ancestors and land spirits

Practices for respectful engagement

Folklore and warnings still told in rural Ireland

Seasonal times when the veil is thinnest

The Sidhe are not characters of story, they are cohabitants of this world. And to understand the Wheel of the Year fully, we must understand the spirits who turn it with us.

Section 1: The Sidhe – Who They Are and Who They Are Not

In modern times, the Sidhe are too often mistaken for the fluttering, winged fairies of Victorian art or sanitized children's tales. But in Irish tradition, the Sidhe are anything but harmless sprites. The word "Sidhe" refers both to the people and the places, the hollow hills or mounds where these beings dwell. The Sidhe are descendants of the Tuatha Dé Danann, a divine race who, after being defeated by the Milesians, withdrew into the Otherworld rather than relinquish their sovereignty.

They did not vanish. They shifted. From that point forward, they became the hidden folk (the People of the Mounds) who walk beside the world of mortals, often unseen, sometimes encountered, and always deserving of respect. The Sidhe are not dead, nor are they gods. They are something in between: noble, prideful, and deeply tied to the fate of the land.

Their nature is elusive. The Sidhe are known for beauty, power, moodiness, and a fierce sense of honor. They are not evil, but they are not bound to human morality either. Crossing them out of ignorance or arrogance can bring illness, misfortune, or spiritual unmooring. Honoring them with sincerity can bring inspiration, protection, and alliance.

They dwell in raths and cairns, in old trees and sacred wells, and sometimes in places so ordinary that only the wise know to tread carefully. Many stories tell of travelers being taken into their world, which may last minutes or years; or a lifetime that turns out to be but a day in human time. Some return with blessings. Some do not return at all.

To truly understand the Sidhe, one must abandon the lens of control. These beings are not for summoning or command. They are for greeting, for honoring, and for avoiding when their mood or message says so. They are sovereign spirits of place and boundary, who demand courtesy and discretion.

Section 2: Encounters, Forms, and Folklore of the Sidhe

Across centuries of oral tradition, the Sidhe have been encountered in countless forms: tall and noble as kings, wild and strange as animals who speak, beautiful as maidens in green cloaks, or shadowy as wailing banshees before death. They are shapeshifters and dreamwalkers, able to bend time, veil vision, and enter the lives of mortals when they choose; or when we wander too close to their domain.

In Irish lore, encounters with the Sidhe are often warnings as much as wonders. They appear on the edges: twilight, crossroads, shores, and mists. They offer riddles or gifts that are never quite what they seem. A silver comb left on a stone. A haunting tune played by unseen hands. A stranger who knows your name.

Many regions of Ireland preserve stories of specific types of Sidhe:

Bean Sidhe (Banshee): A wailing woman who foretells death, particularly for those of ancient lineages. Contrary to popular belief, her cry is not a curse but a lament, a grief older than the one it heralds.

Leannán Sidhe: A fairy lover who inspires artists but drains their life force. Passion and destruction walk hand in hand with her.

The Gentry: A term used in folk speech to refer to the more noble or royal Sidhe, sometimes equated with kings and queens of specific mounds or regions.

Changeling tales: In which human children are swapped for fairy doubles, often as punishment for an offense or in exchange for a destined purpose.

Common signs of a Sidhe presence include strange lights, sudden silence in animals, unusual dreams, the sound of music with no source, or an inexplicable sense of being watched near ancient mounds or groves.

To act carelessly in such places, cutting a fairy tree, building on a known rath, or speaking mockingly of the Good People, invites misfortune. Entire roads in modern Ireland have been rerouted to avoid disturbing known fairy paths. Farmers still leave offerings at boundary stones. The old ways persist not out of superstition, but out of respect.

To walk in this world with awareness of the Sidhe is to walk with humility. You are not alone. The land listens. And in places where the veil thins, the old ones still watch.

Section 3: Honoring the Sidhe in Modern Practice

To honor the Sidhe is to acknowledge that you share the land with other intelligences. It is not worship in the sense of deity devotion, but an ongoing act of respect, reciprocity, and care. In traditional Irish culture, this meant leaving a small portion of food or drink outside at night, avoiding construction near known fairy paths, or whispering a blessing when passing a ringfort. In modern times, the core principles remain the same: live in awareness, offer without demand, and engage the unseen with humility.

Offerings and Acts of Respect

Simple gifts are best: fresh cream, milk, oats, whiskey, water, or bread. Leave them at liminal places, doorsteps, tree roots, stones, or the edge of a field.

Never litter or leave plastic; the Sidhe are of the land, and gifts should return to it.

Offerings should be made with sincerity, not transaction. Do not ask for favors in return; simply acknowledge their presence and goodwill.

Avoiding Offense

Do not mock or speak ill of the Sidhe, even in jest.

Refer to them respectfully, often using euphemisms like The Good People, The Gentry, or Those Who Dwell Below.

If you feel a shift in the air, a prickle of skin, or a sudden hush, quietly excuse yourself and leave the area.

If you take something from the land (flowers, stones, herbs) ask permission aloud and leave something behind.

Tending Sacred Places

If you live near a known rath (fairy mound), ancient tree, well, or other liminal site, care for it.

Keep it free of trash. Offer a prayer or bow when passing.

Even a small act of stewardship can build trust.

In some regions, people still avoid cutting certain trees (especially lone hawthorns) believed to be Sidhe dwellings.

Timing and Thresholds

The Sidhe are most active at dusk, dawn, and midnight; and especially on the liminal days of the year: Samhain, Bealtaine, and the solstices.

If you choose to leave offerings or say prayers, these are potent times to do so.

Spiritual Boundaries

Not all Sidhe encounters are welcome. If you feel overwhelmed, anxious, or spiritually "tangled" after walking a fairy path or entering a misty grove, cleanse yourself with water, salt, or smoke (rosemary or mugwort are good options).

Speak aloud your intention to return fully to the human world.

Regular grounding practices and protective symbols (such as iron or rowan) can help maintain balance.

Section 4: Ancestors, Land Spirits, and Other Hidden Folk

While the Sidhe hold a distinct place in Irish cosmology, they are not the only spirits who dwell in or alongside the land. The ancestors, those of blood, spirit, and tradition, are ever-present, woven into the roots of trees, the walls of old homes, and the prayers of hearth and field. In Irish Paganism, honoring the dead is not an act of mourning alone, but of continuity and respect.

Ancestral spirits are often regarded as guardians of the household or local land, and are especially honored at Samhain, when the veil thins and their nearness is most keenly felt. However, their presence can be acknowledged throughout the year through family stories, offerings, or small altar spaces. To keep their names alive is to keep their wisdom close.

Land spirits are those whose origins may never have been human. They are the animating forces of rivers, stones, forests, and hills, sometimes shy, sometimes fierce, and always deserving of reverence. In ancient times, rivers such as the Boyne were personified as goddesses, and every well or grove had its attending spirit. Modern Pagans can continue this tradition by treating local natural places with the same respect one would offer a sacred site in Ireland.

Other Hidden Folk may include house spirits, hearth guardians, or regional beings preserved in folk belief but not formally named. These spirits, like the Sidhe, are best approached through quiet respect, gentle offerings, and attention to dreams or signs. A chill breeze in a closed room, a sudden scent with no source, or a bird behaving oddly at your window, these may not be random.

Honoring Ancestors and Land Spirits Today:

Create a small ancestral shrine with photos, heirlooms, or candles.

Speak their names aloud, especially during mealtimes, festivals, or rites of passage.

Leave offerings at a tree or stone that feels "watched" or remembered.

Walk the land with reverence, picking up trash, planting natives, or simply listening.

In all these acts, the common thread is relationship. The Irish worldview does not divide spirit from soil, the living from the dead, or the visible from the hidden. It weaves them together. When you walk this path with care, you are never alone.

Section 5: When the Veil Thins – Seasonal Spirit Interactions

There are moments in the year when the boundaries between this world and the Otherworld are more porous, when spirit, memory, and fate interlace more tightly with the rhythm of time. These are the "thin times," where those who listen may hear, and those who reach may be touched in return.

Samhain (October 31 – November 1):

The most well-known liminal festival, when the dead return and the Sidhe walk more freely.

Altars are built, names of ancestors are spoken, and food is left out for wandering spirits.

Divination, trance, and dreamwork are especially potent.

Bealtaine (May 1):

A festival of fire and fertility, but also one of heightened Sidhe activity.

Travelers avoid fairy paths, and protective herbs like rowan or hawthorn are hung on doors.

Offerings are made to ensure harmony and safety for the season ahead.

Winter Solstice (around December 21):

The turning of light in the darkness, and a time for deep ancestral reflection.

Sacred sites like Newgrange align with the returning sun.

Spirits of both land and lineage are honored in quiet rites.

Summer Solstice (around June 21):

A peak of light, often used to commune with nature spirits and local land wights.

Fire rituals and water blessings abound.

Manannán mac Lir is often honored during this time of crossing.

Imbolc and Lughnasadh:

While not as focused on spirit interaction as Samhain or Bealtaine, these points carry their own veils and thresholds.

Imbolc is a time to reach for healing ancestors.

Lughnasadh honors spirits of land, labor, and sacrifice, especially Tailtiu.

By aligning our rituals and awareness with these turning points, we walk more in rhythm with both the land and its unseen kin. The veil is never gone, it only shifts. And in those shifting moments, we are offered the chance to remember: we are not the only ones who turn the wheel.

Chapter 9: Samhain – The Hollow Between Worlds

The Season and Its Significance Samhain (pronounced SOW-in) marks the end of the harvest season and the beginning of the dark half of the year in the Irish calendar. Traditionally observed on or around October 31st, Samhain is both a seasonal and spiritual threshold. It is a time of transition when the boundaries between the worlds of the living and the dead are believed to grow thin. For modern neo-pagans, it offers a deeply meaningful opportunity to honor ancestors, reflect on mortality, and prepare for winter both physically and spiritually.

Historical and Cultural Roots Historically, Samhain was one of the most important festivals in the Irish year. It marked the final harvest, when cattle were brought down from summer pastures and slaughtered for winter. Crops were gathered and stored, and communities began to retreat into the household-centered life of the dark months. It was also a time when great tribal assemblies were held. Legal matters were settled, debts were paid, and kinship ties were reinforced. These practical activities were surrounded by ritual, feasting, and storytelling.

In different regions of Ireland, Samhain was observed with distinct local customs:

In Ulster, great bonfires were lit on hilltops to mark the changing season. Cattle were driven between twin fires as a rite of purification and protection.

In Munster, families engaged in keening (ancestral wailing songs) at burial mounds, evoking both sorrow and communion.

In Connacht, apple bobbing and nut divination were popular, reflecting an intimate relationship with seasonal fruits and symbolic play.

In Leinster, sacred sites like Uisneach saw gatherings where warriors and poets offered tales to honor the dead.

These customs reveal the deep interweaving of land, ancestry, and myth in Irish life.

The Liminal Space and Spiritual Beliefs The spiritual dimensions of Samhain are recorded in both folklore and early literature. It was believed to be a liminal time, when the veil between this world and the Otherworld was at its thinnest. The sidhe, or spirits of the Otherworld, were thought to walk among humans. Ghosts of the dead could return, either as honored ancestors or restless souls. Offerings of food and drink were left at doorways or on altars to appease spirits and welcome beloved dead. Divination was commonly practiced, as the collapse of boundaries made it easier to receive messages from beyond.

Samhain is also closely associated with the festival of the dead. In Irish tradition, there is a strong emphasis on kinship and ancestral memory. Honoring the dead is not a separate religious act but integrated into the cycle of the year. At Samhain, this remembrance becomes central. Candles are lit. Graves are visited. Ancestors are spoken to, not in mourning, but in continuity.

The Role of the Hearth In ancient Irish households, the hearth was not only the center of domestic life but a sacred flame linking generations. At Samhain, the hearth fire was often extinguished and relit, either from a communal bonfire or in solemn ritual, symbolizing a spiritual reset. Today, lighting a new candle from an ancestral flame can recreate this gesture. Sharing a story by firelight or preparing a family dish can be a modern echo of this rite.

Shadow Work Practices Samhain invites deep inner work. Shadow work: exploring one's hidden thoughts, fears, and unresolved grief, is particularly potent during this season. You might write a journal about what you wish to release or forgive. Write a letter to a departed loved one. Burn regrets written on bay leaves or bury them beneath stones. Gaze into a mirror by candlelight and speak affirmations aloud. This is not a season of fear, but of facing what lies beneath, with honesty and compassion.

Tales of Samhain from Myth and Folklore The stories told at Samhain are as haunting as they are illuminating. One such tale is that of Nera, who entered a sídhe mound after witnessing a vision of his town in flames, a warning from the Otherworld. Another speaks of the Morrígan washing bloodied garments at a river ford, foretelling doom. Some tell of travelers who met ghostly herds or were pulled into fairy rings on Samhain night, never to return unchanged. These myths reflect the reality that contact with the Otherworld was both possible and perilous at this time.

Children and Family Traditions Including children in Samhain observances ensures that ancestral practices live on. Families can build simple altars with drawings and family photos, bake oatcakes together, or make lanterns from turnips or pumpkins. Creating ancestor trees or soul candles personalized with names and intentions helps root the celebration in love rather than fear. Stories shared around the fire foster connection and continuity.

Altar Setup and Symbolic Elements Altar setups at Samhain should reflect the solemnity and ancestral focus of the season. Begin with a dark cloth, typically black or deep purple, to ground the altar in the themes of death, reflection, and mystery. At the center, place photographs of departed loved ones, written names of ancestors, or heirlooms that carry personal memory. Surround these with seasonal items such as apples (a symbol of wisdom and the Otherworld), nuts, gourds, and dried autumn leaves. A bowl of water can be added to symbolize the veil between worlds, and a mirror may be included for scrying. Stones or bones may be respectfully included as representations of ancestral presence and the enduring connection to the past.

Candles are a key part of Samhain ritual. Black candles are often used for banishing and protection, cleansing the space and keeping unwanted energies at bay. White candles represent purity and the presence of the dead, serving as a spiritual beacon for ancestors to find their way. Red or deep orange candles evoke the hearth, symbolizing the living flame passed down through generations. Placing a candle in the window (whether real or electric) has become a symbolic gesture of welcome for visiting spirits.

Herbal Allies and Their Uses Herbs used during Samhain carry long associations with death, dreaming, and purification. Mugwort is especially useful for divination and dream work, aiding in spiritual sight and trance states. It has a long history in European folk medicine and is often bundled into smudge sticks or burned in a fire-safe bowl during scrying rituals.

Rosemary is a sacred herb of remembrance. Its sharp, cleansing aroma makes it ideal for ancestral rites. A sprig of rosemary placed on the altar or tucked into clothing helps maintain spiritual clarity while honoring the dead. Boiling rosemary in water can create a purifying steam bath for tools and offerings.

Sage, particularly common sage (Salvia officinalis), is widely used to clear energy, though white sage should be avoided unless cultivated responsibly due to its endangered status and cultural appropriation concerns. European varieties, or native plants such as cedar or pine, offer sustainable alternatives.

Vervain is a traditional herb in Celtic lore, sacred to both druids and poets. Used to protect, bless, and elevate consciousness, it is especially effective when infused into ritual water or sprinkled around the perimeter of sacred space.

Juniper and pine branches offer both spiritual and practical virtues. As evergreens, they symbolize life enduring through death.

Juniper berries can be added to incense blends, while pine needles or cones serve as both decoration and protection. A pine sachet tucked under the pillow may enhance visionary dreaming.

For American practitioners seeking accessible herbal allies with similar spiritual resonance:

Lemon balm offers gentle protection and aids in emotional release

Bay laurel can replace vervain in divination work

Thyme supports ancestral contact and dream clarity

Catnip, despite its mundane connotation, may invite connection with familiar spirits and soft-hearted ancestral presences

Incorporating these herbs thoughtfully (whether by burning, brewing, bathing, or blessing) grounds Samhain rites in both practicality and sacred intention.

Sacred Foods and Offerings Food plays a central role in Samhain practice, serving not just as nourishment but as a bridge between worlds. Meals are a sacred act of remembrance and connection, shared with both the living and the dead. Traditional Irish dishes connect practitioners with ancestral memory, while local adaptations ensure accessibility without losing reverence.

A symbolic meal might begin with the preparation of hearty, seasonal fare. Root vegetables such as turnips, carrots, and parsnips were staples of the Samhain table, dug from the earth just as spirits rise from the underworld. A stew of lamb or beef with barley and onion honors the pastoral rhythms of early Irish life. Fresh bread, often darkened with molasses or rye, ties the feast to the harvest.

The setting of a place at the table for the dead; sometimes called a "dumb supper"; allows the departed to join the living in silence. A plate is laid with intention, filled with food, and left undisturbed. After the meal, it may be respectfully buried, left at the foot of a tree, or returned to the earth with a prayer of gratitude.

Baking specific foods can become ritual acts. Oatcakes, for example, were a rural staple. They represent simplicity, resilience, and nourishment. Adding a protective sigil in honey before baking transforms the mundane into the sacred. Similarly, colcannon (made from mashed potatoes and greens) can include charms or coins wrapped in parchment, echoing the divinatory customs of old.

Desserts often feature fruit and warmth. Apples, deeply linked to wisdom and the Otherworld, were used in games of fate and flirtation during Samhain gatherings. Blackberries, whose harvest traditionally ends with Samhain (when it's said the Púca spoils them), can be combined with apples in crumbles or pies to honor the season's final sweetness.

Libations are a powerful form of offering. Mead, ale, and cider reflect both joy and memory. When poured into the earth or offered on an ancestral altar, they become gifts that nourish the unseen. Tea brewed from rosemary, thyme, or mugwort may also serve as a personal libation; sipped slowly while communing with the dead.

For modern practitioners in North America or other regions, accessible substitutions and additions include:

Cornbread or pumpkin bread, using locally grown grains

Butternut squash or sweet potato dishes, reflecting the harvest of the land

Herbal teas with cinnamon, clove, or ginger to warm the body and spirit

The key is intention. When food is cooked with remembrance, served with gratitude, and shared in silence or song, it transcends its ingredients. It becomes a spell of memory, a communion of lineage, and a celebration of both life and death.

Each dish, each flavor, carries echoes of those who came before, and through them, the cycle continues.

Deities and Ancestral Spirits Samhain is a sacred hinge in the year when deities and the dead draw near. It is a festival not only of endings, but of enduring presence; of those who once walked the earth and those who never left.

Foremost among the deities honored at this time is the Morrígan. Known as a goddess of war, fate, and sovereignty, she moves through Samhain like a shadowed queen. Often appearing as a crow or raven, she is invoked not only for protection but for prophecy, insight, and personal transformation. Standing at thresholds, she guides practitioners through the dying of the year and into the fertile darkness of renewal. Her voice is sharp as truth and deep as earth, fierce, but never cruel.

Rituals to the Morrígan may include black or red candles, crow feathers, bones, or dark berries. Offerings of blood-red wine, iron tools, or spoken oaths align with her themes of power, sacrifice, and sovereignty. One may call her through song, silence, or whispered challenge.

Donn, sometimes known as the Lord of the Dead, is another significant figure. Said to dwell in Tech Duinn; a rocky outpost believed to be the gathering place of souls. Donn reminds us that death is a journey, not a punishment. Honoring him can be as simple as placing a stone at the edge of one's altar, or speaking aloud the names of those who have passed into the unseen realm. In some traditions, a glass of saltwater represents the sea crossing of the dead, and a lantern is lit to guide them.

The Cailleach, the crone of winter, also rises in power at Samhain. She is the bone-mother, the stone of the mountain, the keeper of ice and time. While often feared, she is a guardian of survival and endurance. To work with the Cailleach is to learn to thrive in stillness and to see beauty in decay. Her offerings include stones, cold water, or evergreen boughs. A walk in silence through a winter wood may serve as her invocation.

Beyond gods and goddesses, the ancestors themselves are revered as sacred. This includes not only blood relatives but spiritual forebears, mentors, and cultural heroes. Samhain is the time to honor them all, with stories, songs, offerings, and remembrance. Their presence is invited with gentleness and respect, not summoned or commanded.

A simple ancestor devotion might involve lighting a white candle, placing a token of remembrance on the altar, and reciting: "Those who came before me, Whose blood or spirit flows in mine, I honor your path, I remember your name, And I walk forward with your blessing."

Through honoring these divine and ancestral forces, we anchor ourselves in lineage and mystery. Samhain becomes not merely a night of ghosts, but a time of profound reconnection, with the roots below and the stars above.

Complete Samhain Ritual: A Step-by-Step Ceremony This Samhain ritual is designed for solitary practice but can be easily adapted for a small, focused group. It blends traditional Irish symbolism with practical neo-pagan structure and should ideally take place after dark. Prepare your altar beforehand with ancestral tokens, seasonal offerings, black and white candles, a bowl of water, and incense. Dim the lights or work by firelight if possible.

Preparation Physically clean the space. Spiritually cleanse using smoke from rosemary, mugwort, or juniper. Lay a dark cloth on the altar. Arrange photos, heirlooms, or written names of ancestors alongside offerings of food, drink, or symbolic items.

Grounding and Centering Stand or sit comfortably. Close your eyes. Take slow, deep breaths. Visualize roots growing from your body into the earth, anchoring you. With each breath, feel calm, steady, and present.

Opening the Ritual Light a single white candle and say: "I light this flame to mark the sacred hour, As the veil thins and the year turns to shadow. I stand between the worlds, In remembrance, in reverence, in readiness."

Casting the Circle Walk clockwise around your space (or visualize the motion). Hold a candle, wand, or your hand extended. Say: "With breath and flame, With root and stone, I cast this circle, my sacred home. Let no harm enter, let no fear remain. This space is sealed between worlds."

Invoking the Ancestors Face the altar. Light the black and red candles. Speak: "Ancestors of my blood and spirit, Known and unknown, named and forgotten, I call you now to join me. You whose lives shaped mine, Be present at this hearth. Be honored. Be heard." Place an offering of food or drink. Sit or kneel in silence. Speak to them as if they were present.

Moment of Silence Allow yourself time to be still. Listen with the heart. You may feel a presence, memory, or emotion. Honor what arises. This is sacred time.

Divination Use your chosen tool: tarot, ogham, runes, or mirror. Ask: "What wisdom do the ancestors offer me for the year ahead?" Interpret slowly and intuitively. Write down impressions.

Guided Meditation (Meeting an Ancestor) Close your eyes. Visualize a misty field beneath a silver sky. Walk toward an ancient hill crowned with stones. A doorway opens. Enter. Within, meet a guide, perhaps an ancestor or spirit ally. Listen. When ready, return slowly. Write what you received.

Release and Gratitude Stand and speak: "Spirits of the dead, ancestors of heart and blood, I thank you for your presence. Go if you must, stay if you will, With love, not sorrow." Snuff the black candle. Let the white one burn a while longer.

Closing the Circle Walk counter-clockwise and say: "This rite is ended, the circle released. The veil remains, but so does memory. As the dark half begins, I carry the flame within."

Grounding and Reflection Eat a small piece of bread or sip warm tea. Touch the ground or a stone. Feel your body, your breath. Write down thoughts or sensations in a journal. Let the ritual settle into you.

This ritual honors death not as an end, but as transformation. Whether performed in silence or song, with grandeur or simplicity, its power lies in sincerity. Samhain is not about fear, it is about remembering who we are, where we come from, and what lights we carry forward.

Deepening the Practice: Advanced Samhain Workings

For those who have walked with Samhain for many turnings of the Wheel, the festival can become a portal to deeper communion with the Otherworld. These advanced practices should only be undertaken by those comfortable with liminal work, ancestral contact, and spirit negotiation. They are not meant to frighten, but to honor the profound mystery that exists at this threshold time.

The practice of the Dumb Supper is one of the most potent Samhain rites. A table is set with an extra place for the dead. The meal is prepared in complete silence, with intention and reverence. Participants eat without speaking, allowing the presence of ancestors to fill the space. Food and drink are placed at the empty setting. Some traditions dictate that participants serve themselves backwards, moving counterclockwise, or that they face away from the table while eating to acknowledge the reversed nature of the spirit world. At the meal's end, the offering is taken outdoors and left at a crossroads, at the base of a tree, or buried in the earth. Silence is maintained until dawn.

Another powerful practice is the creation of a Samhain vigil. From sunset on Samhain Eve through sunrise, a candle is kept burning while the practitioner sits in meditation, prayer, or contemplative silence. Some use this time for extended divination sessions, allowing messages to emerge slowly through the long night.

Others journey inward, confronting their own shadows and speaking truth to the parts of themselves they have avoided. The vigil can be broken into watches, with different intentions for each phase: remembrance, release, renewal, and finally, welcoming the dawn.

For those drawn to deeper spirit work, Samhain is an ideal time to establish or strengthen a relationship with a spirit guide or ancestral guardian. This begins with preparation: cleanse yourself and your space, create clear boundaries, and know your lineage as deeply as possible. Light a white candle and speak your intention aloud. Ask to meet a benevolent ancestor or guide who walks with your highest good. Sit in silence. You may feel a presence, see an image in your mind's eye, or simply know that someone has arrived. Offer a gift: food, drink, tobacco, honey, or a pledge of service. Speak respectfully. Ask their name, though they may not give it immediately. Trust takes time, even with the dead. Thank them for their presence and close the working with gratitude. Record everything in your journal. Return to this practice regularly, deepening the relationship over time.

Regional Variations: Samhain Across Ireland

While Samhain was observed throughout Ireland, each province developed its own distinctive customs, shaped by local geography, clan traditions, and the spirits of place. These regional differences reveal the intimate relationship between land and practice.

In County Kerry, along the wild Atlantic coast, fishermen would not go to sea on Samhain Eve. The waters were believed to belong to the dead on this night, and those who ventured out might encounter phantom ships or be lured beneath the waves by the spirits of drowned sailors. Coastal communities lit bonfires on clifftops to guide both living and dead safely home. Offerings of salt and bread were cast into the sea at sunset, a gesture of respect to those who never returned from the deep.

In the Midlands, particularly around County Westmeath, the Hill of Uisneach was recognized as the sacred center of Ireland. Great gatherings were held there, with druids presiding over rituals that honored both the land and the ancestors. The custom of extinguishing all fires and relighting them from a central sacred flame originated here. Families would carry embers home in clay pots, believing that a fire lit from the Uisneach flame carried protection through the dark months. This practice can be adapted today by lighting a central candle during a group ritual and having each participant light their own candle from it to take home.

In Northern Ireland, especially in Counties Antrim and Down, Samhain was a time of storytelling competitions. Families and clans would gather, and the best storytellers would recite tales of heroes, monsters, and the sidhe long into the night. The stories served multiple purposes: they entertained, educated the young about clan history, and honored the dead by keeping their deeds alive in memory. Some tales were deliberately frightening, a controlled way to face fear and death in a communal setting. Others were humorous, reminding listeners that even in darkness, joy and laughter persist.

County Sligo, with its ancient cairns and passage tombs, became a pilgrimage site at Samhain. People would walk to Carrowmore or Knocknarea to leave offerings at the tombs, believing that Queen Maeve herself walked among the stones on this night. Some claimed to hear her laughter on the wind or see her red cloak moving through the mist. Modern practitioners can honor this tradition by visiting local burial mounds, historic cemeteries, or ancient sites in their own regions, leaving biodegradable offerings and speaking words of remembrance.

Omens, Divination, and Samhain Wisdom

The folk wisdom surrounding Samhain is rich with divinatory practices and observations of natural omens. These were not superstitions but sophisticated systems of reading the world, passed down through generations and grounded in careful attention to seasonal patterns.

Traditional Samhain divination practices focused on matters of love, death, and the year ahead. Young people would peel an apple in one long strip and throw it over their shoulder, believing the peel would form the initial of their future spouse. Hazelnuts were placed in the fire, each named for a potential lover; the nut that popped first indicated the truest heart. A person seeking knowledge of their fate might stand at a crossroads at midnight, listening for voices on the wind that would speak their future. Others would look into mirrors or still water by candlelight, expecting to see visions or the face of a spirit guide.

Natural omens were carefully observed. A heavy mist on Samhain morning meant the veil remained thin and spirits still walked. If the wind blew from the west, the winter would be mild; from the north, harsh and long. Finding a white stone on Samhain day was considered a blessing from the ancestors, and the stone would be kept as a protective talisman. Seeing a single crow at dawn suggested a message from the Morrígan; three crows foretold transformation; and a raven circling overhead indicated that a spirit guide was near.

For those who work with dreams, Samhain is a potent time for dream incubation. Before sleep, write a question on a piece of paper and place it beneath your pillow. Anoint your temples with mugwort oil or place dried mugwort in a sachet near your head. As you drift off, repeat your question three times. Keep a journal beside your bed to record any dreams immediately upon waking, before the details fade. Dreams at Samhain often carry messages from ancestors or glimpses of the year to come. Pay attention to recurring symbols, colors, or emotions; these are the language of the Otherworld.

A simple but powerful divination uses three stones. Find three smooth stones of similar size. Mark one with a symbol of the past, one for the present, and one for the future. Hold them in your hands, ask your question, and cast them onto a cloth. The stone that lands closest to you represents the most significant influence. If stones touch or overlap, those time periods are connected. A stone that lands face-down suggests hidden information. This method works well for questions about transitions, decisions, or understanding patterns in your life.

Teaching Story: The Woman at the Ford

There is an old teaching that I carry with me each Samhain, learned not from books but from experience, from watching the land and listening to what moves in the dark.

Years ago, during my first deliberate Samhain vigil, I was young in my practice and uncertain of what to expect. I had prepared everything according to tradition: the altar, the offerings, the candles lit in careful order. But as the night deepened, I felt nothing. No presence. No shift in the air. Just silence and my own doubt.

I left my altar and walked outside, frustrated and feeling foolish. The night was cold and clear, the stars sharp as broken glass. I walked without purpose, just moving, until I found myself at a small stream that ran through the woods near my home. And there, at the ford where the water was shallow enough to cross, I stopped.

Something shifted. The air grew heavier. My skin prickled with the sensation of being watched, not with menace, but with expectation, as though someone waited to see what I would do. I looked across the water and saw, in the way you see things in half-light, a figure. Not solid, but present. A woman, tall and still, wrapped in a dark cloak that moved like smoke.

I knew her. Not by name, not yet, but by presence. The Morrígan. The Washer at the Ford. She who appears before battles, before death, before transformation. She did not speak, but I heard her nonetheless, a voice that was not sound but knowing, placed directly into my mind: "You prepared an altar as though I were a guest at a dinner party. But I do not come when called by candles. I come when you stand at the edge of something and do not turn away."

I stood there, shaking, understanding and not understanding. She remained a moment longer, and then she was gone, not vanishing but simply no longer there, as though she had stepped sideways into a space I could not see.

That moment taught me something essential about Samhain and about working with the gods. Ritual is important. Preparation matters. But it is not the candles or the words or the perfect setup that opens the door. It is presence. It is showing up, not with expectations of how divinity should appear, but with willingness to meet whatever comes. It is standing at the ford, at the threshold, and waiting in the dark without demanding light.

Since then, I have returned to that ford every Samhain. Sometimes I feel her presence. Sometimes I do not. But I have learned to trust the threshold itself, to honor the in-between, and to understand that not every vigil will bring visions, and that is also sacred. The gods do not perform on command. But they are there, in the liminal spaces, waiting for those brave enough to meet them in the dark.

Samhain for Solitary Practitioners

Many who walk this path do so alone, by choice or by circumstance. Solitary practice at Samhain carries its own power and beauty. Without the need to coordinate with others or perform for an audience, the solitary practitioner can sink deeply into personal work, move at their own pace, and follow their intuition without compromise.

If you practice alone, consider creating a Samhain season rather than focusing on a single night. Begin preparations three days before Samhain Eve. Clean your space. Gather your tools. Each evening, light a candle and speak aloud one memory of someone who has died, or one quality you wish to release. Let the season build slowly, naturally, without rush.

On Samhain night itself, honor your practice without pressure to perform elaborate ritual. Sometimes the most powerful work is simple: a candle, a photograph, a whispered prayer. Sit in silence for as long as you need. Write letters to the dead and then burn them, releasing the words to the Otherworld. Walk outside and listen to the night. Stand at your doorway and speak a blessing. Trust that your sincerity matters more than complexity.

In the days following Samhain, tend to the transition. Do not rush back into ordinary life. Let the liminal space linger. Continue to light candles. Pay attention to dreams, synchronicities, and unexpected messages. The veil does not snap closed at dawn on November first; it settles gradually, like mist clearing. Honor that slow return by moving gently between the worlds.

Looking Ahead As the last candle is snuffed and the final prayer offered, we step fully into the dark half of the year. The world grows quieter now. The land rests beneath clouded skies and bare branches. Yet in this deep stillness, the seeds of renewal stir.

The next festival on the Wheel is the Winter Solstice, known in Irish tradition as Midwinter or Mean Geimhridh. It marks the rebirth of the sun and the quiet triumph of light within darkness. It is a time of hope, of hearth, and of holding close those who bring warmth to our lives. As we journey from Samhain's shadowed threshold toward the returning light, we carry our ancestors with us, guiding, watching, and walking beside us.

In the next chapter, we will explore the mysteries and magic of the Solstice fire, and how to honor the still point of the sun's journey with ritual, rest, and radiant intention.

Seasonal Recipes for Samhain

Soul Cakes (Traditional)

These small, spiced cakes were traditionally made to honor the dead and offered to visiting spirits. Soulers would go door to door singing for soul cakes, which were given in exchange for prayers for deceased family members.

Serves: 12 cakes | Prep: 15 min | Cook: 20 min | Total: 35 min

Ingredients

2 cups all-purpose flour

1/2 cup butter, softened

1/2 cup sugar

1 egg

1/4 cup milk

1/2 tsp ground cinnamon

1/2 tsp ground nutmeg

1/4 tsp ground cloves

1/4 tsp allspice

1 tsp baking powder

Pinch of salt

Raisins or currants (optional)

Instructions

1. Preheat oven to 350°F (175°C). Line baking sheets with parchment.

2. Cream together butter and sugar until light and fluffy.

3. Beat in egg, then add milk.

4. In separate bowl, whisk together flour, spices, baking powder, and salt.

5. Gradually mix dry ingredients into wet ingredients until dough forms.

6. Roll dough to 1/2 inch thickness on floured surface.

7. Cut into rounds (about 3 inches diameter). Mark each with a cross using a knife.

8. Place on baking sheets. Press raisins into centers if desired.

9. Bake 15-20 minutes until golden and firm.

10. Cool on wire rack. Offer to ancestors at your altar, share with visitors, or leave outside as an offering to wandering spirits.

The cross marked on top is both protective and symbolic of the four directions. Soul cakes should be made with intention, thinking of those who have passed.

Colcannon (Irish Potato and Kale)

A traditional Irish dish perfect for Samhain feasts. Colcannon combines mashed potatoes with cabbage or kale, representing the harvest and the nourishment needed as winter approaches.

Serves: 6 | Prep: 10 min | Cook: 25 min | Total: 35 min

Ingredients

2 lbs potatoes, peeled and quartered

4 cups kale or green cabbage, chopped

1 cup milk or cream

4 tbsp butter, plus more for serving

4 green onions (scallions), finely chopped

Salt and pepper to taste

Instructions

1. Boil potatoes in salted water until tender, about 20 minutes.

2. While potatoes cook, blanch kale in boiling water for 3-4 minutes until tender. Drain well.

3. In a small pot, warm milk and butter together until butter melts.

4. Drain potatoes and return to pot. Mash thoroughly.

5. Stir in the warm milk mixture, kale, and green onions.

6. Season with salt and pepper.

7. Serve hot with a well of melted butter in the center.

8. Traditionally, small charms were hidden in colcannon for divination: a ring (marriage), a coin (wealth), a thimble (spinsterhood), or a button (bachelorhood).

For Samhain, make this as part of a "dumb supper" where a place is set for deceased loved ones and the meal is eaten in silence, allowing the spirits to join.

Barmbrack (Irish Halloween Bread)

Traditional Irish fruit bread associated with Samhain divination. Objects baked into the bread foretold the finder's fortune for the coming year.

Serves: 8-10 slices | Prep: 15 min + overnight soak | Cook: 1 hour | Total: 1 hr 15 min active

Ingredients

2 cups mixed dried fruit (raisins, currants, sultanas)

1 cup strong black tea, cooled

1/2 cup brown sugar

2 cups all-purpose flour

1 tsp baking powder

1 tsp mixed spice (or cinnamon, nutmeg, allspice)

1 egg, beaten

2 tbsp marmalade or honey

Zest of 1 orange

Instructions

1. Night before: Soak dried fruit in tea and sugar. Cover and leave overnight.

2. Preheat oven to 350°F (175°C). Grease a 9-inch loaf pan.

3. In large bowl, mix flour, baking powder, and spices.

4. Add soaked fruit mixture, beaten egg, marmalade, and orange zest.

5. Mix until just combined—don't overmix.

6. Pour into prepared pan.

7. Bake 1 hour or until a skewer inserted comes out clean.

8. Cool in pan 10 minutes, then turn out onto wire rack.

9. Serve sliced with butter. Best eaten within 2-3 days or freeze.

Traditionally, small, wrapped objects were baked in: a ring (marriage), a coin (wealth), a piece of cloth (poverty), or a stick (unhappy marriage). Modern practice uses only food-safe charms or skips this custom. The bread itself is delicious for Samhain gatherings and keeps well.

Looking Ahead

As the darkness of Samhain settles deep into the land, we move toward the Winter Solstice, when the sun reaches its lowest point and begins its return. In the next chapter, we explore the mysteries of midwinter and the promise of the returning light.

Chapter 10: Winter Solstice – Brú na Bóinne and the Sun's Return

The Winter Solstice, known in Irish as Grianstad an Gheimhridh, marks the longest night and shortest day of the year. Astronomically, it occurs around December 21st in the Northern Hemisphere. Spiritually, it represents the rebirth of light and the enduring power of hope in darkness. For ancient peoples, including those who built Brú na Bóinne (commonly called Newgrange) this was no ordinary date. It was sacred, meticulously observed, and aligned with the sun's return.

At Newgrange, a stone passage tomb older than the pyramids, the winter solstice sun rises and shines through a narrow roof box above the entrance. For just a few minutes, a beam of light pierces the dark interior and illuminates the inner chamber. This annual event demonstrates the builders' astronomical knowledge and their reverence for the sun's rebirth. It is not merely an engineering marvel; it is a profound spiritual statement. Light, long absent, returns to the womb of the earth.

For modern neo-pagans walking the Irish Wheel of the Year, the Winter Solstice is an invitation to stillness, reflection, and quiet celebration. It is a moment to honor survival, both physical and spiritual, and to welcome the promise of brighter days ahead. Though the coldest part of the year lies ahead, the sun has turned. From this night forward, the days will grow longer, even if slowly. In this way, the Winter Solstice marks not an end, but a beginning.

The Mythic Context

In Irish myth and cosmology, the return of the sun at Midwinter echoes deeper themes of renewal, hidden strength, and cyclical restoration. Though there is no single myth explicitly tied to the solstice in surviving texts, several figures and narratives align with the symbolism of this sacred time.

The goddess Danu, considered the divine mother of the Tuatha Dé Danann, is often associated with rivers, fertility, and mystery. At solstice, her energy can be seen in the quiet gestation of light within darkness; the unseen source preparing to give birth to new life. She represents the potential that stirs beneath the surface, invisible but inevitable.

The Dagda, Danu's consort and the great father-god of Irish mythology, is closely tied to both the earth and the sun. His cauldron never runs empty, and his club can kill or revive. In the tale of his union with the Morrígan at Samhain, he is portrayed as a harbinger of cosmic order, fertility, and light. At solstice, he may be honored as the protector of warmth, sustenance, and the promise of spring.

Some modern practitioners also honor Brigid at this time, though her major festival is Imbolc. In her aspect as a bringer of light, healing, and the sacred hearth, Brigid foreshadows the coming turn of the year. Lighting a candle for her at solstice connects the sun's external return with the flame of inspiration and care that burns within.

The mound itself. Brú na Bóinne, is both womb and tomb. It is a threshold space that blurs the line between death and rebirth, silence and song, dark and light. To witness the light enter this space is to witness myth in motion: the sun is reborn, the year turns, and the divine breathes through stone.

Seasonal Signs and Cultural Themes

The Winter Solstice in Ireland would have marked a critical point in the agricultural year. Though little could be planted or harvested in the deep cold, this time was essential for planning, rest, and spiritual renewal. In households and tribal communities, stories were told beside the hearth, tools were repaired, and future crops or journeys were considered in theory if not in motion.

This season was about endurance. The focus shifted from outward work to inward reflection. Livestock were closely watched, fires were maintained around the clock, and resources were rationed wisely. To survive winter was to trust in what had been stored and in the return of what had not yet come. In this way, the Winter Solstice was not just a pause but a quiet act of faith; a belief that what lies buried will rise again.

For modern practitioners, the solstice invites a similar pause. It is a time for deep rest, for letting go of the year's noise, and for planting seeds of intention in the dark soil of the soul. As the ancestors kept fire against the frost, so do we tend the inner flame: our creativity, our devotion, our quiet strength. In this dark, we remember light. In this stillness, we sense movement beginning.

Altar Setup and Seasonal Elements

Creating a Winter Solstice altar allows the practitioner to reflect the sacred themes of rebirth, endurance, and quiet illumination. This altar becomes a symbolic hearth, both a visual focus for ritual and a container for deep seasonal presence. Begin by choosing a base cloth in colors that echo the solstice mood: deep blue for night, white for purity and snow, or gold to honor the returning sun. Layering white over dark fabric can visually represent the light rising from shadow.

Candles play a central role. Use one large white or gold candle as your central "sun candle." This will represent the reborn light of the year and should remain unlit until the moment of ritual culmination. Surround it with smaller candles in red, gold, or even green, colors that symbolize fire, life, and the ever-turning cycle. For safety, LED candles may be substituted in urban or shared environments.

Herbs and incense chosen for this festival should speak to stillness, warmth, and inner clarity. Burn frankincense to invoke sacred stillness and pine or cedar for cleansing and grounding. Rosemary brings memory and peace. Cinnamon or clove, while not native to Ireland, can be used to call warmth and hearth-energy into modern rites. Dried orange peel or a slice of fresh orange may also be added to the altar as a symbol of the returning sun.

Crystals that support solstice energy include clear quartz (for clarity and rebirth), sunstone (for joy and resilience), and black tourmaline (for protection and grounding). Place them in a spiral formation if desired, representing the sun's journey from darkness into light.

Seasonal greenery is especially important. In Ireland, holly and ivy were traditionally brought into the home during winter. Holly, with its blood-red berries and evergreen leaves, symbolizes the survival of life through death. Ivy represents perseverance and rebirth, as it clings and thrives even in cold. A small bundle of both, tied with red thread and placed on the altar, serves as a powerful seasonal charm.

Include symbols of the sun itself, a golden disk, spiral carvings, a handmade sun-wheel, or images inspired by the roof box of Newgrange. These link your personal space to the ancient solar alignments once tracked by your spiritual ancestors.

The altar may also include a bowl of water to represent stillness and reflection, and a piece of bread or cake as an offering to ancestral spirits or solar deities. These elements ensure that the altar does not remain only symbolic, but active, offering touchpoints for real-world practice and devotion.

Sacred Foods, Recipes, and Symbolic Eating
Step-by-Step Solstice Ritual: Rebirth of the Light

This Winter Solstice ritual is designed for solitary practitioners but may be adapted for a household or community group. It draws on Irish cosmology, seasonal rhythm, and the mystery of Brú na Bóinne, where the sun returns to the sacred womb of stone.

Preparation and Centering Choose a quiet space and dim all artificial lights. Let the room hold darkness for a while before you begin. At your altar, place an unlit white or gold sun candle in the center, surrounded by your chosen symbols and offerings.

Sit or stand before the altar. Close your eyes. Breathe deeply, letting the breath fall into rhythm with the silence. Feel the stillness of winter settle around you.

Say: "I enter the stillness of the longest night. Within darkness, I seek light. Within silence, I prepare for rebirth."

Casting the Circle Move sunwise (clockwise) around your space, visualizing a glowing boundary forming in your wake. This is your sacred circle.

Say: "I cast this circle by the breath of night, By stone and frost, by flame and light. Let this space be sealed and sacred. Let only truth and reverence remain."

Invocation of the Sun and Divine Presence Return to the altar. Place your hands near the sun candle.

Say: "Light of the world, child of the sun, You who rise from the womb of stone, Return now, as you have before, Bringing warmth where cold has held."

Optionally invoke a specific deity: "Dagda, guardian of cycles and flame, be with me. Danu, mother of mysteries, hold this space. Brigid, distant flame, stir the spark within."

Lighting the Sun Candlelight the central candle with reverence.

Say: "From darkness you are born, O sun, Not in haste, but in stillness. I welcome your return. May your fire stir the fire within me."

Gaze into the flame. Feel the shift within you. Let the

moment deepen.

Meditation: Within the Womb of Stone Close your eyes and visualize walking the spiral passage of Brú na Bóinne. Feel the stones, the cold air. Reach the chamber's heart and sit in darkness. Overhead, a shaft of light appears. It touches you. What is being reborn in you? What seed stirs?

Remain in stillness. When ready, return slowly.

Statement of Intention Speak aloud your intention for the returning year: • "I welcome clarity into the new year." • "I carry this light into the world with courage." • "I am ready to grow, even in quiet ways."

Write this down and place it beneath a crystal, sun disk, or in your journal.

Offerings and Blessings Place bread, herbs, or a cup of cider at the altar.

Say: "To those who came before, who endured the dark, To those who come after, may they find this flame; I give thanks, I give blessing, I give light."

Releasing the Circle Move counter-clockwise around the space.

Say: "The circle is open, but never broken. The sun returns, and I will return. The flame is kindled. The year begins."

Grounding and Reflection Eat a small piece of bread or sip your warm drink. Touch the earth, floor, or your own body to ground.

Journal your experience. Note visions, emotions, and intentions. Let this entry become your seed.

This ritual does not require grandeur to be sacred. Even a single candle in silence, lit with love and hope, echoes the ritual of Newgrange. In that moment, you are connected to generations past and future.

Modern Practice Tips and City Rituals

While the sacred landscape of Ireland offers a mythic and historical setting for solstice observance, modern practitioners may live in cities, apartments, or suburban areas far removed from the stone circles and mounds of their spiritual ancestors. Yet the magic of the Winter Solstice is not bound by geography. It is carried in the heart, the home, and the flame we choose to tend.

Urban and Indoor Adaptations If you cannot greet the solstice sun on a distant horizon, greet it through ritual and rhythm. Light a single candle before sunrise. Turn off all artificial lights and sit in darkness until the light shifts. Use blackout curtains to simulate the long night, then draw them back ceremonially as you light the sun candle.

Create a ritual corner, a bookshelf, a windowsill, or even a tabletop dressed in seasonal colors. Face it eastward if possible. Use gold or white fabric to reflect light, and a sun symbol you've drawn or crafted by hand. Honor the dawn not just by watching it, but by welcoming it through words, breath, and flame.

Family and Household Rituals The solstice offers a powerful opportunity for shared experience. Involve children or housemates in preparing a special meal or baking sun-themed treats. Let them help shape spiral cookies, draw solar glyphs, or arrange candles in a circle.

In the evening, turn off all lights and gather together. Pass a single flame from person to person, letting each one speak a hope for the coming year. This becomes a household sun rite, where every voice lights the return.

Creating Portable Solar Altars If space is tight or shared, create a portable altar. A wooden box or tin can hold cloths, symbols, candles, herbs, and a small solar charm. Bring it out just for the ritual, and store it afterward with reverence.

Alternatively, make a "sun jar": a clean glass jar painted with golden spirals and filled with a tea light or battery candle. Place it near your bed or on a desk. Let it glow each night of the solstice week.

Solstice Journaling and Reflection Prompts The winter sun invites introspection. These prompts can be written on paper and placed in a jar, drawn randomly during the week leading up to or following the solstice: • What darkness have I endured this year? • What truth emerged in silence? • Where in my life do I seek renewal? • What small light have I kept alive? • What seed am I planting for the new year?

Answer these in writing, art, or spoken prayer. Each reflection is a flame.

Digital and Distant Connection When distance separates loved ones or ritual partners, consider connecting virtually. Host a video call at sunrise or sunset. Light candles together, share a solstice reading, or toast with spiced cider. You can even prepare the same recipes and eat in mirrored ritual spaces.

Some online communities also host virtual Newgrange sunrises, streaming the live solstice alignment from Ireland. Watching together can be a moving way to share ancestral awe.

Above all, remember: the solstice does not demand spectacle. Its greatest lesson is that of the returning light, quiet, patient, and sure. Whether you mark it alone in a city high-rise, with family in a suburban kitchen, or in the wild hills of your homeland, you join an unbroken line of sun-watchers, flame-tenders, and dreamers of dawn.

The Living Stones: Newgrange and the Solar Mysteries

To understand the Winter Solstice in an Irish context is to reckon with Brú na Bóinne, the passage tomb we now call Newgrange. Built over five thousand years ago, this monument stands as one of humanity's most profound acts of devotion to the returning sun. Its builders were not primitive; they were astronomers, architects, and spiritual visionaries who understood the mathematics of eternity.

The roof box above the entrance was engineered with such precision that, for approximately seventeen minutes around dawn on the winter solstice, a shaft of golden light penetrates sixty feet into the inner chamber, illuminating carved spirals and basins that may have held offerings or remains of the dead. This is not accidental architecture. This is a temple. A womb. A declaration that death and rebirth are inextricably bound, and that light will always return from darkness.

The experience of being inside Newgrange during solstice sunrise is described by those fortunate enough to witness it as otherworldly. The chamber is silent, stone-cold, utterly dark. Then the first thread of light appears at the roof box. It grows, widening into a beam that floods the passage with golden warmth. In that moment, the ancestors speak. Not in words, but in presence. The dead are touched by the sun, and the living witness resurrection.

Modern practitioners who cannot visit Newgrange can still honor this alignment. Face east at sunrise on the winter solstice. Stand in silence and watch the sun crest the horizon. Imagine that first beam of light entering the sacred chamber. Feel yourself as part of that lineage: stone-builders, sun-watchers, keepers of the flame.

Speak your intention into the dawn. You are participating in a ritual older than written language, and it recognizes you.

Regional Folk Customs and Solstice Lore

Though the solstices were not as prominently featured in Irish folklore as the cross-quarter festivals, regional customs and folk wisdom still marked this sacred turning point. In rural areas, particularly in the West and Southwest, the solstice was observed as a time to ensure protection through the darkest days.

In County Cork and Kerry, it was customary to keep a candle burning in the window throughout the solstice night as a beacon for any traveler, living or dead, who might need guidance. The candle was never to be extinguished until dawn broke. To let it die early was considered unlucky, as though one had failed to keep faith with the returning light. This practice echoes the ancient belief that the longest night is also the most liminal, when spirits may wander and the living must hold the threshold.

In parts of Ulster, households would gather ivy and holly the day before the solstice and weave them into protective wreaths. These were hung above doorways or windows, with the understanding that evergreens carried the promise of life persisting through death. Holly, with its red berries like drops of blood, represented strength and sacrifice. Ivy, clinging and enduring, symbolized loyalty and resilience. Together, they were a living prayer for survival.

Some families in Connacht would prepare a special solstice bread, baked in the shape of a sun wheel with cuts radiating from the center like rays. This bread was broken and shared at dawn after the longest night, each person taking a piece to symbolize their share of the returning light. Crumbs were scattered outside for the birds, a gesture of reciprocity: as we are fed, so we feed others.

Weather omens were carefully observed around the solstice. A clear dawn on the shortest day promised a harsh but short-lived winter. A clouded or stormy solstice suggested a long, cold season ahead. If snow fell on solstice night, it was considered a blessing; a blanket laid down by the gods to protect the sleeping earth. A red sky at solstice sunset foretold transformation in the year to come, whether in the land, the community, or one's own life.

Devotional Practices: Honoring the Gods of Light and Renewal

The Winter Solstice invites specific devotional work with deities connected to light, rebirth, fertility, and the turning of time. While these gods and goddesses are honored throughout the year, the solstice offers a concentrated moment of contact, when their presence is particularly potent.

The Dagda, the Good God, is perhaps the most fitting deity to approach at this time. As father of the Tuatha Dé Danann and keeper of the great cauldron of abundance, he embodies both nourishment and cyclical renewal. His club can kill with one end and resurrect with the other, a perfect metaphor for the solstice itself: the sun dies and is reborn in a single turning.

To honor the Dagda at solstice, prepare a small feast and offer a portion to him before you eat. Bread, porridge, meat, or stew; simple, hearty food that sustains. Speak to him as you would a grandfather: with respect, affection, and honesty. Ask for his protection through the dark months, for abundance in the coming year, and for the strength to endure. Place your offering outdoors at the base of a tree or stone, or leave it on your altar overnight and return it to the earth the next day.

Brigid, though her primary festival is Imbolc, can also be honored at solstice as a keeper of the sacred flame. She is the light that never goes out, the hearth that warms the home, the spark of inspiration that survives the coldest night. Light a candle in her name and ask her to tend the flame within you through winter. Offer her milk, butter, or a small handmade craft. Brigid appreciates work done with care, and anything made by your hands is a suitable gift.

Some practitioners also work with Lugh at solstice, though his power is strongest at Lughnasadh in summer. At the winter turning, Lugh represents the promise of the sun's eventual return to full strength. He is the distant light, not yet warm, but undeniably present. Offerings of grain, ale, or a pledge of creative work honor his role as patron of skill and mastery.

Finally, do not forget the land itself. The earth is not dead in winter; it is dreaming. Speak to the spirits of place, to the sidhe who dwell beneath hills and stones. Leave offerings of milk, honey, or bread at natural thresholds: the edge of a forest, a stone wall, a crossroads. Ask for their blessing on your work, and promise to tend the land with respect when spring returns.

Teaching Story: The Candle in the Snow

There is a winter I remember, years ago now, when I learned what the solstice truly means.

I was going through a difficult time, the kind where everything feels heavy and the days blur into a monotonous gray. Depression had settled over me like a cold fog, and I moved through my life mechanically, without joy or hope. The solstice approached, and I could not summon the energy to care. What did it matter if the sun returned? Everything still felt dark.

But on the night before solstice, something shifted. I found myself standing at my window, looking out at the snow that had begun to fall. On impulse, I lit a single white candle and placed it on the sill. I had no ritual planned, no elaborate setup. Just one candle in the dark, burning against the glass.

I watched the flame for a long time. I watched the snow fall. And somewhere in that watching, something in me unknotted. I thought about the people who had stood at windows like this for thousands of years, lighting candles, keeping vigil, waiting for dawn.

I thought about Newgrange, that stone womb in the earth, and how the sun finds it year after year, no matter what.

I realized then that the returning of the light is not about feeling better immediately. It is about trust. It is about lighting the candle even when you cannot feel its warmth, about tending the flame because it needs tending, about showing up to the threshold even when you are too tired to cross it. The sun does not ask if we are ready. It returns because that is what it does. That is the promise.

I kept that candle burning through the night. I did not perform a grand ritual. I did not invoke deities or cast circles. I simply sat with the flame and the snow and the darkness, and I let the solstice hold me. By morning, I was not healed. But I was not hopeless. Something small had shifted, a crack in the ice, a single thread of light in a long tunnel.

Since then, I have learned that sometimes the most powerful solstice observances are the simplest. One candle. One breath. One moment of showing up when everything in you wants to hide. The light returns not because we are ready, but because it is time. And we return to ourselves not because we have earned it, but because that, too, is how the Wheel turns.

Solstice for Families and Children

The Winter Solstice offers a beautiful opportunity to introduce children to the cycles of nature and the magic of tradition. Unlike some festivals that focus on the dead or shadow work, the solstice is fundamentally about hope, light, and renewal; themes accessible to young minds and hearts.

Begin by explaining the solstice in simple terms: "Today is the longest night of the year. It's been getting darker for a long time, but after tonight, the days will start getting brighter again. The sun is coming back." Let children help prepare the altar. They can arrange candles, choose symbols, or draw pictures of the sun to place among the offerings.

Create simple crafts together: sun wheels from paper plates and yellow paint, or small lanterns from jars and tissue paper. Bake solstice cookies shaped like suns, stars, or spirals, and decorate them with gold and yellow icing. These activities embed the lesson in joyful, tangible experience.

On the evening of the solstice, gather the family after sunset. Turn off all the lights and sit together in darkness for a few minutes. Talk about what darkness feels like, what it means, how it is not bad but necessary for rest. Then, beginning with the youngest person, let each family member light one candle from the central sun candle, speaking a wish or hope as they do. By the end, the room glows with light, and the lesson is clear: together, we bring back the sun.

Read solstice stories or myths together. Choose tales appropriate to age: younger children might enjoy stories about brave little lights, while older kids can handle more complex myths about solar deities or the building of Newgrange. Storytelling at solstice connects children to an ancient tradition of passing wisdom through the dark.

If possible, wake before dawn on the morning after the longest night and watch the sunrise together. Bring hot chocolate, wrap in blankets, and greet the returning sun as a family. This becomes a memory they will carry: the winter morning when they stood with you, watching light return, knowing that even the darkest night ends in dawn.

Seasonal Recipes for Winter Solstice

Spiced Barley and Root Stew

A hearty winter stew celebrating root vegetables and grains, perfect for the longest night. The warming spices honor the returning sun.

Serves: 6-8 | Prep: 20 min | Cook: 1 hour | Total: 1 hr 20 min

Ingredients

1 cup pearl barley, rinsed

2 tbsp olive oil or butter

1 large onion, diced

3 carrots, peeled and chopped

2 parsnips, peeled and chopped

1 turnip or rutabaga, peeled and cubed

3 cloves garlic, minced

6 cups vegetable or beef stock

2 bay leaves

1 tsp dried thyme

1/2 tsp ground coriander

1/2 tsp smoked paprika

1/4 tsp cayenne (optional)

Salt and pepper to taste

Fresh parsley for garnish

Instructions

1. In large pot, heat oil over medium heat.

2. Sauté onion until softened, about 5 minutes.

3. Add garlic, cook 1 minute more.

4. Add all root vegetables, stirring to coat.

5. Pour in stock, add barley, bay leaves, thyme, coriander, and paprika.

6. Bring to boil, then reduce to simmer.

7. Cover and cook 45-60 minutes until barley and vegetables are tender.

8. Season with salt, pepper, and cayenne if using.

9. Remove bay leaves before serving.

10. Garnish with fresh parsley and serve hot with crusty bread.

This stew represents the earth's stored nourishment sustaining us through winter darkness. Make it as part of a solstice vigil, eating by candlelight while awaiting dawn.

Honey-Glazed Winter Vegetables

Roasted root vegetables with honey represent the sweetness of the returning light and the earth's golden gifts.

Serves: 6 | Prep: 15 min | Cook: 45 min | Total: 1 hour

Ingredients

3 large carrots, peeled and cut into chunks

2 parsnips, peeled and cut into chunks

1 small butternut squash, peeled and cubed

1 large beet, peeled and cubed

3 tbsp olive oil

2 tbsp honey

1 tbsp fresh rosemary, chopped

1 tsp fresh thyme leaves

4 cloves garlic, whole

Salt and pepper to taste

1 tbsp balsamic vinegar (optional)

Instructions

1. Preheat oven to 400°F (200°C).

2. In large bowl, toss vegetables with olive oil, salt, and pepper.

3. Spread on large baking sheet in single layer.

4. Add whole garlic cloves.

5. Roast 30 minutes, stirring halfway.

6. Drizzle with honey, sprinkle with herbs.

7. Return to oven for 10-15 minutes until caramelized and tender.

8. Remove from oven, drizzle with balsamic if using.

9. Serve hot, garnished with extra fresh herbs.

The golden color of these vegetables honors the sun. Serve as offering on your Solstice altar before the feast, speaking prayers for the sun's return.

Mulled Wine (Wassail)

A traditional warming drink for winter gatherings, spiced wine honors the season and toasts the returning light.

Serves: 8-10 | Prep: 5 min | Cook: 30 min | Total: 35 min

Ingredients

1 bottle (750ml) red wine

2 cups apple cider

1/4 cup honey or brown sugar

2 oranges, sliced

2 cinnamon sticks

6 whole cloves

4 star anise

3 cardamom pods, crushed

1 piece fresh ginger, sliced (1 inch)

1/4 cup brandy (optional)

Instructions

1. Combine wine and cider in large pot.

2. Add honey or sugar, stirring to dissolve.

3. Add orange slices and all spices.

4. Heat gently over medium-low, do not boil.

5. Simmer 20-30 minutes to meld flavors.

6. Strain out solids or leave them floating for presentation.

7. Add brandy if using.

8. Serve warm in mugs.

9. Save some to pour as libation to the gods and spirits.

Toast the sun at midnight or dawn with this warming drink. Traditional wassailing involves singing to apple trees, but any joyful honoring of the season works. Non-alcoholic version: use only apple cider and double the amount.

All recipes follow a consistent format: headnote, timing, ingredients, numbered instructions, and ritual context connecting each recipe to spiritual practice.

Closing Reflection

The Winter Solstice is a paradox, deep stillness paired with quiet momentum, the longest night pregnant with the promise of dawn. To stand within this moment, as our ancestors once did before sacred mounds and hearths, is to witness the oldest magic: the returning of the light.

We do not light candles to banish the dark, but to remember that light has always lived within it. In Irish tradition, light is not a victory over dark, but its complement. The two spiral around one another, each giving shape to the other, just as life and death define the turning year.

At Brú na Bóinne, where stone and sun meet only for a moment, we see the wisdom of waiting. That which is most sacred arrives not in haste but in rhythm. The same is true of our inner lives. Renewal cannot be rushed. Hope, like the sun, rises in its time.

So as you step from the longest night into the lengthening days, may you carry this knowing with you:

That stillness is fertile. That the flame you tend is ancient. That your light, however small, is part of a vast and timeless dawn.

May the return of the sun bring warmth to your hearth, vision to your path, and clarity to your spirit. And may you walk this next cycle with reverence, courage, and joy.

The solstice has turned. The year begins anew.

So be it. So it is. So it shall return.

Looking Ahead

With the sun reborn at Winter Solstice, we journey forward to Imbolc, the festival of Brigid and the first stirrings of spring. The next chapter guides you through the quickening season and the return of hope.

Chapter 11: Imbolc – Brigid's Fire and the First Light of Spring

The Season and Its Significance Imbolc, celebrated around February 1st, signals the first true stirring of spring in the Irish seasonal cycle. The word Imbolc is often interpreted as "in the belly," referring to pregnant ewes whose lambs will soon be born; a natural symbol of new life waiting beneath the surface. In older agrarian societies, this was a time of quiet optimism. Though the landscape remained stark, subtle signs appeared: buds on blackthorn, lengthening days, and the distant bleat of lambs.

To the Irish, this moment was not only seasonal but spiritual. Imbolc was a time to bless the hearth, purify the home, and light the first ritual flames that would carry the promise of renewal into spring. Just as Samhain was the beginning of the dark half of the year, Imbolc is the threshold into light. It is a feast of beginnings, of whispered awakenings, and of honoring the flame that lives within.

Brigid's presence is woven through every part of this celebration. The hearth goddess of healing, poetry, fertility, and the forge, she is both gentle and powerful; protector of the home and guardian of the sacred fire. The returning sun is still faint at Imbolc, but the fire of Brigid is strong. She does not wait for warmth to arrive; she makes warmth by tending what is vital. That is the essence of this sabbat: not waiting for change, but preparing for it with devotion, clarity, and quiet strength.

Mythic Context and Deity Association Brigid (Bríde, Bríg, or Brigantia) is one of the most beloved deities in the Irish pantheon, and Imbolc is her sacred festival. Her influence extends across poetry, smithing, healing, midwifery, and domestic craft. She embodies the spark of life in its many forms, creative inspiration, the fire of transformation, and the sacred warmth of care.

Brigid's name may come from the Old Irish root brígh, meaning "strength" or "exalted one." She is often viewed as a triple goddess: one face for healing, one for poetry, and one for smithcraft. These aspects are not divided but unified, reminding us that transformation (whether of metal, body, or word) requires the same inner fire.

In mythology, she is the daughter of the Dagda and closely linked with the Tuatha Dé Danann. She is said to have keened the first mourning song when her son Ruadán was slain, and thus became patroness of lamentation and grief's expression through art. She is both hearth and forge, tender of flame and wielder of it.

Brigid's sacred flame was once kept perpetually lit by nineteen priestesses at Kildare (Cill Dara; "Church of the Oak"). Even after Christianization, the cult of Brigid continued as Saint Brigid, a syncretic figure who retained many of the goddess's attributes, including the sacred fire, the healing well, and the protection of livestock and crops.

To call on Brigid at Imbolc is to call on transformation guided by grace. She lights the inner path forward when outer signs are faint. Her fire is the oath to persevere, to create, to care, and to begin anew.

In every flickering candle, in every crafted word or healed wound, in every act of compassion or creativity, Brigid lives. At Imbolc, we invite her in; not only to bless our hearths, but to rekindle the flame in our hearts.

Step-by-Step Imbolc Ritual: Flame of the Hearth

This ritual is designed for solitary practitioners but may be easily adapted for small groups or households. It honors Brigid in

her aspects as healer, poet, and flame-bringer, and invites her
blessing into your home and heart as the year's light begins to return.

Preparation and Cleansing

Tidy and clean your ritual space with intention. Sweep the
floor, dust surfaces, and smudge the area with smoke from rosemary,
cedar, or juniper. Open a window briefly to release stagnant energy.

Say aloud:

"I cleanse this space in Brigid's name;
With air and flame, with ash and grace.
Let all that is weary be released.
Let all that is sacred now take root."

Setting the Altar

Arrange your Imbolc altar as previously described. Light the three
Brigid candles but leave the central flame unlit. Place the dish of
water beside it and a token of your craft or healing art nearby.

Casting the Circle

Walk clockwise around your space, tracing a circle in the air with
your hand, wand, or candle.

Speak:

"By Brigid's hearth, I cast this ring;
Of flame and breath and blossoming.
This space is sealed. This moment true.
No harm may enter. Only blessing may pass."

Invocation   of   Brigid

Stand before the altar and raise your arms or hands.

Say:

"Brigid of the flame, come now.
Brigid of the forge, be with me.
Brigid of the well, flow through me.

Bright one of wisdom, strength, and healing;
Lady of flame and flowering earth;
Enter this space. Enter this heart."

Offer milk, honey, or bread on the altar. Let silence follow.

Lighting the Sacred Flame
Light the central candle.

Say:
"This is the fire that does not falter.
This is the flame that warms the seed.
This is the light of Brigid's blessing;
Within my hearth and within my need."

Gaze into the flame. Reflect on what is awakening within you.

Guided Meditation: Tending the Inner Flame
Close your eyes. Envision sitting beside a hearth in a stone cottage.
Brigid enters, cloaked in white and red. She places a small flame
into your hands. Feel its warmth, its steadiness.

She speaks: "What will you tend this year? What will you heal? What
will you create?"

Hold the flame to your chest and breathe deeply. Sit with this vision
for several minutes.

Statement of Intention
Open your eyes. Write or speak a clear intention for the coming
season. Example:

"I will protect the sacred time I need to create."

"I will nourish what is tender in me."

"I will let light return slowly and without fear."

Place the written intention beneath Brigid's cross or under a small bowl of herbs on the altar.

Water Blessing and Anointing
Touch the water dish on your altar.

Say:
"Well of Brigid, source of song,
Bless this water, make it strong."

Anoint your forehead, heart, and hands. If performing the ritual with others, offer the bowl in silence to pass from hand to hand.

Gratitude and Closing
Thank Brigid for her presence.

Say:
"Brigid of the mantle, Brigid of the flame,
I honor your gift. I carry your name."

Snuff or let candles burn safely down. Share bread or drink. Offer any remaining food to the earth.

Opening the Circle
Walk counter-clockwise and say:
"The circle opens, but the flame remains.
Blessings of Brigid in all my days."

After-Ritual Reflections
Journal your impressions. What came forward? What must be protected and nurtured in the light to come?

This ritual need not be grand to be profound. A single candle, lit with love and purpose, becomes a sun to guide your next turning of the wheel.

Modern Practice Tips

In modern life, we often find ourselves far from stone hearths and sacred wells. But Brigid's presence can still be felt in city apartments, suburban homes, and digital spaces. Imbolc remains a deeply accessible sabbat, quiet, reflective, and adaptable to all kinds of modern pagan paths.

Urban and Apartment-Friendly Adaptations

If you live in a small space or an apartment with no outdoor access, set up a miniature altar on a shelf, desk, or windowsill. Use LED candles if open flame isn't safe. A bowl of tap water blessed with intention can substitute for a sacred well. Place a small plant or sprig of rosemary as your living green presence. What matters most is reverence.

Family and Children's Participation

Involve children or family members by weaving Brigid's crosses together, blessing household candles, or baking bannocks as a shared ritual. Let children craft simple "flame jars" using orange tissue paper and battery tea lights. Explain Brigid as a protector and teacher of healing, creativity, and kindness.

Remote and Virtual Gatherings

If you are part of an online community or coven, consider holding a virtual Imbolc ritual. Share poems, blessings, or photos of your altars. Synchronize a time to light candles together. Distance does not lessen the sacred; intention bridges all.

Tending the Hearth Through Daily Acts

Brigid's fire burns not only in ritual but in every loving act. Tend your hearth by making a nourishing meal, writing a heartfelt letter, cleaning your space with gratitude, or creating art. These are sacred gestures. Declare them offerings.

Blessing Tools of Craft and Care

Lay out tools you use to heal, create, or serve, pens, pots, herbs, thread, instruments. Sprinkle them with blessed water and speak a short prayer over them:

"May these hands create in Brigid's name.
May this work serve life and beauty.
May this path be lit by fire that heals."

In honoring Brigid in the context of modern life, we affirm that the sacred does not live only in the past. It lives in how we rise to meet each day, with gentleness, courage, and devotion.

Brigid's Many Faces: The Triple Goddess Explored

Brigid is often described as a triple goddess, but this tripling is not simply a division of labor. It is a recognition that transformation, the core of her power, takes many forms. To understand her fully is to meet her in each of her faces and to see how they weave together into a single flame.

Brigid the Healer tends wounds both seen and unseen. She is the midwife at the threshold of birth, the herbalist gathering yarrow and comfrey at dawn, the keeper of wells whose waters restore. Her healing is not passive; it requires engagement, reciprocity, and trust. To call on Brigid for healing is to commit to the work of tending yourself or another with patience and reverence. She does not fix; she accompanies. She holds space for the slow mending that cannot be rushed.

Brigid the Poet is the voice that sings truth into being. She is the bard composing praise songs, the keeper of stories, the one who transforms grief into art. Poetry, in her hands, is not decoration but necessity; it is how we make sense of joy and sorrow, how we honor what was and call forth what will be. She is invoked by writers, musicians, and anyone who works with words as sacred tools. An offering to Brigid the Poet might be a poem written in her honor, a song sung at dawn, or simply the act of speaking truth when silence would be easier.

Brigid the Smith wields the transformative fire of the forge. She is the blacksmith shaping iron, the metalworker turning raw ore into something useful and beautiful. In her aspect as smith, she teaches that creation is often violent, loud, and demanding. The hammer must strike. The metal must be heated until it glows. But from this intensity comes form, function, and strength. Modern practitioners working with difficult personal transformation; breaking old patterns, forging new identities, enduring the heat of necessary change; can call on Brigid the Smith. She does not shy from the hard work. She stands at the anvil and waits for you to join her.

Together, these three faces form a whole. Brigid teaches that healing, art, and transformation are inseparable. To heal is to create. To create is to transform. To transform is to heal. The sacred flame at her shrine burned for all three reasons at once, and when you light a candle in her name, you invoke all of her power, not just one aspect.

Sacred Wells and Healing Waters

Throughout Ireland, sacred wells dedicated to Brigid are sites of pilgrimage, healing, and prayer. These wells are not mere tourist attractions; they are living shrines where people still come to seek blessing, leave offerings, and drink the waters that flow from deep within the earth. The tradition of well-veneration predates Christianity and was seamlessly absorbed into the cult of Saint Brigid, ensuring its survival.

Among the most famous is Brigid's Well at Kildare, where the perpetual flame once burned. Pilgrims tie ribbons, called clooties, to nearby trees as prayers for healing, each strip of cloth representing a petition or gratitude. The well water is collected in bottles and taken home to bless family members, livestock, or land. To drink from such a well is to take the goddess into yourself, to let her waters cleanse and renew from within.

Other wells dedicated to Brigid can be found throughout the country: Liscannor in County Clare, Faughart in County Louth, and many smaller springs and streams marked only by local memory. Each carries her presence, and each is approached with respect. Visitors leave coins, flowers, stones, or written prayers. Some wells have stone basins where people wash their faces or hands, seeking healing for specific ailments. Others are simply places to sit in silence and listen to the sound of water moving through rock.

For those far from Ireland, you can create your own well shrine. Find a natural spring, creek, or even a fountain in your area. Visit it at Imbolc with an offering: milk, honey, bread, or a handmade token. Speak a prayer to Brigid and ask her to bless the waters. If no natural water source is accessible, place a bowl of fresh water on your altar and dedicate it as a temporary well. Change the water daily and use it to anoint yourself, bless your home, or water plants. The act of tending water with intention makes it sacred.

The Art of Brigid's Crosses

One of the most enduring symbols of Imbolc is Brigid's cross, a woven charm traditionally made from rushes, reeds, or straw. The cross has four arms radiating from a woven square center, creating a shape that resembles both a sunwheel and a protective talisman. Though it carries the name "cross," its origins are pre-Christian, likely connected to solar symbolism and the turning of the seasons.

Traditionally, a new Brigid's cross is woven on Imbolc Eve and hung above the door or hearth for protection throughout the year. The previous year's cross is either burned in the Imbolc fire or buried in the garden to return its blessing to the earth. This cycle of making, hanging, and releasing mirrors the seasonal rhythm: what is created must be tended, honored, and eventually released so that new growth can begin.

To make a Brigid's cross, gather long, flexible reeds or rushes; or use wheat stalks, straw, or even sturdy dried grasses. Soak them in water for a few hours to make them pliable. Begin with one piece bent in half, then weave additional pieces through, folding each new strand around the previous one and turning the cross as you work. The rhythm of folding, turning, weaving becomes meditative, a prayer in motion. As you work, speak your intentions aloud: protection for your home, blessing for your family, healing for those in need.

When finished, tie the ends with red thread or natural twine. Hold the cross in both hands and say: "Brigid, bless this work of my hands. May it guard this threshold, may it hold your flame, may it remind me that protection and beauty are woven together." Hang it with reverence, knowing that it is not just decoration but a living charm, a physical embodiment of devotion.

Regional Customs and Folk Traditions

Imbolc was observed across Ireland with customs that varied by region but shared common themes: purification, protection, and the welcoming of Brigid into the home. These practices offer rich material for modern adaptation.

In many households, particularly in the West of Ireland, a Brídeog; a small doll or effigy of Brigid; was fashioned from straw, rushes, or cloth. Young women or girls would carry the Brídeog from house to house on Imbolc Eve, singing songs and asking for offerings of food, coins, or blessings. Each household welcomed the Brídeog inside, offered hospitality, and received a blessing in return. The doll was then placed in a small bed near the hearth, and a wand or stick was laid beside her, symbolizing Brigid's power to bring fertility and protection. In the morning, ashes from the hearth were examined for signs: if a mark resembling a wand or footprint appeared, it was believed Brigid had visited during the night.

Another widespread practice was the creation of a Brat Bríde; Brigid's Mantle. A piece of cloth, often white or undyed, was left outside on Imbolc Eve, draped over a bush, fence, or windowsill. It was believed that Brigid would pass by during the night and bless the cloth, imbuing it with healing properties. The blessed cloth was then kept throughout the year and used to treat illness, ease childbirth, or comfort the dying. Pieces might be cut from it and given to those in need, extending Brigid's blessing far beyond a single household.

In some areas, divination was practiced on Imbolc, particularly regarding weather and the timing of spring planting. If the weather was fair and mild on Imbolc, it was said that winter would return with force; the old woman (the Cailleach) was gathering firewood for a long cold spell. But if the day was stormy and harsh, it meant winter was nearly over, for the Cailleach had overslept and would soon relinquish her hold on the land. Farmers watched for these signs carefully, planning their work accordingly.

Teaching Story: The Flame That Does Not Go Out

I once knew a woman who tended a flame for Brigid every day, without fail, for more than twenty years.

She was not a priestess in any formal sense. She had no temple, no congregation, no public role. She simply kept a candle lit on a small shelf in her kitchen, replacing it when it burned down, lighting a new one from the dying flame. Every morning, she would stand before it and speak a prayer, thanking Brigid for the day and asking for guidance. Every evening, she would return and offer gratitude for what had passed.

I asked her once why she did it. She smiled and said, "Because someone must. The old flame at Kildare was tended for hundreds of years by nineteen women who took turns so it never went out. I can't do that, but I can do this. One flame. One prayer. Every day."

What struck me was not the ritual itself, though it was beautiful in its simplicity. It was her consistency. Through illness, grief, joy, exhaustion; through days when nothing made sense and days when everything did; she kept the flame. It became her practice, her anchor, her way of saying to Brigid: I am here. I remember. I honor you.

Years later, when she was dying, I visited her in the hospital. She was weak, but her mind was clear. She asked me to continue the flame. "It doesn't have to be my candle," she said. "But someone should keep it. Pass it on. Let Brigid know she's not forgotten."

I promised I would. And I have. Not every single day; I am human, and sometimes I forget. But most days, I light a candle for Brigid, and when I do, I think of that woman and the unbroken thread of devotion she carried. She taught me that the sacred does not require perfection. It requires presence. It requires showing up, even when it feels small or insignificant, and trusting that your offering matters.

The flame at Kildare may have been extinguished by history, but it burns in a thousand small ways: in kitchens, on altars, in hearts. Brigid does not need grand temples. She needs people who remember. She needs hands willing to strike the match, day after day, and say: this light will not go out.

Seasonal Recipes for Imbolc

Oat and Honey Bannocks

Warm spiced cider evokes the hearth and the comfort of fire at the darkest time of year. This drink bridges seasons, honoring the apples of autumn and the spices of distant lands. Sipped slowly by candlelight, it becomes a ritual of warmth and hope.

Serves: 6 | Prep: 5 min | Cook: 30 min | Total: 35 min

Ingredients

1 liter apple cider or mead

1 orange, sliced

2 cinnamon sticks

4 whole cloves

1 star anise (optional)

Honey to taste

Instructions

1. Pour cider or mead into a saucepan.

2. Add orange slices, cinnamon sticks, cloves, and star anise.

3. Heat gently over medium-low heat, simmering for 20–30 minutes.

4. Do not boil—maintain a gentle steam to preserve the aromatic oils.

5. Taste and add honey if desired for additional sweetness.

6. Strain into mugs and serve hot.

Ritual Context

Serve this as a blessing cup at the height of your winter solstice ritual. Sip slowly, feeling the warmth move through your body as the sun's promised return. Pass cups to ritual partners to affirm your shared commitment to the turning year.

Spiced Apple Cider

In early Ireland, bread was sacred, offered to the gods and baked to mark seasonal rites. This dense, fragrant loaf incorporates barley flour and honey, evoking both earth and light. Simple to make and deeply nourishing, it connects us to ancestral kitchens and the fire of home.

Serves: 8 | Prep: 15 min | Cook: 40 min | Total: 55 min

Ingredients

2 cups barley flour

1 cup whole wheat flour

1 teaspoon baking soda

1/2 teaspoon salt

1/4 cup melted butter

1/3 cup honey

1 cup buttermilk or milk with 1 tablespoon vinegar

Instructions

1. Preheat oven to 375°F (190°C). Grease a loaf pan or baking sheet.

2. In a large bowl, combine barley flour, wheat flour, baking soda, and salt.

3. Stir in melted butter and honey, then add buttermilk.

4. Mix until just combined—do not overmix.

5. Pour into prepared pan and bake 35–40 minutes until a skewer comes out clean.

6. Cool slightly before slicing.

Ritual Context

Break this bread at the solstice table with intention and gratitude. Share pieces with loved ones as a blessing for the year ahead. Leave an offering at the roots of a tree or on your altar as thanks to the sun for its promised return.

Honeyed Barley Bread

Barley, one of the oldest cultivated grains in Ireland, symbolizes endurance and grounding. Root vegetables dwell in the earth through frost, representing gifts drawn from the dark. Simmered together with herbs, they become a warming invocation of survival and connection to the land's hidden treasures.

Serves: 6 | Prep: 15 min | Cook: 60 min | Total: 75 min

Ingredients

1 cup pearl barley, rinsed

2 carrots, diced

2 parsnips, diced

1 small turnip or rutabaga, peeled and cubed

1 onion, chopped

2 cloves garlic, minced

6 cups vegetable broth

1 teaspoon dried thyme

1/2 teaspoon rosemary

1/4 teaspoon ground cloves

Salt and pepper to taste

Olive oil or butter for sautéing

Instructions

1. In a large pot, sauté onion and garlic in oil or butter until soft.

2. Add root vegetables and cook for 5 minutes, stirring occasionally.

3. Stir in barley, herbs, and broth. Bring to a boil, then reduce heat.

4. Simmer for 45–60 minutes until barley and vegetables are tender.

5. Add salt, pepper, and cloves during the last 10 minutes.

6. Serve hot with crusty bread.

Ritual Context

Serve this stew at your solstice altar as an offering to the returning sun. Each spoonful carries the warmth of earth and the promise of light's return. Share with those you love, knowing that together, you have endured the dark and now feast in hope of the coming year.

Closing Reflection

Imbolc is a promise whispered through cold soil and grey sky. It is the breath that begins to warm the frost, the silent fire in the heart, the gentle stirring of things not yet seen. In honoring this festival, we are not rushing toward spring; we are learning to witness its first breath.

Brigid, with her eternal flame, teaches us that tending is sacred. The healing that begins now may be slow. The poems written may be raw. The seeds of change may still be underground. But none of that lessens their power. In fact, it deepens it.

To celebrate Imbolc is to step into quiet intention. It is to declare that the sacred is here, in the washing of a floor, the baking of bread, the lighting of a single candle in the hush of morning. It is to say: this, too, is worthy.

As we move forward from this festival, let us carry Brigid's mantle with us: in our acts of healing, in our daily devotion, and in our unwavering protection of that which is tender and new.

Light returns. And so do we.

Looking Ahead

From Imbolc's gentle flames, we move toward the Spring Equinox, the moment of perfect balance when day and night stand equal. The next chapter explores this threshold of renewal and the surge of life returning to the land.

Chapter 12: The Spring Equinox – Balance Beneath the Blossoms

The Season and Its Significance The Spring Equinox, known in some traditions as Alban Eilir or the Light of the Earth, marks a moment of rare equilibrium. On this day, light and dark are held in perfect balance. In Ireland, where seasonal rhythms guided planting and harvest alike, the equinox signals a threshold: the pivot from winter's slow breath to spring's awakening surge. It typically falls around March 20th–21st in the northern hemisphere.

For those living close to the land, the Spring Equinox is not only a solar event but a moment of inward poise. It is a pause between extremes; a sacred stillness between inhale and exhale, calling for both reflection and readiness. With the lengthening days, warmth begins to seep into the soil. Fields are prepared. Seeds are sown. The promise of life no longer sleeps beneath frost, but stretches upward.

This sabbat carries a gentle wisdom: balance is not stasis, but motion held in grace. We honor both the light and the dark, not favoring one over the other, but recognizing their interdependence. To celebrate the equinox is to walk the edge between inner and outer, between idea and action. It is the threshold between dreaming and doing.

For Irish-inspired pagan practice, this is a time to welcome fertility in its many forms, creative, agricultural, spiritual. It is a time to bless the soil, plant our hopes, and name what we wish to cultivate in the season ahead. We stand between what was and what will be, arms open to both blossom and burden, knowing that the wheel turns with or without us. Choosing to move with it, we do so in reverence and renewal.

Step-by-Step Spring Equinox Ritual: Weaving Light and Shadow This ritual is designed to honor the balance between light and dark, calling upon the energies of Danu, Aengus, and the fertile turning of the year. It may be done alone or with a group, indoors or outdoors, adapted to the tools and space you have.

Preparation and Cleansing

Begin by cleaning your space, physically and energetically. Sweep, dust, and tidy with intention. Smudge using juniper, rosemary, or a spring floral incense.

Say:

"By air and seed, by light and stream,
I clear this space to hold the dream."

Creating the Altar and Casting the Circle

Set your altar as described previously. Light two candles (one white, one black) and place them on opposite ends of the altar. Walk clockwise to cast your circle, saying:
"I draw this circle to hold the turning;
Of balance, breath, and bold returning."

Invocation of the Season and Spirits

Stand at your altar and raise your hands.

Say:
"I call to Danu, mother of the land.
I call to Aengus, whose song is new light.
I honor the spirits who stir and rise;
Let this space be made sacred in sight and soul."

Offer water and honey to the earth or altar.

Blessing the Seeds (Literal or Symbolic)

Hold seeds in your hands or place them in a small bowl on the altar. Speak your intentions aloud or write them down, one by one, placing each written word beneath a small stone or bowl.

Say:
"What I plant now, I tend with care.
What I speak now, I make sacred air.
May this season bring balance to blossom."

Guided Meditation: Meeting the Balanced Self

Sit comfortably and close your eyes. Breathe deeply.

Imagine yourself standing at the edge of a forest, where light and shadow meet. From the forest emerges two forms, one cloaked in sunlight, the other in night. They are both you. You watch as they step toward one another and join hands. In their unity, a third version of you is born: whole, present, and strong.

Receive whatever message or symbol they offer. Stay in this vision for a few minutes.

Statement of Balance and Vow

Open your eyes and write or say your vow for balance this season.

Examples:

"I will give as much as I receive."

"I will let joy and rest share space in my days."

"I will honor both the seen and the unseen."

Place this written vow on your altar.

Offering and Gratitude

Pour spring water into the soil (or a plant). Leave a piece of bread, honey, or egg outdoors or in a sacred dish as offering.

Say:

"To the spirits, the land, and the season;
Thank you for this turning, this lesson, this breath."

Closing the Circle

Extinguish one candle, then the other.

Say:

"The balance is honored. The work is begun.
The circle opens but remains unbroken."

Post-Ritual Integration

Eat something grounding. Journal your experience. Tend your planted seeds or symbolic intention daily with care.

This ritual is a mirror, held gently to yourself and the world. In light and in shadow, you are whole.

Modern Practice Tips

Balcony and Indoor Gardens

If you don't have land to plant in, use pots, window boxes, or even jars. Herbs like basil, mint, or thyme do well in small spaces and bring green life indoors. Planting a single seed with intention can transform your living space into a sacred grove.

Sun Salutations and Body Movement

Celebrate balance through physical practice. Simple yoga flows, Tai Chi, or walking meditations at sunrise can center you in your body. Each breath can become a prayer. Mark sunrise and sunset on the equinox with movement or stillness.

Equinox Journaling Prompts
Reflect on balance in your own life:

- What parts of me are growing? What parts are still in rest?
- Where can I make space for stillness?
- What does balance feel like, and how can I return to it? Write your answers with honesty, without needing resolution.

Creating Symbols of Balance

Craft a personal symbol of light and dark, perhaps a small mandala, a painted stone, or a cloth with dual tones. Place it on your altar or in a visible space as a daily reminder of harmony.

Sharing Sacred Meals

Invite friends or family to a spring meal. Use seasonal ingredients. Share blessings before eating, or pass a candle clockwise before the meal begins. Even a simple loaf of bread broken in gratitude becomes ritual.

Honoring Both Joy and Grief

Let this be a season where both are welcome. Hold space for celebration and for the gentle shadows we carry. Balance includes contrast. Speak your truth aloud, or offer your emotions to a bowl of spring water, then return it to the earth.

No matter how small the act, your observance of the Spring Equinox roots you in the sacred rhythm of the turning year.

The Sacred Egg: Symbol of Potential

The egg is one of the most ancient and potent symbols of spring, and its connection to the equinox runs deep across cultures. In Irish tradition, eggs represented fertility, new life, and the promise of abundance. They were painted, blessed, rolled down hillsides, and buried in fields to ensure a good harvest. The egg holds all potential within its shell; life waiting, protected, ready to emerge.

Decorating eggs at the Spring Equinox is a practice that predates Christianity and has been carried forward through time. Natural dyes can be made from onion skins (gold and rust), beets (pink), red cabbage (blue), turmeric (bright yellow), or coffee (brown). Boil the eggs in water infused with these materials, or paint them by hand with plant-based pigments. Some practitioners inscribe symbols onto the eggs: spirals for growth, suns for warmth, seeds for intention, or ogham for specific blessings.

Once decorated, these eggs can be used in several ways. Place them on your altar as offerings to the season. Give them as gifts to friends or family, blessing them as you do. Bury them in your garden or at the base of a tree, returning their potential to the earth. Or save them through the season, then crack them and eat them at Beltane, consuming the energy of growth you have tended for two months.

The tradition of egg rolling; where decorated eggs are rolled down hills; was practiced in many parts of Ireland and Britain. The first egg to reach the bottom unbroken was said to bring luck for the year ahead. This playful custom can be adapted for modern use: gather with friends or family, create a gentle slope, and roll your eggs while speaking wishes aloud. The act itself becomes a spell, releasing intentions into motion.

Aengus Óg: The Young God of Love and Renewal

Aengus Óg, whose name means "Young Son," is one of the most fitting deities to honor at the Spring Equinox. He is the god of love, youth, poetry, and beauty, often depicted with birds circling his head; symbols of the soul, inspiration, and the sweetness of spring. In mythology, he is the son of the Dagda and Boann, born through cunning and desire, and his presence brings warmth, charm, and creative vitality.

His most famous tale is that of his search for Caér Ibormeith, a maiden who appeared to him in a dream. After a year of longing, he found her at Loch Bél Drágan on Samhain, when she and her companions took the form of swans. Aengus transformed into a swan as well, and together they sang a song so beautiful that all who heard it fell into a peaceful sleep for three days and nights. This story speaks to the power of longing, transformation, and the willingness to change oneself for love.

At the Spring Equinox, Aengus represents the youthful energy of awakening, the stirring of desire, and the courage to pursue what calls to us. He reminds us that spring is not only about planting seeds in the soil, but about planting dreams in the heart. To work with Aengus, offer him beauty: fresh flowers, honey, sweet cakes, or handwritten poetry. Light a green or pink candle in his name and speak to him about what you long to create, to attract, or to become.

A simple prayer to Aengus might be: "Aengus of the sweet voice, Aengus of the birds, I call to you in this season of opening. Teach me to pursue what I desire with courage and grace. Help me to transform when transformation is needed. May I sing my own song into the world, and may it bring beauty." Leave your offerings outdoors or on your altar, and pay attention to signs in the days that follow: birds appearing unexpectedly, dreams of flight, sudden inspiration, or the pull toward something new.

Planting the Sacred: Agricultural and Magical Practices

The Spring Equinox in Ireland was a time of intense agricultural preparation. Fields were turned, manure spread, and the first seeds sown. This was not merely practical work; it was sacred labor. Every action in the field was a prayer, every seed planted a negotiation with the spirits of the land. Farmers would walk the boundaries of their fields sunwise, speaking blessings and leaving offerings at corner stones or hawthorn trees.

Before planting, seeds might be blessed with water from a sacred well or mixed with ashes from the Imbolc fire. Some farmers would carry a piece of iron or a blessed stone in their pocket while sowing, believing it would protect the crop from blight and ensure a strong harvest. Others spoke charms over the seeds: "In the name of the earth, in the name of the sky, in the name of the seed that does not die, I plant you now. Grow strong. Grow true. May your roots hold and your branches reach."

For modern practitioners without access to land, this practice can be adapted in powerful ways. Plant seeds in pots with intention, speaking your wish into the soil as you cover them. Bless the seeds before planting by holding them in your hands and breathing onto them, imbuing them with your energy. Choose plants that resonate with your goals: basil for prosperity, lavender for peace, rosemary for memory, mint for healing. Tend them with care, speaking to them regularly, and watch as your intention grows alongside the green shoots.

If you have a garden or yard, dedicate a small corner to the spirits of the land. Leave this space wild and untended, a refuge for insects, birds, and small creatures. Place a stone or marker there and leave regular offerings: water, breadcrumbs, wildflower seeds. This reciprocal relationship honors the truth that we do not own the land; we are guests, and we must act accordingly.

Folk Wisdom and Omens of Spring

Irish folk tradition is rich with signs and omens observed at the equinox, practical wisdom passed down through generations of farmers, shepherds, and weather-watchers. These observations helped communities predict the season ahead and plan accordingly.

If the first swallows returned before the equinox, it was said the summer would be long and warm. If they arrived late, expect a cool, wet season. The direction of the wind on equinox morning was also telling: wind from the south brought warmth and growth; from the north, a late spring with potential for frost; from the east, steady weather; from the west, changeable conditions and rain.

The blooming of specific plants served as natural calendars. Blackthorn blossoms appearing before the equinox meant an early spring; after, a cautious one. If dandelions bloomed in great profusion, the year would be abundant. Scarce dandelions suggested a lean harvest. Watching for these signs was not superstition but close observation of natural patterns, an intimate knowledge of how one element connected to another.

Animals, too, were watched carefully. The first lamb born in spring was considered especially lucky and often given a blessing or a red ribbon tied around its neck for protection. If hares were seen boxing in the fields near the equinox, it was a sign of fertility and abundance. Birds nesting early indicated a safe spring; late nesting suggested storms ahead.

Modern practitioners can revive this practice by paying attention to the natural world around them. Keep a journal of when you first see certain flowers blooming, when birds return, when trees leaf out. Notice patterns over years. This kind of observation deepens your connection to place and attunes you to the subtle shifts that mark the turning of the Wheel.

Teaching Story: The Garden That Grew in Shadow

I once knew a man who spent years chasing balance and never finding it. He would swing between extremes: working until exhaustion, then collapsing into rest so complete he could barely rise. Pursuing joy with manic intensity, then sinking into despair when it faded. He came to me one spring, frustrated and defeated, asking how to find the equilibrium everyone spoke of.

I did not have an answer in words, so instead I invited him to help me in my garden. It was early spring, just past the equinox, and the ground was still cold. We worked together in silence, turning soil, pulling weeds, planting seeds. The work was steady, rhythmic, neither frantic nor lazy. Just movement. Just presence.

At one point, he stopped and said, "Half of this garden is still in shade. Should we move the plants to where there's more sun?" I looked at him and smiled. "No," I said. "Some things grow best in shade. Some need full sun. Some need both at different times of day. The garden doesn't chase the light. It works with what it has."

He was quiet for a long time after that. We finished the planting, washed our hands, and shared tea. Before he left, he said, "I think I've been trying to be all light. But I need the shade too, don't I?"

"Yes," I told him. "Balance isn't about being fifty percent light and fifty percent dark all the time. It's about knowing when to step into the sun and when to rest in the shade. It's about not forcing growth when the ground is still cold, and not refusing to bloom when the time is right."

He came back many times that spring and summer, working in the garden, learning to read the needs of different plants, understanding that care is not one-size-fits-all. By autumn, he had started his own small plot, and though he still struggled, he no longer swung so wildly between extremes. He had learned to tend himself the way he tended the garden: with attention, patience, and trust in the natural rhythms of growth and rest.

The Spring Equinox teaches this: balance is not static. It is not a destination. It is a practice, a returning, a constant adjustment to the conditions of your life. Some seasons ask you to grow. Some ask you to rest. Some ask you to stand in the uncomfortable middle and simply be. And that, too, is sacred.

Seasonal Recipes for Spring Equinox

Spring Greens Soup

Brigid is the patroness of dairy, craft, and the hearth's flame. This soft bread, enriched with milk and butter, honors her presence as spring begins. The sweetness of honey and the warmth of spices speak to healing and inspiration.

Serves: 8 | Prep: 20 min | Cook: 35 min | Total: 55 min

Ingredients

1 1/2 cups whole wheat flour

1 cup white flour

1 teaspoon baking powder

1/2 teaspoon salt

1/4 teaspoon ground ginger

3 tablespoons butter, melted

2 tablespoons honey

1 cup milk

Instructions

1. Preheat oven to 350°F (175°C). Grease a round baking dish.

2. Mix flours, baking powder, salt, and ginger in a bowl.

3. Combine melted butter, honey, and milk in another bowl.

4. Stir wet ingredients into dry until just combined.

5. Press into baking dish and score the top lightly.

6. Bake 30–35 minutes until golden and a skewer comes out clean.

7. Cool and cut into wedges.

Ritual Context

Bake this bread on Imbolc morning or the night before, infusing it with intentions of healing, creativity, and renewal. Share it at the table with milk or herbal tea, honoring Brigid's sacred fire and her blessing of new beginnings.

Brigid's Milk Bread

These traditional flatbreads honor the grain of the land and the sweetness of Brigid's fire, marking the first stirrings of spring. Simple and nourishing, they connect us to hearth and awakening. Serve them warm with butter and honey at gatherings or as a solo meditation on renewal.

Serves: 12 | Prep: 15 min | Cook: 20 min | Total: 35 min

Ingredients

2 cups oat flour or rolled oats, ground fine

1/2 teaspoon salt

1/4 teaspoon baking soda

1 tablespoon honey

3 tablespoons butter, melted

1/2 cup buttermilk or milk with 1 teaspoon vinegar

Instructions

1. Preheat oven to 375°F (190°C). Grease a baking sheet or cast iron pan.

2. In a bowl, mix oat flour, salt, and baking soda.

3. Add melted butter and honey, then stir in buttermilk to form a soft dough.

4. Knead gently on a floured surface until just combined.

5. Press or roll dough into 12 small rounds about 1/4 inch thick.

6. Place on prepared baking sheet and bake for 15–20 minutes until golden.

7. Serve warm with butter or honey.

Ritual Context

Serve warm with butter and honey at Imbolc to celebrate spring's first light, still tender and new. Share with a circle to mark the quickening of the year. Each bannock represents the spark of Brigid's fire beginning to warm the earth.

Closing Reflection The Spring Equinox reminds us that equilibrium is not a final destination but a living, breathing process. It is the delicate art of returning, over and over, to center; especially as the world pulls us in many directions.

In this season, we are invited to open both hands: one to release the quiet of winter, the other to receive the stirrings of spring. What was dreamt in darkness now seeks sunlight. What rested in silence now longs to grow.

To live in balance is not to deny difficulty or chase perfection. It is to stand between light and shadow with awareness and compassion, to honor both, and to grow through their meeting.

As you walk forward from this turning, may you carry the seeds of your intention with care. May your rituals become roots. May your words bloom.

And may the balance you seek be the balance you become.

Looking Ahead

As the Spring Equinox tips toward summer, we approach Beltane, the fire festival of passion, fertility, and the full flowering of life. The next chapter celebrates the height of spring and the gateway to summer.

Chapter 13: Beltane – Fire at the Threshold

The Season and Its Significance Beltane, celebrated on May 1st, marks the midpoint between the Spring Equinox and the Summer Solstice. It is a festival of fire, fertility, passion, and blooming abundance. In ancient Ireland, it was a time to light sacred fires, drive cattle between flames for protection, and bless the land and animals for the fertile season ahead. As a cross-quarter day, Beltane ushers in the bright half of the year. Where Samhain honored descent and death, Beltane celebrates ascent and life.

This is a time to embrace vitality, to move from the inward reflection of winter and early spring into embodied joy. Flowers bloom, animals mate, and the days grow warmer and longer. Rituals during this time are sensual and celebratory, focusing on union, of lover and beloved, of spirit and flesh, of self and season. Beltane reminds us that desire is sacred, pleasure is holy, and creation is the divine act of living fully.

Mythic Context and Deity Association In the Irish mythological cycle, Beltane resonates with tales of sacred unions and transformative love. The Dagda, the powerful god of abundance and fertility, is often invoked at this time, along with his consort, the Morrígan, in her spring aspect as life-bringer and protector of land.

Aengus Óg, the youthful god of love, music, and poetic inspiration, is another key figure for this sabbat. His stories of longing, beauty, and magical courtship remind us of love's power to awaken the soul. In some traditions, Brigid is honored again for her connection to healing and inspiration, especially as the fires of Beltane echo her eternal flame.

In many folkloric traditions, the May Queen and the Green Man are archetypes who represent the union of earth and sun, body and spirit. The May Queen embodies blooming life, while the Green Man brings the vital, untamed energy of nature into the circle of celebration. Their symbolic union is reenacted in Maypole dances, wreath offerings, and sometimes in sacred rites of love.

Seasonal Signs and Cultural Themes The natural world during Beltane is alive with movement. Birds are nesting, blossoms unfurl in hedgerows and meadows, and dawn arrives with songs of courtship. In early Irish society, Beltane was a time to bring herds to summer pasture. Fires were kindled on hilltops, particularly at Uisneach, considered the mythic center of Ireland.

In the cultural calendar, Beltane represented a liminal point, a threshold between seasons. Such thresholds were considered magically potent, times when the veil between worlds thinned and spirits moved freely. Protective charms were made, boundaries blessed, and the fertility of animals and land was ritually ensured.

Modern pagans and Irish-inspired practitioners carry these themes forward by honoring sensuality, connection, and joyful embodiment. Beltane becomes not only a seasonal celebration, but a reminder to embrace the sacredness of the body, the warmth of the sun, and the beauty of desire without shame.

Altar Setup and Seasonal Elements A Beltane altar is a riot of color, fragrance, and symbolism. Begin with a red, green, or gold cloth to represent fire, fertility, and growth. Add fresh flowers such as hawthorn, primrose, or rose. If hawthorn is blooming, a sprig may be placed in a vase or laid on the altar, but do so respectfully, as this tree is sacred to the sidhe.

Candles are central, choose red, orange, or gold. A cauldron, fire-safe dish, or lantern may be used as the hearth of your ritual fire. Ribbons, bells, and garlands add a festive air.

Suggested altar items: • A small Maypole or braided ribbons to honor union • A bowl of fresh cream or honey for offering • A chalice with water infused with flower petals • Representations of the May Queen and Green Man (figurines, masks, or drawings) • A phallic and yonic symbol to represent sacred polarity (optional)

Crystals like carnelian, garnet, and rose quartz support Beltane's themes of passion and vitality. Herbs such as mugwort, hawthorn, thyme, and vervain can be used in incense or sprinkled on the altar. Some practitioners also include a mirror to reflect the beauty and joy of the season back upon themselves.

Step-by-Step Beltane Ritual: Fire at the Threshold This ritual is designed to honor the fire of life, sensual vitality, and sacred union. It may be done alone or in a group. Outdoor settings near nature or a bonfire are ideal, but a candlelit space indoors is equally powerful with the right intention.

Preparation and Cleansing Cleanse your space physically and energetically. Sweep, tidy, and burn sage, mugwort, or hawthorn if available. Say: "By bloom and blaze, I clear this ground, To call the fire that circles round."

Creating the Altar and Circle Dress your altar in red, gold, or green. Place fresh flowers, a candle, and offerings of honey, cream, or bread. Cast the circle clockwise: "By fire and earth, by sun and stone, This circle turns, this space is grown."

Invocation of Deities and Spirits Stand before your altar. Say: "I call to the Dagda, the fertile father. I call to the Morrígan, fierce and free. I call to Aengus Óg, singer of hearts. I call to Brigid, bearer of flame. Come now through blossom and breeze. Bring your fire to awaken me."

Lighting the Beltane Flame Light your central candle or fire. Say: "This is the fire of sacred joy. This is the flame that quickens. By its light, I step forward. By its heat, I am reborn."

Jumping the Fire (or Symbolic Leap) If safe, leap over a small flame or step through a symbolic threshold. Say: "I cross from longing into life. I leap from hope into becoming."

Dance or Movement Dance, sway, or move freely to music. Let the body express delight, desire, and release. Offer your movement as prayer.

Making a Vow or Declaration Speak aloud: "This I tend. This I call. This I offer." Name what you are ready to birth, whether it be love, art, courage, or healing.

Offering and Gratitude Leave flowers or food outdoors. Say: "To the land, the spirits, and the fire; Thank you for this blessing."

Closing the Circle Walk counter-clockwise and say: "The fire fades, but the vow remains. The joy returns with every flame."

After-Ritual Reflections Eat something sweet or rich. Write your experience. How did your body feel? What are you ready to embody?

Modern Practice Tips

Craft a flower crown with wild blooms or herbs

Create a mini bonfire in a fire-safe dish

Braid red and white ribbons to symbolize union

Spend time in joyful, embodied activity: dance, sing, kiss, touch nature

Make love with sacred intent, alone or with a partner; inviting spirit into the body

The Sacred Marriage: Hieros Gamos and Union

At the heart of Beltane lies the concept of sacred union; the marriage of opposites, the blending of energies, the moment when two become one and create something greater than alone. This theme appears throughout Irish mythology and folklore, often symbolized by the union of gods and goddesses, or the marriage of the land to its king.

The most famous of these sacred unions is that between the Dagda and the Morrígan, which takes place at Samhain in some tellings, but whose energy flows through to Beltane. In the tale, the Dagda encounters the Morrígan washing herself in the river, and they come together in a powerful act that ensures the fertility of the land and the success of the Tuatha Dé Danann in battle. This union is not gentle or romantic; it is fierce, primal, and necessary. It reminds us that sacred sexuality is not always soft; sometimes it is raw, wild, and transformative.

In Irish kingship traditions, the king was symbolically married to the land, represented by a sovereignty goddess such as Maeve or Ériu. This marriage was not merely political but deeply spiritual, binding the king to the welfare of the land and its people. If the king ruled justly, the land flourished; if he failed, the land would sicken. This concept of sacred responsibility between ruler and realm can be adapted by modern practitioners to understand their own relationship with place, body, and community. We are all, in a sense, married to the land we live on, and our choices affect its health.

For those who work with a partner, Beltane is an ideal time to consecrate or renew a relationship through ritual. This can be as simple as lighting candles together and speaking vows of mutual support, or as elaborate as a handfasting ceremony where your hands are bound with ribbon while you speak your commitment. The key is intention: approach the act as sacred, not merely romantic. Ask for the blessing of the gods. Offer your union as a reflection of the divine marriage that sustains the world.

For solitary practitioners, the sacred marriage can be understood as the union of different parts of the self: masculine and feminine energies, light and shadow, conscious and unconscious. A simple ritual might involve lighting two candles; one representing each polarity; and bringing them together to light a third candle that represents wholeness. Speak aloud what you are bringing into union within yourself, and let the flame witness your integration.

The Hawthorn and the Fair Folk

No discussion of Beltane is complete without addressing the hawthorn tree, known in Irish as sceach gheal (bright thorn). In folklore, hawthorn is one of the most sacred and dangerous trees, beloved by the sidhe and protected by ancient taboos. To cut a hawthorn, especially a lone tree growing on a fairy mound, was to invite disaster: illness, bad luck, or the wrath of the Good Folk themselves.

Hawthorn blooms around Beltane, its white flowers covering the tree like snow in spring. The blossoms have a distinctive scent, sweet but with an undertone of decay, as though beauty and death walk hand in hand. In folk belief, bringing hawthorn flowers indoors was considered unlucky; they belonged outside, in the realm of the fey. Yet gathering a small sprig with respect and leaving an offering in return was acceptable, even blessed, as long as one asked permission first.

The connection between hawthorn and the sidhe is deep. Hawthorn trees often mark boundaries between fields or grow at crossroads, liminal spaces where the Otherworld presses close. It is said that if you sit beneath a hawthorn on Beltane Eve, you may see the sidhe pass by in procession, or you may be taken into their realm and not return. The tree is both protection and portal, guardian and gateway.

For modern practitioners, working with hawthorn at Beltane requires respect and reciprocity. If you wish to gather blossoms, approach the tree with humility. Speak to it, asking permission aloud. Leave an offering of milk, honey, or a coin. Take only what you need, and never strip a branch bare. Use the flowers on your altar, in flower crowns, or as decorations for your Beltane fire, but be mindful of their power. They are not merely pretty; they carry the presence of the Fair Folk.

The Beltane Fires: History and Practice

The most iconic image of Beltane is the bonfire, blazing on hilltops across the Irish landscape. These were not small domestic fires but great communal conflagrations, built with wood gathered by the entire community and lit at sunset on May Eve. The fires served multiple purposes: they were protective, purifying, celebratory, and deeply symbolic of the sun's growing strength.

In historical practice, twin fires were often lit, and cattle were driven between them as a blessing and protection against disease. The smoke and flame were believed to carry away sickness and ill fortune, while imbuing the animals with vitality for the summer months. People, too, would leap over the flames or walk between the fires, seeking purification and blessing. Young couples might jump together, holding hands, as a form of handfasting or pledge of commitment.

The hilltop location of these fires was deliberate. Lighting a fire on high ground made it visible for miles, connecting communities across the landscape in a shared act of celebration. As one fire was lit, others would answer, until the whole countryside blazed with light. This network of fires created a web of protection and blessing that extended across the entire land.

For modern practitioners, lighting a large outdoor bonfire may not be feasible, but the spirit of the practice can be honored in other ways. Gather with friends or coven-mates and light a fire in a safe container or fire pit. Use this fire as the center of your celebration: dance around it, sing to it, offer herbs and flowers into it. If even a small fire is not possible, a ring of candles can serve. The important thing is the intention: you are calling the power of the sun, blessing your community, and marking the threshold into summer.

Pleasure as Prayer: Embodied Spirituality

Beltane challenges the dualistic thinking that separates spirit from flesh, the sacred from the sensual. In many religious traditions, the body is viewed with suspicion, and pleasure is considered a distraction from the divine. But Irish paganism, and neo-paganism more broadly, offers a different vision: the body is sacred, pleasure is a form of prayer, and the erotic is a pathway to the divine.

This does not mean Beltane is about hedonism or indulgence without awareness. Rather, it is about approaching pleasure; whether sexual, sensory, or joyful; with consciousness and reverence. When you eat a ripe strawberry at Beltane, do so slowly, tasting every note of sweetness. When you dance, let your body move without self-consciousness, offering the motion as devotion. When you make love, do so with presence, recognizing the divine spark in yourself and your partner.

For those who are not partnered or who do not engage in sexual practice, embodied spirituality can be expressed in other ways. Walk barefoot on grass. Feel the sun on your skin. Swim in a river or lake. Sing at the top of your lungs. Cook a meal with your hands and eat it with gratitude. Touch yourself with love, not as indulgence but as sacred self-care. These acts, when done with intention, are prayers. They say: I am here. I am alive. I am grateful for this body and this moment.

Teaching Story: The Fire That Would Not Die

I once attended a Beltane celebration where everything went wrong. The gathering was held on a farmer's land, and we had planned a grand bonfire, a Maypole dance, and a feast. But when Beltane Eve arrived, the weather turned. Rain came in sheets, cold and relentless, soaking the wood we had gathered and turning the field into mud.

Half the group gave up and went home. The rest of us huddled under a tarp, debating whether to cancel. But one woman, a priestess who had been practicing for decades, stood up and said, "The fire is not the wood. The fire is us. If we choose to burn, we will."

She walked out into the rain, arms open, and began to sing. It was a Beltane song, old and half-forgotten, but she sang it anyway. One by one, we joined her. We stood in the rain, singing, and then someone started to dance. And then we were all dancing, slipping in the mud, laughing, shouting into the storm.

We never lit the bonfire that night. But we were the bonfire. We were the flame that would not be extinguished by rain or cold or disappointment. We celebrated Beltane not with perfect conditions, but with fierce joy in the face of imperfection. And it was one of the most powerful rituals I have ever experienced.

When we finally went inside, soaked and muddy, someone said, "That wasn't what we planned." And the priestess smiled and replied, "No. It was better. It was real."

Beltane teaches this: the sacred does not require perfection. It requires presence. It requires willingness. The fire you carry within is more important than any external flame, and no weather, no circumstance, can put it out unless you let it. When you celebrate Beltane, you are not performing a script. You are igniting something true, something alive, something that burns regardless of conditions.

Seasonal Recipes for Beltane

Honeyed Oat Cakes

Symbolizing both the egg and the sun, this bright tart is ideal for both ritual and feasting. The custard's golden hue and gentle sweetness celebrate balance and the sun's return to equal power with the night.

Serves: 8 | Prep: 15 min | Cook: 40 min | Total: 55 min

Ingredients

1 pre-baked tart shell

3 egg yolks

1/4 cup honey

1 1/2 cups whole milk

1/4 teaspoon nutmeg or cinnamon

Pinch of salt

Instructions

1. Warm milk gently in a saucepan.

2. Whisk egg yolks, honey, salt, and spice together in a bowl.

3. Slowly add warm milk, whisking constantly.

4. Pour into pre-baked shell and bake at 325°F (160°C) for 30–40 minutes, until just set.

5. Chill before serving.

Ritual Context

Serve this tart as a centerpiece to your spring table, honoring both the balance and the sweetness of the season. Let its golden hue remind you of the sun's growing strength.

Honey Custard Tart

Traditional seed cakes are a nod to fertility and the planting season. These sweet, aromatic cakes are often offered to land spirits and shared at spring gatherings. Caraway or fennel seeds link them to ancient Celtic traditions of blessing.

Serves: 12 | Prep: 15 min | Cook: 12 min | Total: 27 min

Ingredients

1/2 cup butter, softened

1/2 cup sugar or honey

2 eggs

1 1/2 cups flour

1/4 teaspoon salt

1 teaspoon caraway or fennel seeds

1/2 teaspoon baking powder

Splash of milk if needed

Instructions

1. Preheat oven to 350°F (175°C).

2. Cream butter and sugar together.

3. Add eggs and mix well.

4. Stir in flour, salt, seeds, and baking powder until just combined.

5. Drop spoonfuls onto a greased baking sheet.

6. Bake 10–12 minutes until lightly golden.

7. Cool before serving.

Ritual Context

Bake these cakes to honor the earth's fertility and your own creative power. Offer them at your altar or leave small portions at the roots of trees. Share with loved ones to bless their endeavors.

Seed Cakes

As the earth awakens, so does the appetite for light, green fare. This nourishing soup welcomes the body back into balance and honors the season's first edible greens. Made with wild or cultivated leaves, it becomes a blessing to both body and the land.

Serves: 4 | Prep: 10 min | Cook: 25 min | Total: 35 min

Ingredients

1 tablespoon butter or oil

1 small onion, diced

2 cloves garlic, minced

4 cups fresh greens (nettles, spinach, kale, or dandelion)

3 cups vegetable broth

1 medium potato, peeled and diced

Salt and pepper to taste

Cream or fresh herbs for garnish

Instructions

1. In a pot, sauté onion and garlic in butter until soft.

2. Add potato and broth. Simmer until potato is tender.

3. Stir in greens and cook just until wilted.

4. Blend until smooth.

5. Season with salt and pepper.

6. Serve with a swirl of cream or a sprinkle of fresh herbs.

Ritual Context

Serve this soup at your spring table as a welcome to the growing season. Each spoonful carries the green promise of the earth reawakening. Offer a portion to the land as gratitude for its renewal.

Closing Reflection

Beltane is a threshold of delight. It does not demand solemnity, but invites celebration. In the blooming of the land, we are reminded that joy is sacred, that love is transformative, and that our desires are part of the world's unfolding song. May we honor this fire with laughter, courage, and the beauty of our becoming.

Looking Ahead

From Beltane's fires, we journey to the Summer Solstice, the longest day when the sun reaches its zenith. The next chapter explores midsummer's power and the turning point when light begins its slow decline.

Chapter 14: Summer Solstice – The Sun at Full Power

The Season and Its Significance

The Summer Solstice, known in some Irish traditions as "Grianstad" or the "standing still of the sun," marks the apex of the solar year. Occurring around June 20–22 in the Northern Hemisphere, it is the longest day and the shortest night; the moment when the sun hangs highest in the sky, drenching the world in light. In Ireland, this sacred turning was marked by rituals on high places, such as hilltops and cairns, where the sun could be seen to rise in alignment with ancient stones. It was a time to honor the power of the sun as a divine and life-giving force.

This season is associated with strength, fullness, and radiance. Crops are maturing. Flowers are in bloom. Bees hum and fields sway with golden promise. At the solstice, the energy is not just of growth, it is of culmination. What was planted in spring now shows its form. What was kindled at Imbolc, balanced at the Equinox, and flamed at Beltaine now reaches its zenith.

But this peak also holds its turning. The solstice is not only celebration; it is also recognition that from this moment on, the days will begin to shorten. There is wisdom in this: that even in the fullness of light, the shadow is born. This is the sacred pause between rising and falling, between ripening and harvest.

To celebrate the Summer Solstice is to honor abundance and gratitude, to bless the light within and without, and to hold awareness that no season lasts forever. It is a time for revelry, yes, but also reflection. The sun at full power is both a crown and a mirror. What will you do with your light before it begins to wane?

Mythic Context and Deity Association

The Summer Solstice is not explicitly named in surviving Irish mythological texts, yet its essence pulses through tales of radiant gods, sovereignty rites, and midsummer quests. This is the time when solar deities shine at their brightest and when the interplay between strength and wisdom becomes essential.

Lugh, the warrior of many skills, is often associated with the high sun. Though his primary festival, Lughnasadh, occurs later in the wheel, midsummer is when his presence begins to stir in earnest. His solar attributes (brilliance, mastery, and leadership) align with the full force of the sun. He reminds us that light must be wielded with integrity and focus.

Brigid, goddess of fire, fertility, and inspiration, also stands powerfully at this season. As a goddess of both the hearth and the forge, she embodies the constructive use of fire; the sustaining flame of creativity and the burning away of what is no longer needed. Her light is not harsh, but illuminating.

Danu, as the ancestral mother and embodiment of the land's vitality, is present in every field and flowering branch. At the solstice, she may be honored in her full, mature aspect, giver of abundance, nourisher of all things rooted and rising.

Other beings (like the sidhe) are said to be most visible in the high light of midsummer and then begin to withdraw. This is a final moment of openness before their realm folds back in upon itself. Gifts of honey, bread, or flower garlands may be left to honor them and thank them for their presence in the first half of the year.

The Summer Solstice invites us to look to the sky and the stories that live there, to see in the bright arc of the sun not only mythic figures, but our own capacity for radiance and right action.

Step-by-Step Solstice Ritual: Crown of Light

This ritual honors the radiant fullness of the sun and your own inner light. It is best performed at sunrise, noon, or sunset on the longest day of the year. You may perform it indoors or outdoors, alone or with a group.

1. Preparation and Cleansing

Create sacred space by tidying your area and lighting incense (such as frankincense or rosemary). Place a gold or yellow cloth on your altar. Arrange candles, a small mirror, fresh flowers, and a bowl of water charged in the sun.

Say aloud: "I cleanse this space with smoke and song, To welcome light where it belongs."

2. Circle Casting and Intentions

Cast a circle by walking sunwise (clockwise) and envisioning golden light encircling you.

Say: "From dawn to dusk, this space I claim, To call the light and speak its name."

Place your hands over your heart. Speak clearly your intention for the coming season.

3. Solar Invocation

Light a central candle or stand in direct sunlight.

Say: "O Sun, bright eye of the sky,
At your crown I lift my voice.
Shine within me, golden flame,
That I may live with purpose and choice."

4. Crown of Light Creation

Using flowers, herbs, or ribbons, create a simple crown. As you work, speak: "This crown I weave with joy and might,
A garland born of sacred light."

Place the crown on your head or hold it above in blessing.

5. Water and Fire Blessing
Dip your fingers in the sun-charged water. Touch your brow, heart, and hands.

Say: "By fire and water I am made whole.
In light, I remember my soul."

6. Offerings and Gratitude
Offer a portion of your food, flowers, or honey to the earth or a nearby tree.

Say: "To all who grow and guard the land,
I offer thanks with open hand."

7. Closing the Circle
Blow out the candle or raise your arms to the sky.

Say: "The light remains, though day will end;
I walk with fire as my friend."

8. Celebration
Dance, feast, sing, or simply sit in silence and watch the light. Let joy fill the sacred space you've created.

This ritual may be adapted to suit your setting or needs. Its heart remains: the honoring of light as sacred, alive, and present within you.

Modern Practice Tips
Not all solstice observances require access to ancient cairns or wide green fields. The essence of this celebration (the honoring of light, fullness, and turning) can be lived meaningfully in everyday spaces and lives. Here are ways to bring the Summer Solstice into modern, American, or urban Pagan practice:

1. Sunrise or Sunset Observation

If you cannot see the full arc of the sun, choose a time (dawn or dusk) to pause and consciously greet or release the sun. Watch the sky change. Reflect. Offer a few words of thanks to the light.

2. Apartment and Balcony Altars

Place a sun altar on your windowsill, kitchen counter, or balcony railing. Use solar-colored candles, seasonal herbs, and fruits. Include a small mirror to reflect light and remind you of your own.

3. Solar Sigil Crafting

Draw or paint a personal sun sigil using gold ink, yellow chalk, or natural pigment. Hang it near your workspace or front door. Charge it with intention during the solstice.

4. Herbal Baths and Self-Anointing

Infuse a bath or foot soak with rosemary, lemon balm, or chamomile. Add a drop of essential oil if desired. Soak in silence or with light music. Speak affirmations of fullness, vitality, and clarity.

5. Community and Family Feasts

Host a solstice meal with loved ones; even if they're not Pagan. Share seasonal foods, tell stories, light candles, and toast to life's sweetness. Let joy be your offering.

6. Digital Altars and Photo Shrines

Create a digital altar background or folder of solar-themed images. Light a candle and open it with intention. Even in digital space, energy can be focused and sacredness cultivated.

7. Journaling Prompts for Solstice Reflection

Where am I at my fullest right now?

What have I grown that I can now harvest?

How can I share my light more freely?

The Summer Solstice is not bound by place, it is carried in intention, in practice, and in the small, sacred ways you meet the turning of the year.

Lugh Lamhfada: The Long-Armed God of Light

Though Lugh's primary festival is Lughnasadh in early August, his presence begins to build at the Summer Solstice, when the sun reaches its greatest power. Lugh Lamhfada, the Long-Armed One, is a god of mastery, skill, light, and righteous kingship. He is called Samildanach, "skilled in all arts," for he possesses every craft and talent to perfection: warrior, poet, smith, musician, healer, and more.

Lugh's most famous entrance into Irish mythology comes at the court of the Tuatha Dé Danann, where he arrives at the gates of Tara and demands entry. When asked what skill he possesses, he names his talents one by one, only to be told each time that the court already has someone with that skill. Finally, he asks: "Do you have one person who possesses all of these skills?" They do not. And so Lugh is admitted, bringing his mastery and brilliance into the hall of the gods.

At the Summer Solstice, Lugh represents the fullness of potential realized. This is the moment when skills, honed through practice, shine at their brightest. If you have been working on a craft, a project, or a personal goal, the solstice is the time to honor how far you have come. Light a candle for Lugh and speak your accomplishments aloud, not in pride but in acknowledgment. Offer him ale, bread, or a token of your own work: a poem written, a drawing made, a tool you have mastered.

Lugh also teaches discernment. Not all light is beneficial; some is harsh, blinding, or destructive. To work with Lugh is to learn how to wield power responsibly, how to shine without scorching, how to lead without dominating. His light is not ego; it is excellence in service of something greater. When you invoke him, ask: "How can I use my gifts to serve? What is mine to do, and what is mine to release?"

Sacred Sites and Solar Alignments

Ireland is home to numerous ancient sites aligned with the summer solstice sunrise or sunset, evidence that this solar turning was observed with great reverence by the Neolithic peoples who built them. While Newgrange is most famous for its winter solstice alignment, other sites honor the midsummer sun.

The Hill of Tara, seat of ancient kings and spiritual center of Ireland, has alignments that mark the summer solstice. The Mound of the Hostages, a passage tomb on Tara's slopes, is illuminated by the rising sun at both the summer and winter solstices, linking the two turning points in a sacred symmetry. Standing at Tara on the longest day, one can feel the power of the sun as it was felt by kings and druids thousands of years ago.

Loughcrew, another major cairn complex in County Meath, has chambers that align with the equinoxes, but its positioning on high ground makes it a powerful place to observe the solstice as well. The view from the cairns extends for miles, and at midsummer, the sun seems to hang suspended above the landscape, reluctant to set.

For modern practitioners unable to visit these sites, you can create your own alignment practice. Find a place where you can observe the sunrise on the solstice, a hilltop, a beach, a park, or even a rooftop. Mark the position of the sun as it rises, perhaps by placing a stone or making a note in your journal. Return to this spot at subsequent solstices and observe how the sun's position shifts over the years. This practice connects you to the cyclical nature of time and to the ancient observers who marked these changes with stone and story.

Herbal Allies and Midsummer Magic

The Summer Solstice is a peak time for gathering herbs, when their essential oils and magical properties are at their strongest. In Irish folk tradition, herbs gathered on Midsummer's Eve or Day were believed to carry extra potency, particularly for healing and protection.

St. John's Wort, named for the Christian saint whose feast day falls near the solstice, is one of the most powerful midsummer herbs. Its bright yellow flowers seem to capture sunlight itself, and it has been used for centuries to treat depression, wounds, and nervous system issues. In magic, it offers protection against negative energy and banishes darkness, both literal and metaphorical. Hang bundles of St. John's Wort above doorways or burn it in ritual to invoke solar blessings.

Yarrow, with its feathery leaves and white or pink flowers, is another traditional midsummer herb. It was used in divination, healing, and love magic. Young women would sleep with yarrow beneath their pillows on Midsummer's Eve, hoping to dream of their future spouse. Warriors carried it for protection in battle. Modern practitioners can use yarrow in teas for psychic opening or place it on the altar for courage and clarity.

Elderflower, blooming in creamy white clusters at midsummer, was believed to offer protection from malevolent spirits and was used in blessings for home and family. The flowers can be made into cordials, syrups, or infused into water for ritual baths. Elder is sacred and should always be approached with respect; some traditions say you must ask the Elder Mother's permission before harvesting.

Mugwort, vervain, and lavender are also at their peak. Gather them with gratitude, dry them in bundles hung in a dark, airy place, and use them throughout the year in incense, teas, or sachets. The act of harvesting itself is a ritual: move slowly, speak to the plants, leave offerings of water or a strand of your hair, and take only what you need.

Sovereignty and Self-Mastery

The Summer Solstice is a time to contemplate sovereignty, not just political power, but personal sovereignty over your own life, choices, and energy. In Irish tradition, a true king was one who ruled with justice, wisdom, and care for the land. His sovereignty was not about domination but about right relationship with all he governed.

At the height of the sun's power, ask yourself: Where am I sovereign in my life? Where do I give my power away unnecessarily? What boundaries need to be set or reinforced? Sovereignty is not about controlling others; it is about knowing yourself deeply enough to stand firm in your truth, even when the world asks you to bend.

This is also a time to assess self-mastery. Lugh, as master of all skills, reminds us that excellence requires discipline, practice, and humility. Have you been honing your craft? Have you been consistent in your spiritual practice? The solstice asks us to be honest about where we shine and where we still have work to do. There is no shame in acknowledging areas for growth; in fact, doing so is an act of sovereignty.

A simple exercise: write two lists. On the first, name the areas of your life where you feel strong, clear, and in control. On the second, name the areas where you feel scattered, overwhelmed, or compromised. Do not judge either list. Simply witness. Then ask: What is one small step I can take to reclaim sovereignty in the places where I have lost it? Make that your solstice vow.

Teaching Story: The Crown That Burns

A student once came to me at the Summer Solstice, exhausted and burned out. She was a leader in her community, someone everyone turned to for guidance, energy, and support. But she had been shining so brightly for others that she had nothing left for herself. "I thought this was what it meant to be of service," she said. "But I feel like I'm dying inside."

I asked her to join me for a solstice ritual, and together we built a small fire. As the flames grew, I handed her a flower crown she had woven earlier in the day. "This is your light," I said. "The light everyone sees. The crown you wear for them." She held it, and I could see tears forming in her eyes.

"Now," I said, "burn it."

She hesitated, then placed the crown into the fire. It caught quickly, petals curling and blackening, smoke rising. We watched it burn in silence. When it was ash, I said, "That crown was beautiful, but it was not you. It was a performance. And performances end."

She nodded, crying now. "What do I do instead?"

"You tend the fire," I said. "Not the crown. The fire is steady. The fire does not perform. It simply burns. And when it needs fuel, you feed it. When it needs rest, you bank it. You do not let it consume you, and you do not demand it burn forever at full strength."

Over the following months, she slowly rebuilt her practice, learning to say no, to rest, to tend her own light before offering it to others. She is still a leader, but now she leads from a place of fullness rather than depletion. The Summer Solstice taught her what it teaches us all: that the brightest light is not the one that burns itself out, but the one that knows when to shine and when to rest in shadow.

Seasonal Recipes for Summer Solstice

Golden Grain and Herb Bread

May Wine is a traditional spring drink that blends the freshness of woodruff or mint with wine and strawberries. This light, fruity blend honors the season's union of fire and flower, perfect for Beltane gatherings and celebrations.

Serves: 8 | Prep: 10 min | Cook: 0 min | Total: 10 min

Ingredients

1 bottle white wine

A few sprigs fresh sweet woodruff or mint

Strawberries, halved

Instructions

1. Combine wine, woodruff, and strawberries in a pitcher.

2. Chill overnight to allow flavors to meld.

3. Stir gently before serving.

4. Serve chilled in cups, with a strawberry in each glass.

Ritual Context

Toast the season with this fragrant wine, honoring the union of fire and flower. Share toasts of love, joy, and passion with those gathered. Let each sip remind you that pleasure and connection are sacred.

May Wine

Flowers bloom with wild abundance at Beltane, and this infused cream captures their delicate essence. Used to top cakes, fruit, or served alone, it speaks to sensuality and the beauty of the blooming season.

Serves: 6 | Prep: 10 min | Cook: 5 min | Total: 15 min

Ingredients

1 cup heavy cream

1 tablespoon edible flower petals (rose, violet, or elderflower)

1 teaspoon sugar or honey

Instructions

1. Gently warm cream in a saucepan—do not boil.

2. Add flower petals and sugar.

3. Steep for 10 minutes while warm.

4. Chill completely before serving.

5. Strain if desired, or serve with petals intact.

Ritual Context

Crown your Beltane feast with this delicate cream, letting its floral essence awaken the senses. Use it as a blessing, anointing desserts and loved ones with its beauty.

Flower-Infused Cream

Beltane feasts are sweet, spiced, and sensuous. These honeyed cakes evoke fertility, pleasure, and abundance. Made with oats and the golden sweetness of honey, they become offerings of joy and sexual vitality.

Serves: 12 | Prep: 10 min | Cook: 20 min | Total: 30 min

Ingredients

1 1/2 cups rolled oats

1/4 cup honey

1/2 cup butter

Pinch of salt

1/4 teaspoon cinnamon

Instructions

1. Preheat oven to 350°F (175°C).

2. Melt butter and honey together.

3. Stir in oats, salt, and cinnamon.

4. Press mixture firmly into a greased pan.

5. Bake for 18–20 minutes until golden.

6. Cool slightly, then cut into squares.

Ritual Context

Serve these cakes at your Beltane feast as a celebration of joy, abundance, and embodied pleasure. Share with loved ones as a blessing of desire and connection.

Closing Reflection

The Summer Solstice is a threshold bathed in brilliance. It is the high point of the sun's journey, and also the first step into its decline. This balance of light and loss, of fullness and fading, teaches us how to live with reverence for the moment.

We are reminded that joy must be embraced while it is here. That our inner fires must be tended before the dimming days return. That what has blossomed in us deserves celebration, and what begins to wane still carries wisdom.

To stand in the solstice sun is to stand in your power, knowing it will not last forever, and loving it all the more for that.

Carry this light with you. Let it glow in your words, your choices, your craft. You are part of the wheel, the flame, the song.

And when the days begin to shorten, remember: you once stood crowned in golden light, and that crown lives still within you.

Looking Ahead

As summer peaks at Solstice, we move toward Lughnasadh, the first harvest festival honoring Lugh and the sacrifice that sustains us. The next chapter celebrates the gathering of grain and the gifts of the land.

Chapter 15: Lughnasadh – The First Harvest

The Season and Its Significance

Lughnasadh (pronounced LOO-nuh-suh), also known as Lammas in some traditions, is the first of the three harvest festivals on the Wheel of the Year. Celebrated around August 1st, it marks the beginning of the grain harvest in Ireland and across much of the Northern Hemisphere. Its name honors the god Lugh, but its heart is agricultural, ancestral, and deeply practical: a time of gratitude for what is growing, and sober awareness of what must be gathered before it fades.

This is not a season of abundance without labor; it is the moment when the fruits of our efforts begin to show, but must still be brought in with care. It is a time to acknowledge the work already done, and the work still required. It is the turn from wild summer joy to conscious preparation for the dark.

Historically, Lughnasadh was marked by communal gatherings, fairs, athletic games, matchmaking, and ritual bread-making. People climbed sacred hills to feast and compete. Handfastings were made. First fruits were offered to the land and gods in thanks.

Spiritually, this is a time to assess what has grown in your life, both outwardly and within. What seeds you planted in Imbolc, Beltaine, and the Summer Solstice may now begin to bear fruit. It is also a time to ask: what must I release to ensure a full harvest? What inner labor still remains?

To celebrate Lughnasadh is to step into sacred responsibility. We honor the bounty not as entitlement, but as the result of cycles, care, and the grace of the land. We begin to reap, to bake, to give thanks, and to prepare for what comes next.

Mythic Context and Deity Association

At the heart of Lughnasadh lies a myth of devotion, sacrifice, and skill. The festival takes its name from Lugh, the many-skilled god of light, craftsmanship, and oath keeping. But it is not a celebration of his birth or his victories, instead, it is a commemoration of his foster-mother Tailtiu.

Tailtiu, a noblewoman of the Fir Bolg or a goddess in her own right, cleared the great plain of Ireland so that crops could be sown. The labor broke her body, and she died of exhaustion. Lugh established the festival in her honor, calling for games and feasts in remembrance of her sacrifice. Thus, Lughnasadh is not only a harvest celebration, it is an act of ancestral gratitude.

Lugh himself is the patron of many things: smithing, poetry, warfare, healing, and truth. At Lughnasadh, his spirit reminds us that excellence, effort, and skill are sacred. Competitions, performances, and shared labors honor him.

The festival also invokes the spirits of the land; the sovereign earth that gives grain and fruit, but requires care and offering in return. In some traditions, the grain itself is personified as a spirit or god who must be ritually cut and honored. This act is not taken lightly: the first sheaf is sacred.

Other deities sometimes honored at this time include Danu (as ancestral earth), Brigid (as protector of the hearth and home's bounty), and even darker figures who remind us of sacrifice and transition. All are bound to the turning of the land.

To honor the gods at Lughnasadh is to honor what has been given; and to commit yourself anew to the labor that keeps the wheel turning.

LUGHNASADH

Seasonal Signs and Cultural Themes

In the Irish landscape, early August is a time of subtle yet unmistakable change. Grains turn from green to gold. Blackberries ripen in the hedgerows. The brightness of summer deepens into something more grounded, heavier, richer, and edged with the first whispers of decline.

Farmers begin their most critical work, cutting, collecting, and storing the first harvest. In the past, a successful Lughnasadh was not guaranteed; poor weather or pests could still destroy the crop. The community held its breath as the first sheaves were taken in. Joy and solemnity walked hand in hand.

Communal gatherings during this time served not only as celebration but as preparation. Marriages were contracted. Disputes were settled. Feats of strength and wit were displayed in Lugh's name, reinforcing social bonds and individual excellence.

Herbs gathered at Lughnasadh, such as meadowsweet, heather, and mugwort, were considered especially potent for healing and protection. They were often dried and stored for use through the winter. Wildflowers were braided into garlands or corn dollies as offerings to the land.

Weather magic and augury were also practiced. The shape of clouds, behavior of birds, or condition of early grain could predict the harvest's fate. People read the land like a living book.

In the heart of the season, we are asked to give thanks, not just for what has been received, but for what still requires care. The harvest has begun, but it is far from complete. Lughnasadh calls us to act with awareness, to honor the labor of the land and of the soul, and to participate fully in the turning of the year.

Altar Setup and Seasonal Elements

To prepare a Lughnasadh altar, begin with natural textures, wood, burlap, wheat stalks, and woven cloth in gold, brown, and rust tones. This is a working altar, full of gratitude and intention. Set it up in a sunny place or near a window where the warmth of the season can reach it.

Central to the altar is bread. A loaf you've baked yourself is ideal, shaped in a spiral, sheaf, or even a simple round to symbolize the sun and the cycle of life. Beside it, place grains, oats, barley, or corn. A few ripe berries or apples, if available, represent the fruits of labor beginning to emerge.

Include tools, symbols of your own work and craft. This could be a pen, a hammer, a kitchen spoon, or a needle. These represent the labors you honor, just as Lugh honored the skills of every craft.

Candles in gold, amber, and red can flank the altar, along with sunflowers, marigolds, or wildflowers gathered from the field or roadside. A small bowl of water and a stone may be placed to represent the grounded balance of the harvest season, rooted, yet flowing.

Images or symbols of Lugh, Tailtiu, or Danu may be added, as well as a small token of something you are ready to release in exchange for growth.

Finally, leave a space for an offering (a piece of bread, honey, or milk) to be placed outside at the end of your ritual. The altar should feel lived in, present, and honest. This is not a time for polished beauty, it is a time for meaningful connection.

Step-by-Step Lughnasadh Ritual: Offering of the Loaf

This ritual honors the first harvest, the god Lugh, and the ancestral labor of the land. It can be done alone or in a group. Bread, grain, and offerings are central to this rite, and the ritual is best held outdoors or near a window at sunset.

LUGHNASADH

1. Preparation and Cleansing
Set your altar with bread, grains, a candle, and a symbol of your craft. Clean the space with a sweeping motion or incense.

Say: "I clear this space with breath and hand,
To honor grain, to bless the land."

2. Casting the Circle
Walk sunwise around your space, imagining golden light enclosing it.

Say: "With wheel of fire and ring of stone,
This circle stands, this space is known."

3. Invocation of Lugh and Tailtiu
Light the candle.

Say: "Lugh of skill, of shining art,
Be welcome here with open heart.
Tailtiu, who gave her strength to sow,
May your memory here grow."

4. Blessing and Offering of the Loaf
Hold the loaf in both hands. Reflect on your labor, your growth, and what you are ready to harvest.

Say: "This bread is made with hand and will,
Of grain and ground, of strength and skill.
I bless this loaf in honor of toil,
In reverence to seed and soil."

Break the loaf. Offer a piece to the earth or a bowl.

Say: "To the land I give what first was mine,
In thanks, in trust, in sacred time."

5. Meditation or Reflection

Close your eyes. Breathe deeply. Ask: What have I grown? What must I protect? What must I release?

Let images or thoughts rise and fall like golden fields in wind.

6. Gratitude and Release

Give thanks aloud for three things that have grown in your life. They may be physical, emotional, creative, or spiritual.

Say: "I give thanks for what is full and true.
I walk with harvest strong and new."

7. Closing the Circle

Walk counterclockwise.

Say: "The wheel turns on, the sun shall fade,
But gratitude and seed remain.
This circle opens but is not broken."

8. Feast and Celebration

Eat your bread. Share it with others if possible. Tell stories. Sing. Bake. Let your ritual end in joy and nourishment.

This is the sacred act of receiving and returning; of taking in the grain and giving back your thanks.

Modern Practice Tips

Lughnasadh need not be celebrated on a hillside or at a great communal fair to be meaningful. Modern Pagans can honor this turning of the wheel in small, intentional ways that bring the spirit of the season into home and heart.

1. Bake and Break Bread at Home

Even if you are alone or new to baking, making a simple loaf connects you directly to the ancient rhythms of harvest. Use local grains if possible. Speak gratitude as you mix, knead, and share, even if the sharing is with yourself.

2. Set a Skill-Based Intention

Lugh is the master of many crafts. Choose one skill, writing, cooking, gardening, repairing, parenting, organizing; and dedicate time this month to improving or honoring it. This is a sacred act.

3. Create a Jar of Gratitude

Each day around Lughnasadh, write down something you are grateful for that has grown in your life. Use a small jar or bowl. On the day of the ritual, read them aloud before your altar or meal.

4. Kitchen Altar and Daily Offering

If a full altar isn't feasible, create a small space in your kitchen. Light a candle. Place a bowl of grain. Offer a pinch of salt or a word of thanks each day. Let your cooking be part of the practice.

5. Backyard or Balcony Harvesting

If you grow herbs, flowers, or vegetables, harvest something intentionally. If not, bring home fresh produce from a farmer's market or nearby orchard. Let each act of washing, slicing, or storing be sacred.

6. Modern Games and Creativity

Host a small Lughnasadh gathering with friends or children that includes games, storytelling, or art-making. These echo the fairs of old and help keep the joy and skill of the festival alive.

7. Journaling Prompts for the First Harvest

What in my life is reaching maturity?

What effort am I proud of?

What needs to be completed or protected in the coming weeks?

Your modern Lughnasadh does not need to mimic ancient rites, it only needs to carry their heart. Give thanks, honor effort, and celebrate what is ready to be received.

The Games of Lugh: Competition as Sacred Practice

One of the most distinctive aspects of Lughnasadh was the holding of funeral games in honor of Tailtiu. These were not somber events but lively gatherings where people competed in feats of strength, skill, and wit. Contests included racing, wrestling, hurling, horse racing, and tests of archery or spear-throwing. Poets competed in verse, musicians in song, and storytellers in the telling of ancient tales.

These games were sacred, not frivolous. They honored Tailtiu's sacrifice by celebrating human excellence and community bonds. To compete was to demonstrate that her labor had not been in vain; that the people she made space for had grown strong, skilled, and worthy. Winners received honor and sometimes material prizes, but the true reward was the recognition of mastery.

Modern practitioners can revive this tradition by hosting skill-sharing gatherings at Lughnasadh. Invite friends or coven-mates to demonstrate their crafts: cooking, music, storytelling, crafting, gardening. Hold friendly competitions: who can bake the best bread, write the most moving poem, create the most beautiful altar? The point is not to establish hierarchy but to celebrate what each person has cultivated, to witness each other's growth, and to honor the diversity of talents within a community.

If you practice alone, the competition can be internal. Challenge yourself to complete a project by Lughnasadh, whether it's finishing a book, mastering a new recipe, or refining a spiritual practice. Set a goal at Imbolc or Beltane, work toward it through summer, and present it to Lugh at the first harvest. Your offering is your effort, and the gods witness your dedication.

LUGHNASADH

Corn Dollies and Grain Spirits

The cutting of the grain at harvest was understood as a ritual act with spiritual consequences. It was believed that a spirit lived within the grain, sometimes called the Corn Mother, the Grain Spirit, or the Cailleach of the Harvest. This spirit moved through the field as it was cut, retreating into the final standing stalks. The last sheaf to be harvested was therefore sacred, and special care was taken with it.

From this final sheaf, a corn dolly was fashioned; a small figure woven from the stalks and dressed with ribbons or cloth. The corn dolly represented the captured spirit of the grain and was kept in the home throughout winter as a protective charm and a promise of next year's harvest. In spring, it would be plowed back into the earth or burned in the Beltane fire, releasing the spirit to begin the cycle anew.

Making a corn dolly at Lughnasadh connects you to this ancient practice. Use wheat stalks, oat stalks, or even dried grasses. Soak them in water to make them pliable, then braid and weave them into a simple figure. As you work, speak to the spirit of the grain: thank it for its sacrifice, ask for its protection, promise to honor the cycle. Place the dolly on your altar or hang it in your kitchen. Treat it with respect throughout the year, knowing it carries the blessing of the harvest.

If wheat or oats are not available, you can create a symbolic grain spirit from other materials: twisted cloth, braided yarn, or even folded paper. The act of making is the magic. What matters is your intention and your recognition that the harvest is not merely material but spiritual, and that what we take, we must honor.

Sacrifice and Gratitude: The Ethical Harvest

Lughnasadh forces us to confront an uncomfortable truth: we live by consuming what was once alive. The grain was a living plant. The fruit was part of a tree's body. Even the vegetables we harvest were growing, breathing beings. To eat is to participate in a cycle of life and death, and to do so consciously is to engage in a sacred exchange.

Our ancestors understood this. They knew that every harvest was a form of sacrifice, and they honored the spirits of the plants and animals who gave their lives so that humans could continue. Offerings were made. Prayers were spoken. Nothing was taken for granted. This is the ethical core of Lughnasadh: recognizing that abundance is not an entitlement but a gift that requires reciprocity.

How do we practice this today? Begin by being conscious of where your food comes from. If possible, buy from local farmers who treat the land and animals with care. Grow some of your own food, even if it's just herbs on a windowsill. When you harvest or prepare food, pause and acknowledge its origin. Speak aloud: "Thank you for this gift. I honor your life. I will not waste what you have given."

Leave offerings for the spirits of the harvest. Before you eat, place a small portion of food outside or on your altar. Pour a libation of water or wine onto the earth. Compost food scraps mindfully, returning them to the soil. These small acts cultivate a relationship of respect with the more-than-human world, and they align your practice with the ancient wisdom that all life is interconnected.

Teaching Story: The Bread That Saved a Village

An elder once told me a story about his grandmother, who lived through the difficult years of the early twentieth century in rural Ireland. One year, the harvest was poor. The grain came in thin and sparse, and the community feared they would not have enough to last the winter.

On Lughnasadh, his grandmother baked a loaf from the first of the grain, as was traditional. But instead of eating it herself or offering it to the gods alone, she took it to the center of the village and broke it into pieces, giving a portion to every family. "This bread is ours together," she said. "What we have, we share. What we lack, we endure together."

The gesture was small, but it changed everything. Other families began to share what they had: potatoes, eggs, preserved fruits. No one hoarded. No one went hungry. They rationed carefully, helped one another, and when spring came, they planted together, ensuring that the next harvest would be stronger.

The elder looked at me and said, "That loaf saved us, not because it was magic, but because it reminded us what Lughnasadh truly means. The harvest is not yours or mine. It is ours. And when we act as though it is ours, we survive."

This story has stayed with me for years. It teaches that gratitude is not enough if it ends with us. The harvest calls us to generosity, to community, to the recognition that what we have been given is meant to be shared. Whether we break bread literally or metaphorically, the principle is the same: abundance is a collective gift, and we honor it by ensuring others are fed.

Seasonal Recipes for Lughnasadh

Lughnasadh Oat and Honey Loaf

Mead, the honey wine of the ancients, celebrates the sun's fullness when infused with summer herbs. This warming drink honors the Celtic connection between the divine and the earth's generous gifts.

Serves: 8 | Prep: 10 min | Cook: 20 min | Total: 30 min

Ingredients

1 bottle dry white wine (750ml)

1/4 cup honey

3 sprigs fresh mint

2 sprigs fresh lavender or chamomile

1 cinnamon stick

2 whole cloves

Instructions

1. Combine wine and honey in a saucepan.

2. Add herbs, cinnamon, and cloves.

3. Heat gently for 15–20 minutes—do not boil.

4. Remove from heat and let cool.

5. Strain into a pitcher and chill.

6. Serve in small cups or goblets.

Ritual Context

Serve this mead at your solstice celebration as a libation to the sun and the land. Each sip carries the warmth of summer and the blessing of the season's height.

Herbal Mead

Lugh, the warrior god of many skills, reaches his height at the summer solstice. These honey cakes, golden and radiant, honor his presence and the sun's zenith. Each cake carries the light of the season into the darker months ahead.

Serves: 12 | Prep: 15 min | Cook: 15 min | Total: 30 min

Ingredients

1/2 cup butter, softened

1/3 cup honey

LUGHNASADH

2 eggs

1 1/2 cups flour

1/2 teaspoon baking powder

1/4 teaspoon salt

1 teaspoon vanilla extract

Instructions

1. Preheat oven to 350°F (175°C).

2. Cream butter and honey until light.

3. Beat in eggs one at a time.

4. Mix in flour, baking powder, salt, and vanilla.

5. Drop spoonfuls onto a greased baking sheet.

6. Bake 12–15 minutes until golden.

7. Cool on a wire rack.

Ritual Context

Bake these cakes on the solstice morning or the night before. Present them as offerings to Lugh, the warrior of many skills. Share them with those you love as blessings of strength, skill, and radiant power.

Lugh's Honey Cakes

Summer brings an abundance of ripe fruit, and this vibrant compote celebrates that fullness. Served warm or chilled, it honors the season's peak and the gifts of the earth at its most generous.

Serves: 6 | Prep: 10 min | Cook: 15 min | Total: 25 min

Ingredients

2 cups mixed fresh berries (strawberries, raspberries, blueberries)

1 cup stone fruit, pitted and chopped (peaches or apricots)

2 tablespoons honey

1 tablespoon lemon juice

1 cinnamon stick

3 whole cloves

Instructions

1. Combine all fruit in a saucepan.

2. Add honey, lemon juice, cinnamon, and cloves.

3. Simmer gently for 12–15 minutes until fruit softens and juices flow.

4. Remove cinnamon stick and cloves.

5. Serve warm over cake or ice cream, or chilled on its own.

Ritual Context

Offer this compote at your solstice altar as gratitude for the season's abundance. Let its jeweled colors and sweet taste remind you of the sun's blessing on the land.

Summer Fruit Compote

At the sun's height, golden grains reach their peak. This bread, infused with fresh summer herbs, celebrates the fullness of light and the earth's generosity. Simple yet sacred, it honors the sun's blessing at its most powerful moment.

Serves: 8 | Prep: 20 min | Cook: 40 min | Total: 60 min

LUGHNASADH

Ingredients

2 cups white flour

1 cup whole wheat flour

1 teaspoon baking powder

1/2 teaspoon salt

1 tablespoon fresh thyme or rosemary, finely chopped

3 tablespoons olive oil

1 tablespoon honey

3/4 cup warm water

Instructions

1. Preheat oven to 375°F (190°C). Grease a baking sheet.

2. Mix flours, baking powder, salt, and herbs.

3. Combine oil, honey, and water.

4. Stir wet ingredients into dry until just combined.

5. Form into a round loaf and place on baking sheet.

6. Score the top with a cross or sun pattern.

7. Bake 35–40 minutes until golden.

Ritual Context

Present this bread as an offering to the sun at the height of the solstice. Bake it with gratitude and intention, knowing that its golden form mirrors the sun's power. Share it with community as a blessing of light and vitality.

Closing Reflection

Lughnasadh is a moment of balance between joy and responsibility. It reminds us that behind every feast is a field, behind every loaf a labor, and behind every blessing a body that gave of itself so that others may thrive. The harvest is not a gift freely given, it is a relationship, a cycle, a covenant.

To walk the path of Lughnasadh is to walk with eyes open to what has grown and what is still needed. It asks us to meet our lives with honesty, to honor the work we've done, and to prepare for the seasons of decline and quiet that follow.

Gratitude is not passive. It is an action. An offering. A turning of the heart toward what matters. Whether you bake, gather, write, speak, plant, or simply pause with awareness, you are participating in this sacred turning.

May your first harvest be full of meaning. May your hands know their worth. And may you walk onward with grain in your bag, strength in your step, and a song in your soul.

Looking Ahead

From Lughnasadh's first harvest, we arrive at the Autumn Equinox, the second harvest and moment of balance before the descent into darkness. The next chapter explores gratitude, balance, and the preparation for winter.

Chapter 16: Autumn Equinox – The Second Harvest

The Season and Its Significance

The Autumn Equinox, observed around September 21st–23rd, is a time of equilibrium. It is one of two points in the year when day and night share equal time, perfectly balanced. This sacred symmetry marks the second harvest and signals the shift from abundance toward descent. In Irish climates, the winds turn cooler, the light softens, and the air carries the scent of change.

This equinox, sometimes referred to in modern Pagan traditions as Mabon, does not have a direct counterpart in the ancient Irish calendar, but the themes of balance, thanksgiving, and preparation are deeply rooted in the land's seasonal rhythms. In the older Irish agricultural year, this would have been a time to gather the last of the grain and begin preserving fruit and root crops, to store what must last through the coming dark.

Culturally and spiritually, this is a moment of reckoning. What have we reaped? What must be put aside? What must be let go? The equinox invites stillness and stock-taking, not only of pantry and storehouse, but of the soul.

It is a time to honor reciprocity. To recognize the balance between light and shadow, giving and receiving, fullness and release. As the year wanes and the nights begin to overtake the days, the equinox opens a door to reflection. In that doorway, we pause, not to hold the light forever, but to learn what it has illuminated.

The Autumn Equinox arrives not with fanfare but with a whisper. It does not announce itself like the fire festivals of Samhain or Bealtaine. It simply is, a pivot point inscribed by the sun's arc across the horizon, where the axis of day and night achieves a fleeting equilibrium. In agricultural societies, this was not a festival day in the formal sense, but a marker, a moment to assess and adjust. The grain had been threshed, the hay baled, the apples picked. What remained was the steady work of preservation and preparation.

In Ireland, where rain is frequent and seasons shift gradually rather than dramatically, the equinox could pass unnoticed if one were not paying close attention. But for those who lived by the land's rhythms, who rose and slept by the sun's light, this turning was felt in the bones. The morning mist lingered longer. The evening chill crept in earlier. The hedgerows, once bursting with late-summer blooms, began to brown and seed.

This is the second harvest, a harvest of reflection as much as of grain. Where Lughnasadh celebrated the cutting of the first fruits and the community's survival assured for another year, the Autumn Equinox asks us to consider what we have truly gathered, not only in basket and barrel but in experience, in wisdom, in relationships tended and tasks completed. It is a time to look at the year's work with honest eyes. What flourished? What withered? What lessons did the land teach, and did we listen?

There is a solemnity to this season that differs from the joyful abundance of high summer or the protective urgency of Samhain. The equinox is calm, measured, neither exuberant nor mournful. It holds space for gratitude without pretense, for acceptance without despair. It teaches us that balance is not a static state but a momentary grace, a breath held between inhalation and exhalation, before the rhythm continues.

Mythic Context and Deity Association

Though no explicit Autumn Equinox festival survives in early Irish sources, the spiritual undertones of the season echo through Irish mythology. It is a time ruled not by a single deity but by the interplay of forces, sovereignty, fate, memory, and descent.

The Mórrígan, goddess of prophecy, battle, and the land itself, becomes especially resonant. She is the voice that warns of change, that sees what lies ahead when others are too full of harvest to notice the withering edge. At this point in the cycle, her presence becomes less as a war-bringer and more as the whisperer of truths we must face. Her connection to the dying year reminds us that decline is sacred, not a failure, but a return.

Danu, as the great mother and fertile source, is also honored in her mature aspect. Her gifts are evident in every basket of apples, every jar of jam, every seed stored for spring. She is the land's memory and its wisdom, quiet, enduring, essential.

Manannán mac Lir, god of the sea and the mists between worlds, also walks closer as the veil begins to thin. He is the liminal one, the guide to the places in-between. In this season of balance and turning, his energy prepares us for what comes after light.

This is a time to honor the gods of threshold and reckoning. They teach us that harvest is not just about gain, it is about preparation, discernment, and trust in the darkening path ahead.

In broader Celtic tradition, this liminal time between harvest and descent also evokes the presence of the Cailleach, the divine hag who claims sovereignty over winter. Though she is most powerfully associated with Samhain and the colder months, her approach can be felt as early as the equinox. She is the one who measures the stores, who knows what will last and what will fail. She is not cruel, but she is truthful. Her gaze is the gaze of necessity.

The equinox is also a time when the ancestors draw near. Not yet fully present as they will be at Samhain, but stirring, beginning their slow return from the Otherworld. Some practitioners light candles at dusk during this season, not for specific ritual but as a simple acknowledgment: we remember you. We honor what you gave. We walk the path you walked.

The Tuatha Dé Danann, those bright gods of skill and sovereignty, also fade slightly at this time. Their power does not vanish, but it withdraws, moving from the surface of the land into its depths. They retreat to the hollow hills, to the sidhe mounds, where they will wait through winter's dark before returning with the spring. This is not abandonment but transformation. The gods do not leave; they descend, as we must also learn to do.

Seasonal Signs and Cultural Themes

As the equinox nears, the Irish landscape shifts from late-summer fullness to early-autumn quiet. Hedgerows droop with blackberries. Apples fall heavy from the branch. Bracken begins to bronze, and the long light of evening stretches further into dusk.

This is the season of second chances and final gatherings. In traditional communities, this time was used to complete what was unfinished. The last sheaves were bundled. Root crops were lifted and cellared. Jams and preserves simmered in hearth-warmed kitchens. What could not be used was dried, stored, or shared.

It was also a time of accounting. Herds were counted, debts were weighed, and contracts were considered for the year ahead. As in the land, so in the spirit; this was a time to examine one's choices, to measure not just results but integrity.

Themes of fairness and balance surface everywhere: in folklore, in the judgments of wise chieftains, and in the stories of those who stepped beyond the veil only to return changed. Equinoxes often signify thresholds in myth, the moment when a hero returns, or a warning comes, or an ancestor's voice is heard in a dream.

Even the weather speaks of this balance. Some days blaze like summer's final song. Others whisper of frost. Rain feeds the roots, and wind strips the leaves. We are reminded that this is a world always in motion.

To live with the Autumn Equinox is to live in readiness and respect. We honor the fruits of what we've done, yes, but also prepare the ground for silence. The dance of plenty is nearly done. Now, we gather what we can, and learn to walk with what is fading.

In older Irish practice, the equinox marked a time of settling accounts not only in grain and coin but in social bonds. Fostering arrangements were renewed or concluded. Marriages contracted at Bealtaine were evaluated for their strength and harmony. Disputes unresolved during the harvest months were brought before brehons or community elders, who judged with the understanding that winter's hardship made social cohesion essential.

This was also a season of hospitality and generosity tempered by wisdom. Excess grain might be gifted to a neighbor whose crop failed, but only if one's own stores were secure. Acts of charity were framed not as selflessness but as an investment in community survival. What you gave in autumn might return to you in spring, through labor shared or seeds loaned or a meal offered when your own pantry ran thin.

The landscape itself becomes a teacher during this season. Trees demonstrate the wisdom of release, letting go of leaves to protect their living core. Animals gather and store, or else prepare for migration or hibernation. Everything in nature models the lesson of the equinox: hold what is essential, release what is not, and trust the cycle to return.

For modern practitioners, these themes translate into questions of sustainability and boundaries. What commitments are worth keeping through the dark months? Which relationships nourish you, and which drain you? What projects deserve your winter's energy, and which should be composted like spent plants, returning their nutrients to the soil for future growth? The equinox offers time to discern these answers before the rush of Samhain and the introspection of winter claim our full attention.

Altar Setup and Seasonal Elements

The Autumn Equinox altar is one of balance and preparation. Begin with cloth in deep red, rust, gold, or dark green, colors of the shifting land. Place two candles of equal size at the center, one white and one black, to represent day and night in equal measure.

Apples, gourds, blackberries, and hazelnuts are traditional offerings. Include items from the final harvest: grains, onions, root vegetables, or corn. A jar of jam or dried herbs may symbolize the work of preserving.

Symbols of duality are powerful here: sun and moon tokens, a feather beside a stone, or a bowl of water next to a dish of salt. These elements speak to the balance between what nourishes and what endures.

Add an image or token representing The Mórrígan, Danu, or Manannán mac Lir if you feel called. You might include a mirror or an acorn as a symbol of inner reflection and seeds for the future.

Your altar should invite both stillness and gratitude. Let it hold space for what is complete, and also what remains unknown. Light both candles at dusk to mark the moment of turning; and let their glow remind you of the power held in equal parts.

Consider adding representations of both abundance and scarcity to your altar. A full bowl of grain beside an empty bowl. Fresh apples next to dried apple rings. This juxtaposition reminds us that both states are sacred, both necessary. Abundance without awareness breeds waste; scarcity without preparation breeds desperation. The altar teaches balance through its very arrangement.

If you work with ogham or runes, Tinne (Holly) or Muin (Vine) are appropriate for this season. Holly represents protection and foresight, the evergreen that endures through winter's darkness. Vine represents harvest, intoxication, and ecstasy, but also the wisdom that comes from fermentation, transformation through time and darkness. Both carry the energy of preservation and endurance.

Some practitioners include scales or a balance beam on their altar, a literal representation of the equinox's central theme. This can be as simple as two stones of equal weight on either side of a candle, or an actual small scale used to weigh offerings. The physical act of balancing objects becomes a meditation on balance in all its forms.

Water and earth elements deserve special attention at this time. A bowl of soil from your garden or a local place you love, paired with a bowl of water, represents the marriage of growth and nourishment that made the harvest possible. As the season progresses, you might let the water evaporate naturally, watching the earth remain, enduring and patient until spring's return.

Step-by-Step Ritual – Equal Light, Equal Shadow

This ritual honors the balance of the Autumn Equinox and invites you to recognize both the abundance in your life and the truths that must now be faced as the light wanes. It is best performed at twilight, as day and night begin to trade places.

1. Preparation and Cleansing

Clean your ritual space physically and spiritually. Use herbal smoke or sprinkle blessed water.

Say: "As the light fades and balance reigns,
I cleanse this space of all remains."

2. Setting the Altar and Casting the Circle

Place your altar elements, balanced candles, seasonal fruits, and a mirror.

Walk sunwise, envisioning a soft golden light forming a circle.

Say: "From dusk to dawn, from seed to stone,
This circle holds me. I stand alone;
Yet joined with sky, with root, with flame,
In balance, I speak my sacred name."

3. Lighting the Candles

Light the white candle.

Say: "I honor the light, the growth, the flame."

Light the black candle.

Say: "I honor the dark, the rest, the grave."

Together: "Day and night, I hold both true;
One cannot be without the two."

4. Invocation of the Deities

Call upon the deities of the threshold.

Say: "Mórrígan, voice of knowing and night,
Danu, earth-mother of yielding and right,
Manannán, walker between wave and mist;
Stand with me now, in balance kissed."

5. Mirror Reflection and Offering

Gaze into the mirror.

Ask:

What truth have I harvested?

What weight must I release?

What must I carry into the dark?

Hold a fruit or small stone and whisper your answers into it. Place it on the altar.

Say: "What is gathered, I bless.
What is fading, I honor.
What is uncertain, I trust."

6. Libation and Toast

Pour a sip of blackberry cordial into a bowl for the land.

Say: "For the spirits, for the land, for those who came before."

Drink your portion and sit in stillness.

7. Closing the Circle

Thank the deities.

Say: "Dark and light, I thank you both.
The turning comes, and I stand whole."

Walk counterclockwise.

Say: "This rite is ended, the wheel moves on.
From balance born, from balance drawn."

8. Feast or Silence

Enjoy a ritual meal, or rest in quiet. Journal, dream, or walk under the stars. Let the moment linger.

In doing this rite, you've honored not just the changing sky; but the sacred tension within your own soul, as it prepares to carry the final harvest into the waiting dark.

Modern Practice Tips

The Autumn Equinox offers modern Pagans a moment of sacred pause. You need not live on a farm or host a full ritual gathering to honor its energy, simple, intentional acts can bring this turning of the wheel into everyday life.

1. Create a Balance Journal

Use the days around the equinox to reflect on areas of imbalance in your life. What receives too much of your energy? What have you neglected? Write one page each day for a week, exploring how you can return to equilibrium.

2. Preserve Something Seasonal

Make a jar of blackberry jam, pickle onions, or dehydrate apple slices. Preserving food connects you to ancestral rhythms and reminds you to prepare for leaner times. Label each jar with a blessing.

3. Create a Day and Night Meditation Space

Set up two candles in a quiet place, one light, one dark. Meditate in their glow, reflecting on what in your life is growing and what is fading. This small practice anchors the season's meaning.

4. Equal Giving and Receiving

Offer something anonymously (a donation, a helping hand, a kind word) and consciously accept help from another. The balance of giving and receiving is central to the equinox. Both are sacred.

5. Nature Walk and Offering

Walk through a natural area near sunset. Gather a fallen leaf, acorn, or small stone. Leave an offering in return: a bit of bread, a whispered blessing, or a heartfelt thought. Notice the shifting air, the slant of the light.

6. Host a Silent Meal

Prepare a meal with autumn ingredients and eat in silence by candlelight. Use this time to notice your food, your breath, and your inner voice. Invite family or friends if desired; but speak only at the meal's end.

7. Dedicate a New Intention

As the wheel turns toward darkness, dedicate yourself to a quiet project: journaling, mending, inner work, or learning. Let this intention grow as the light recedes, so it may emerge ripened by winter.

These quiet practices (gentle, sacred, and sincere) remind us that we are part of the great turning. Even in modern life, the balance of the earth can still live in our hands, homes, and hearts.

8. Shadow Work and Inner Balance

The equinox's theme of balance between light and dark makes it an ideal time for shadow work. Set aside time for honest self-reflection. What parts of yourself have you been avoiding? What truths have you been unwilling to face? Journal on these questions without judgment. The equinox teaches us that darkness is not evil; it is simply the other half of existence, equally necessary and equally sacred.

9. Release and Gratitude Ritual

Write down on separate pieces of paper what you are grateful for from the past year and what you are ready to release. Place the gratitude papers on your altar to honor them throughout the season. Burn the release papers safely in a cauldron or fireplace, offering them to the element of transformation. As they burn, speak aloud: "I release what no longer serves. I honor what remains."

10. Community Gratitude Gathering

If you practice with others, host a simple gratitude circle. Each person brings a seasonal food to share and speaks briefly about one thing they've harvested this year, whether literal or metaphorical. Keep the gathering low-key and intimate, focused on presence rather than performance. Let the shared meal become a living altar to community and reciprocity.

11. Prepare Your Winter Workspace

As the light decreases, your workspace will need adjustment. Clean and organize your ritual space, your study area, or your creative corner. Add lamps or candles to compensate for shorter days. This practical act honors the coming darkness while asserting your intention to remain active and engaged throughout winter.

12. Seasonal Skill Renewal

Choose one skill or practice to deepen during the dark months ahead. This could be learning a traditional craft, studying Irish mythology more deeply, developing your divination practice, or mastering a new cooking technique. The equinox is the time to commit; winter is the time to practice. By spring, you'll have grown in ways you couldn't have anticipated.

Seasonal Recipes for Autumn Equinox

Roasted Apple and Grain Bowl

Berries and apples mark the transitional spirit of Lughnasadh, when summer begins its turn toward autumn. This crisp celebrates the fruits that have ripened under the sun and the gratitude we feel for the land's generosity.

Serves: 6 | Prep: 15 min | Cook: 35 min | Total: 50 min

Ingredients

2 cups blackberries (fresh or frozen)

2 apples, peeled and chopped

1/4 cup brown sugar

1/2 cup rolled oats

1/4 cup flour

1/4 cup butter, melted

1/2 teaspoon cinnamon

Instructions

1. Preheat oven to 350°F (175°C).

2. Combine blackberries, apples, and brown sugar in a baking dish.

3. Mix oats, flour, cinnamon, and melted butter until crumbly.

4. Sprinkle topping evenly over fruit.

5. Bake for 30–35 minutes until golden and bubbly.

6. Cool slightly before serving.

Ritual Context

Present this crisp as an offering to the gods of the harvest and to Tailtiu, honored at Lughnasadh for her sacrifice. Serve it warm to those gathered, sharing the fruits of summer's labor.

Blackberry and Apple Crisp

Simple, fragrant, and grounding, this dish captures the essence of the early harvest. Root vegetables—gifts from the earth's depths—are blessed with fresh summer herbs and golden butter.

Serves: 6 | Prep: 10 min | Cook: 35 min | Total: 45 min

Ingredients

2 carrots, sliced

2 parsnips, sliced

1 small beet, cubed

1 tablespoon olive oil

Salt and pepper to taste

2 tablespoons butter

1 teaspoon fresh sage, finely chopped

1 teaspoon fresh thyme, finely chopped

Instructions

1. Toss vegetables with oil, salt, and pepper.

2. Roast at 400°F (200°C) for 30–35 minutes until caramelized.

3. Melt butter with sage and thyme.

4. Pour herb butter over hot vegetables before serving.

Ritual Context

Serve these vegetables at your Lughnasadh feast as a blessing of abundance and gratitude. Each bite honors the work of the land and the generosity of the harvest.

Roasted Root Vegetables with Herb Butter

This rustic bread honors the earliest grains and the sacred role of bees in the harvest. Oat flour connects us to one of Ireland's most ancient grains, while honey sweetens with the gratitude of summer's work.

Serves: 8 | Prep: 10 min | Cook: 40 min | Total: 50 min

Ingredients

2 cups oat flour or finely ground rolled oats

1 cup whole wheat flour

1 teaspoon baking soda

1/2 teaspoon salt

1 3/4 cups buttermilk

2 tablespoons honey

Instructions

1. Preheat oven to 375°F (190°C). Grease a loaf pan.

2. Mix dry ingredients in a bowl.

3. Combine buttermilk and honey.

4. Stir wet ingredients into dry until just combined.

5. Pour into pan and bake 35–40 minutes until a skewer comes out clean.

6. Cool before slicing.

7. Offer the first slice outdoors with gratitude.

Ritual Context

Bake this loaf on Lughnasadh morning as an offering to Lugh and a thanksgiving for the harvest. Break the first slice at your altar and place it at the roots of a tree or on the earth as gratitude.

Closing Reflection

The Autumn Equinox is not merely a calendar date or symbolic alignment. It is a lived experience; a breath between the fullness of summer and the quiet hush of winter. It asks nothing but presence, and yet it offers everything: perspective, humility, and a renewed sense of grace.

We stand, for a moment, between day and night. Not clinging to the light, not fearing the dark, but holding both. This is the wisdom of the equinox. It is not perfection but wholeness. We are invited to accept our contradictions, our incompletions, our ripened gifts, and our tender unknowns.

As you walk forward from this threshold, may you carry with you the lessons of equal light and equal shadow. May you remember that every harvest is both culmination and beginning. And may your steps, from this season onward, be guided by the calm clarity that only balance can bring.

The wheel turns. And with it, so do we, grateful, grounded, and never alone.

In honoring the Autumn Equinox, we practice a deeper form of thanksgiving than simple gratitude for abundance. We thank the year for its lessons, both bitter and sweet. We thank the failures as well as the successes, recognizing that both taught us something essential about ourselves, our communities, and our relationship with the land and the sacred.

This is also a time to acknowledge that balance is temporary. The equinox lasts only a moment before the darkness begins to dominate. This is not cause for mourning but for recognition. All things that rise must fall. All things that grow must rest. All light must eventually yield to shadow, and all shadow must eventually yield to light again. The wheel turns because it must, because that turning is the very nature of existence.

For those who walk an Irish Pagan path, the Autumn Equinox reminds us that our practice is not separate from our daily lives but woven through them. Every apple cut and stored, every jar sealed, every candle lit against the early dusk is an act of devotion. The sacred is not elsewhere, waiting to be discovered in ritual alone. It is here, in the turning of the season, in the work of our hands, in the choices we make about what to keep and what to let go.

May you find in this season's balance a mirror for your own life. May you discover what is worth preserving and what is better released. May you stand in the threshold between light and dark with courage and clarity, knowing that both are necessary, both are sacred, and both are home. And may you trust, as the earth trusts, that the wheel will turn again, that spring will return, and that what seems like ending is always, in truth, transformation.

Walk gently into the darkness. It is not empty but full, not barren but waiting, not an ending but a beginning of a different kind.

Looking Ahead

As the Autumn Equinox tips toward darkness, we return to Samhain, completing the cycle of the Wheel. The year turns, and we find ourselves once more at the threshold between worlds, ready to honor the ancestors and the eternal return.

Chapter 17: Sacred Craft of the Seasons – Herbs, Foods, and Tools of the Irish Year

Across Ireland's sacred calendar, the land itself offers gifts: herbs with healing and magical properties, foods with ceremonial significance, and tools fashioned from stone, wood, bone, and fire. These were not arbitrary choices. Each object and plant belonged to its season, ripened by time, climate, and need.

For those living in the modern world, especially across the American landscape, many of these traditional plants may be difficult to access or endangered. This chapter offers not only a deep look into the original Irish materials but also accessible American equivalents for those practicing far from the misty hedgerows of Éire.

Samhain (October 31 – November 1)

Seasonal Invocation: As the veil thins and shadows deepen, I call to the blood, to memory, to the hearth behind the stars. Ancestors, draw near. This fire is for you.

Harvesting Note: If foraging herbs like mugwort or elder, always ask permission from the land. Take only what is needed. In urban settings, ensure plants are free from pesticides and pollution.

Ritual Tool Use Tip: Keys and nails are not only symbolic; they can be ritually charged by burying them in earth for three days, then placing them in moonlight or beside an ancestral photo overnight.

Cross-Reference: For the full Samhain ritual and meditation, see Chapter 6.

Key Herbs:

Mugwort (Artemisia vulgaris) – For dreamwork and ancestor contact. Common in Ireland and grows wild across North America.

Yew (Taxus baccata) – Sacred tree of death and rebirth; extremely toxic and not for internal use. Symbolic branches may be used on altars.

Elder (Sambucus nigra) – Used in protection rites and honoring the dead. In the U.S., black elder grows in temperate zones.

Substitute/Local Options:

Juniper – Spirit-cleansing smoke.

Black walnut hull – Used in protection and ending cycles.

Foods & Offerings:

Colcannon (mashed potatoes with kale or cabbage)

Soul cakes (buttery cookies for the dead)

Roasted squash and dark bread

Tools:

Iron keys or coffin nails for the threshold

Black candles or bone-white tapers

Ancestral altar cloths and photos

Winter Solstice (Around December 21)

Seasonal Invocation: In the hush of darkest night, I tend the ember. Light returns, not as firestorm, but as whisper. May this candle be the promise that warmth and growth will come again.

Harvesting Note: If you gather evergreens or pine needles, be sure to clip gently and never take from young or sparse trees. Offer thanks with breath, water, or song. Avoid overharvesting from a single grove or patch.

Ritual Tool Use Tip: Solar wheels can be made from grapevines, straw, or crafted twigs tied into a circle. Charge the wheel by setting it in sunlight during the day, then using it to crown your altar.

Cross-Reference: See Chapter 7 for Winter Solstice myth, ritual, and meditative practices.

Key Herbs:

Holly (Ilex aquifolium) – Protection, winter strength, resilience. American holly can be used with care.

Mistletoe (Viscum album) – Rare and sacred in Ireland. Use symbolic sprigs; avoid ingestion.

Substitute/Local Options:

Pine resin or needles – Purification and renewal.

Rosemary – Associated with remembrance.

Foods:

Seed cakes and oat bread

Mulled wine or cider with clove and cinnamon

Winter root vegetable stew

Tools:

Solar wheel symbols

Gold and white candles

Evergreen wreaths

Imbolc (February 1 – 2)

Seasonal Invocation: I kindle the flame in the belly of winter. Brigid of the well and flame, guide my hand and hearth. Let what has been frozen begin to flow again.

Harvesting Note: Dandelions and chamomile often appear near roads or sidewalks, avoid areas with heavy pollution. Harvest with respect, ideally in the early morning, and leave a strand of hair, a drop of milk, or a quiet word in thanks.

Ritual Tool Use Tip: A Brigid's cross should be woven with intention. As you fold the reeds or straws, whisper a blessing or personal prayer into each arm of the cross. Leave one at the hearth and one at the door.

Cross-Reference: See Chapter 8 for Imbolc's full ritual and seasonal rites.

Key Herbs:

Snowdrop – First flower of spring; poisonous, used symbolically.

Angelica – Protection, light, sacred feminine.

Dandelion root – Cleansing and internal renewal.

U.S. Equivalents:

Milk thistle – Liver cleansing and renewal

Chamomile – Soft rebirth and restful integration

Foods:

Dairy-based dishes (milk, cheese, cream)

Seed bread

Fresh butter

Tools:

Brigid's cross (woven from rushes or straw)

Silver bowl with sacred water

White altar cloth

Spring Equinox (Around March 20–22)

Seasonal Invocation: Day and night walk side by side. I breathe in balance, plant hope, and honor both seed and soil. Let growth come gently and wisdom rise like light.

Harvesting Note: Early spring herbs like nettles and violets are often found at the edge of tree lines and moist, fertile soil. Wear gloves for nettles and harvest with gratitude, never clearing more than a third of a patch.

Ritual Tool Use Tip: Eggshells used in Equinox rituals may be inscribed with runes or intentions and returned to the soil to fertilize new growth. A birch wand can be consecrated by passing it through early morning dew.

Cross-Reference: See Chapter 9 for Spring Equinox rituals and offerings.

Key Herbs:

Nettles – For cleansing, growth, awakening.

Cleavers – Detoxification, purification of the blood.

Substitute/Local Options:

Chickweed – Widely available; used in spring healing tonics.

Violets – Heart-opening and gently cleansing.

Foods:

Fresh greens and young root vegetables

Hard-boiled eggs dyed naturally

Honey oatcakes

Tools:

Eggshell charms

Green candles

Birch or ash wand

Bealtaine (May 1)

Seasonal Invocation:

Twin fires blaze across the threshold. I leap with joy, with longing, with renewal. Brigid's flame, flaring now to meet the green of the land, guide me through the veil of blossoms and desire.

Harvesting Note:

When gathering blossoms such as hawthorn or dogwood, do so gently, taking only what is abundant and leaving plenty for pollinators and the land. Offer a token (such as a hair, breath, or whispered song) as part of the exchange.

Ritual Tool Use Tip: Ribbon for the Maypole may be anointed with scented oil or infused water before ritual use. Floral garlands can be woven while singing or reciting prayers for fertility, union, and joy.

Cross-Reference: For full Bealtaine rites and faery lore, see Chapter 10.

Key Herbs:

Hawthorn blossom – Faery magic and boundary keeping (not to be brought indoors).

Woodruff – Love and fertility rites.

Substitutes in North America:

Dogwood blossoms – Gentle spring blooming, protective.

Daisy or red clover – Love, healing, balance.

Foods:

Strawberry honey cakes

Grilled meats or halloumi over open fire

Floral mead or lemonade

Tools:

Maypole ribbon

Garland of flowers

Bonfire ash in a protective pouch

Key Herbs:

Hawthorn blossom – Faery magic and boundary keeping (not to be brought indoors).

Woodruff – Love and fertility rites.

Substitutes in North America:

Dogwood blossoms – Gentle spring blooming, protective.

Daisy or red clover – Love, healing, balance.

Foods:

Strawberry honey cakes

Grilled meats or halloumi over open fire

Floral mead or lemonade

Tools:

Maypole ribbon

Garland of flowers

Bonfire ash in a protective pouch

Summer Solstice (Around June 21)

Seasonal Invocation: The sun stands high, and all the world hums. I gather the golden light, not to keep, but to bless. Let joy fill the field and warmth linger in my bones.

Harvesting Note: Harvest herbs like calendula, lavender, and St. John's Wort in the late morning sun after dew has dried. Choose flowers in full bloom and speak your gratitude aloud.

Ritual Tool Use Tip: Sun-charged water can be made by placing clean water in a glass jar and leaving it in direct sunlight with a gold coin or clear quartz inside. Use this water to anoint candles or sprinkle around thresholds.

Cross-Reference: See Chapter 11 for the full Summer Solstice ritual, hilltop practices, and solar blessings.

Key Herbs:

St. John's Wort – Joy, solar blessing, protection.

Lavender – Peace, clarity, sacred sleep.

American Gatherables:

Calendula – Light-bringing and soothing.

Echinacea – Strength, solar immunity.

Foods:

Honey bread

Sun-dried tomato and basil dishes

Herbal teas (lemon balm, mint, calendula)

Tools:

Gold sun disk

Sun-charged water

Fire-touched herbs hung on the door

Lughnasadh (August 1)

Seasonal Invocation: The sun begins its descent. I gather what has grown, offering thanks with each cut. May the fruits of labor feed more than hunger, may they nourish the spirit.

Harvesting Note: When collecting goldenrod or corn husks, do so on a dry day when the plant is thriving. Avoid wet or mold-prone specimens. Give thanks by returning a seed, song, or hair to the field.

Ritual Tool Use Tip: A corn dolly is more than decoration, it is the spirit of the grain. Weave it with clean hands, whispering a word of thanks with each twist. Place it in the kitchen or hearth until Samhain.

Cross-Reference: See Chapter 12 for Lughnasadh's rituals, games of Lugh, and harvest feast customs.

Key Herbs:

Wheat and barley sheaves – Abundance and gratitude.

Heather – Courage, transition, endings.

Available in the U.S.:

Goldenrod – Early harvest symbolism.

Corn silk and husks – Offerings and dollies.

Foods:

First bread from freshly milled flour

Cornbread or bannock

Blackberry pie

Tools:

Scythe or sickle replica

Corn dolly

Harvest basket

Autumn Equinox (Around September 21–23)

Seasonal Invocation: I stand at the threshold of descent, arms full of what the light has given. With every falling leaf, I remember: to let go is also to honor what was.

Harvesting Note: Apples and nuts should be gathered only once they fall naturally or are ready to be picked without force. Share the bounty, leave a few behind for the animals, for the spirits, and for next year's promise.

Ritual Tool Use Tip: Create an offering bowl from a natural material (clay, wood, or even a carved gourd) and dedicate it to the equinox. Fill it with shared food, fallen leaves, or small charms and place it on your altar.

Cross-Reference: See Chapter 13 for Autumn Equinox rituals, feast traditions, and hearth preparations.

Key Herbs:

Apple – Wisdom, wholeness, and the Otherworld.

Hazel – Inspiration and ancestral lore.

U.S. Equivalents:

Crabapple – Useful for charms.

Hickory or walnut – Nut harvest rites.

Foods:

Apple cider or apple butter

Nut and oat cakes

Roasted root vegetable medley

Tools:

Offering bowls

Acorn charms

Hearth stone or small cauldron

Final Note

The journey through the sacred year is not only marked by festivals and rituals but by a deepening intimacy with the land, the elements, and the unseen world. Each season teaches a different kind of listening: Samhain whispers in memory, Imbolc hums in hope, and Bealtaine sings in celebration. The turning of the wheel is not just a cycle of dates, it is a pattern woven into your bones, one that reawakens when you light a candle, gather a herb, or kneel before your altar.

In America and beyond, practicing Irish Paganism means bridging the ancestral with the immediate. When you swap pine for rowan, or offer tobacco in place of mead, you are not failing; you are forging a living link between old ways and your lived world. This sacred craft is not about perfect replication, but honest presence. Let your rituals grow roots in the land beneath your feet.

The herbs, foods, and tools of the year are not merely symbolic; they are embodied spells, offerings of time and patience. Tending them with care across the seasons is an act of devotion that honors the land of Ireland and the spirit of wherever you stand.

So ask yourself each season: What am I harvesting? What am I tending? What am I willing to let fall away?

The wheel turns. The work begins again.

Chapter 18a: Seasonal Devotionals and Daily Practices

The Wheel of the Year is not made solely of fire festivals and great rites. Between the thresholds and holy days, there is the quiet rhythm of daily life, morning and evening, light and dark, breath and stillness. It is in these ordinary moments that the Irish Pagan path is most often walked. This chapter provides guidance for those seeking to live the sacred year not just in ritual, but in rhythm. Living devotionally means letting the seasons shape your days like water shaping stone.

Morning and Evening Routines

In traditional rural Ireland, the day often began with a blessing at the hearth or a word to the land before the first task. Morning light was seen as a liminal moment, when blessings could be set upon the day. Likewise, the twilight hours were a sacred threshold when prayers were offered to the spirits of place, the ancestors, or the gods.

Morning Devotion:

Light a candle or open a window to greet the day.

Speak a simple prayer such as: "May the light rise before me, may my words carry kindness, and may I walk this day in honor."

Take three mindful breaths and give thanks aloud or silently for something present.

Wash your face or hands with herbal water (such as rosemary or mint infusion) to welcome freshness.

Evening Devotion:

Dim the lights or extinguish your altar candle with care.

Offer a word of release from the day: "May all that is unfinished rest. May my spirit ease into the night."

Place a hand on your heart or the earth, and breathe into stillness.

Journal a brief thought, dream, or gratitude from the day.

These small acts, repeated, become threads in the great spiral of the year. You may not always notice the change, but it will notice you.

Prayers in the Old Style

Prayer in the Irish tradition was often poetic, metaphorical, and deeply embedded in the cycles of land and life. The Caithréim Cellaig and other medieval sources reveal that everyday tasks (milking, spinning, baking) were often begun and ended with spoken blessings.

You may craft your own prayers using these time-honored structures:

1. Invocation of the Elements:

Land beneath me, Sky above me, Sea around me, guide my step.

2. Threefold Structure:

A prayer to the day or time of day

A prayer to your patron or seasonal deity

A prayer to the ancestors or local land

3. Rhymed or metered style:

By flame and well, I rise and speak, My path is strong, my heart is meek.

Examples of Devotional Phrases:

"With oak for strength, and ash for knowing, I walk the path the wise are showing."

"Bless this threshold and those who pass. Let joy be planted and sorrow pass."

You need not be fluent in Old Irish to pray in an Irish style. The essence is reverence, rhythm, and relationship. A murmured thanks to the river is as sacred as a memorized liturgy.

Keeping a Personal Almanac

A devotional almanac is a spiritual record of your journey with the Wheel. It may contain:

Seasonal journal entries

Dreams, omens, or signs

Phases of the moon and local weather

Daily devotions and reflections

Herbs gathered, foods made, rituals performed

Sacred encounters or notable animal sightings

This becomes a deeply personal grimoire; one that reflects both the old ways and your lived place. It is not meant to be perfect. It is meant to be true.

Almanac Practice Tips:

Use a bound journal or digital document; whichever you'll return to.

Mark the eight festivals with a full page or spread each.

Include entries for equinoxes, solstices, and other astronomical events.

Record how each season feels in your body, your home, your dreams.

Add photos, pressed herbs, recipes, and snippets of ritual text.

With time, this almanac becomes a mirror of your sacred journey; your own scripture written in ink and mud and memory.

Weaving the Sacred Into the Everyday

The sacred does not only arrive with incense and chant. It is found in the sweeping of a floor, the stirring of a pot, the brushing of hair, the tending of a fire.

Here are ways to ritualize the everyday:

1. Meal Blessings:

Before eating, place a hand on the food and whisper: "May this food nourish body, spirit, and heart. May those who lack be fed in turn."

2. Altar Offerings:

Place a small stone, shell, or leaf from your day on your altar.

Rotate these with the seasons or with the cycles of the moon.

3. Sacred Chores:

Sweep from east to west with intention, whispering: "With every stroke, may heaviness leave and clarity enter."

Stir your tea or soup clockwise, speaking a word of blessing or a wish.

4. Portal Moments:

Pause at doorways and gates. These are thresholds where spirits and blessings may gather.

Touch the frame and say: "As I pass, may peace walk with me."

Over time, these practices become anchors. They teach the body what the spirit already knows, that every moment is a doorway.

Honoring the Day's Shape with the Sun and Moon

The cycle of the sun and moon was central to Irish timekeeping. You can attune to these energies by observing:

Morning Sun: Bless beginnings, light candles, tend the hearth. Midday Sun: Act with clarity and strength. Sunset: Reflect, bless the harvest of the day. Moonrise: Invoke dreams, release fears, sow intentions.

Even indoors, you can keep a small sun token near your workspace and a moon token near your resting place.

Sacred Space in Any Setting

Whether you live in a rural cottage or a studio apartment, you can create sacred space:

In Small Places:

A window altar with a candle and seasonal token

A bowl of water and sprig of rosemary on a shelf

In Shared Spaces:

A stone or charm carried in your pocket

A blessing drawn with your finger in steam or dust

In Nature:

Speak aloud to a tree, even in a city park.

Trace a sigil with your foot in the dirt.

Sacred space is not defined by walls, but by intention.

Closing Reflection

To live in alignment with the Wheel of the Year is to make the sacred ordinary and the ordinary sacred. Through morning breath and evening stillness, through weathered hands stirring bread or herbs steeping in jars, you participate in a rhythm that is older than empire, older than even myth.

You are not only observing the sacred year. You are becoming it.

You do not need to be on a mountaintop to find the divine. The Morrigan may appear in your morning dishwater. Brigid may whisper through the steam of your kettle. The land spirits may bless your sidewalk with a single bloom growing through concrete.

Live it daily. Let each breath carry prayer. Let each footfall echo the spiral path.

Let the Wheel turn within you.

Chapter 18b: Folk and Hearthcraft Year-Round

Introduction

The sacred was never far in traditional Irish life. It was in the bowl of milk left on the doorstep, the charm knotted into a child's belt, the whispered blessing over bread. Folk magic was not a separate practice, it was the heartbeat of the home. This was not magic of grand rituals or ceremonial robes. It was the magic of hands at work, of intention spoken aloud over simple objects, of protection woven into the daily rhythms of living.

In Irish households across centuries, the hearth held the spiritual and physical center of family life. It was where prayers were spoken, omens read in the flames, and stories passed down. To tend the hearth was to tend the soul of the home. Meals were cooked with prayer, ashes were gathered for blessings, and fire was kept alive from season to season. Hearths were not just sources of warmth; they were witness to all that transpired within the home's walls.

This tradition did not end with modernization or emigration. The magic lives on wherever people choose to tend it: in city apartments, suburban homes, and rural gardens. You do not need to live in rural Ireland to practice folk magic. You need only the willingness to see the sacred in the ordinary and to tend it with sincerity.

Section 1: Hearth As Sacred Center

In Irish homes, the hearth held multiple roles simultaneously. It was a place of nourishment, where the body was fed. It was an altar, where offerings were made and blessings spoken. It was a gathering place, where family and community drew close. It was a sacred threshold; the boundary between the wild outside world and the protected interior of the home. To sit by the hearth was to sit at the center of all things.

In many Irish homes, the hearth was never fully extinguished. Peat was banked with ash each night to preserve the flame through darkness. If the fire died entirely, it was considered a spiritual emergency; a sign that the home's protection had lapsed. A new fire would be kindled from a neighbor's hearth or from a sacred bonfire, restoring the connection.

How to Tend Modern Hearth

If you don't have a traditional fireplace, your hearth can be:

- The stove or oven where you prepare meals

- A candle kept in a central location

- A small oil lamp or electric light

- Even a dedicated space on your kitchen altar

Daily Hearth Tending Practice:

Light a candle on your stove or near your oven with each meal you prepare. Speak a brief blessing as you light it: "May this flame warm body and spirit. May this home be a sanctuary."

Sweep your kitchen space clockwise weekly with intention, asking for protection and nourishment. Keep a small token (a Brigid's cross, a stone, or shell) above your stove or in your cooking area.

You can create a hearth bowl, a vessel that contains a small flame, a sacred object, or seasonal token, to serve as your focus. Refresh this seasonally, changing the contents to reflect the turning year.

Seasonal Hearth Blessings

Speak these blessings aloud as you light your candle, tend your fire, or even as you stand before your stove. Over time, these words become a prayer embedded in your daily life.

Samhain Hearth Blessing (October 31 – November 1):

"As the veil thins and the year darkens, I tend this flame in honor of those who came before. May the hearth be a beacon for wandering spirits. May ancestors find warmth and welcome here."

Winter Solstice Hearth Blessing (December 20-23):

"In the longest night, this fire holds the promise of returning light. I keep the flame alive, as my ancestors did. May hope glow in every shadow."

Imbolc Hearth Blessing (February 1-2):

"Brigid of the fire, Brigid of the well, stir the spark within this hearth. As lambs are born and the world awakens, let healing and inspiration kindle here."

Spring Equinox Hearth Blessing (March 19-21):

"In balance, I tend this fire. May the hearth be a place where old and new meet. May seeds of intention be planted in ash and ember."

Bealtaine Hearth Blessing (April 30 – May 1):

"Twin fires blaze at this threshold between seasons. May passion, joy, and sacred union warm this home. May all who gather here be blessed."

Summer Solstice Hearth Blessing (June 20-22):

"The sun stands highest, and this hearth mirrors its radiance. I honor the light within and without. May this flame shine with strength and generosity.

Lughnasadh Hearth Blessing (August 1):

"Lugh of skills, Tailtiu of labor. I honor the work that feeds this home. May the hearth be blessed with gratitude and the fruits of honest effort."

Autumn Equinox Hearth Blessing (September 20-23):

"As the year tilts toward darkness, I gather what sustains. May this hearth hold both harvest and memory. May balance and wisdom guide all who warm themselves here."

Section 2: Protective Charms and Thresholds

Every home deserves boundaries, not just locks and keys, but spiritual protections that affirm safety, wellness, and clarity. In Irish folk tradition, these protections were not elaborate; they were woven into everyday objects and actions, placed with intention at vulnerable points in the home's spiritual geography.

The threshold is the most critical protective point. It is a liminal space where the outside world meets the inside sanctuary. It is a place where spirits, both helpful and harmful, may attempt to enter. Traditional Irish households often marked thresholds with symbols, charms, or offerings to establish spiritual clarity: "This boundary is known. This space is protected."

Iron Nails and Rowan Berries

Iron was believed to have protective power against faery interference and malevolent spirits. Iron nails, especially old ones, salvaged from abandoned buildings or ancient sites; were sometimes buried beneath doorways or hammered into the frame above a door. The act of placing iron was itself protective; it declared a boundary.

Rowan berries, red as blood, were gathered in autumn and strung on red thread to create protective garlands. These were hung above doors, in windows, or placed in bowls near thresholds. The color red, like iron, was believed to have protective and clarifying properties. Some families kept a rowan branch dried and hanging year-round, replacing it each Lughnasadh.

Modern Application:

- Collect old iron nails or purchase new ones.

- Bury three nails beneath your front doorstep with a spoken intention: "Iron marks this threshold. No harm may pass."

- String rowan berries (or red beads as substitute) on red thread and hang above your door.

- If rowan is unavailable, dried red chili peppers or pomegranate seeds can serve similar purposes.

Evil Eye and Protective Symbols

While not exclusively Irish, the concept of the "evil eye" (harm sent through jealousy, envy, or ill-wishing) was understood in Irish folk tradition as a real spiritual danger. Protections against it were common in households, particularly those with children or recent good fortune (births, marriages, successful harvests).

Traditional Irish Protections:

Red Thread: Tied to a child's wrist, worn under clothing, or knotted around the wrist at night for protection. The knot could be tied nine times while whispering a protection prayer. Some families kept a red thread tied to the bedpost or hidden in the pillowcase.

Brigid's Cross Variations: The traditional Brigid's cross (woven from rushes) was standard protection. But variations existed:

- A cross made from white thread and hung in windows

- A cross carved into the hearth lintel

- A cross drawn in ash on the threshold on protective days (Imbolc, Samhain)

Horseshoe Above the Door: While often associated with broader European tradition, horseshoes were used in Irish homes too. The iron was protective, and the U-shape was believed to catch and hold blessings, preventing them from flowing out of the home. The horseshoe was always hung with the opening facing upward, like a cup catching luck.

Salt Lines at Thresholds: A line of salt placed just inside a doorway created a spiritual boundary. Malevolent entities or heavy energies were believed unable to cross salt. This was refreshed monthly or after a difficult visitor.

Rowan Berries in a Pouch: A small cloth bag filled with rowan berries, hung near the entrance or placed on a windowsill, offered continuous protection. Some families added other herbs: vervain, St. John's Wort, or dried mugwort.

Knotted Cord with Nine Knots: A cord knotted nine times, with each knot tied while speaking a specific protection (health, joy, clarity, etc.), was hung above the bed or worn on the person. This combined knot magic with the power of the number nine, sacred in Celtic tradition.

Create Your Own Protection Packet

1. Gather: red thread, salt, rowan berries (or substitute), a small cloth or paper

2. Wrap the items together or place in a small pouch

3. Tie with red thread, speaking: "This home is protected. Harm cannot enter. Only blessings cross this threshold."

4. Place above or beside your front door, or bury it beneath the doorstep

5. Refresh annually at Samhain or when you feel the need

Threshold Crossings with Intention

A threshold is more than a physical door, it is a spiritual boundary. Crossing it with awareness transforms the act into ritual.

Morning Threshold Blessing (Leaving Home):

As you step through the door, pause. Place your hand on the frame and say: "I cross this threshold with clear intention. May I walk in safety. May I return to this sanctuary renewed."

Evening Threshold Blessing (Returning Home):

Before entering, pause outside. Touch the door or frame and say: "I return to this threshold. I shed the day's weight here. I enter renewed and protected."

Blessing for Visitors:

When someone new enters your home, mentally or quietly speak: "You cross our threshold as a guest. You are welcomed with sincerity. May your presence honor this space."

Blessing When Someone Leaves:

As they depart, speak (aloud or in thought): "You carry our blessing with you. Go in safety. Return when you will."

Blessing for New People in the Home:

If someone moves in or a baby is born, formally bless their crossing: "You are welcomed here. This threshold honors your presence. May you find safety, joy, and belonging."

Section 3: Broom and Sweeping Magic

The broom, or besom, was more than a cleaning tool. It was a boundary-setter, a protector, and a purifying charm. A new broom might be passed over a threshold three times before use. Sweeping was not just practical, it was spiritual. Energy lingers where dust gathers.

In Irish homes, sweeping was often done with intention and rhythm. The direction mattered: sweeping from back to front (toward the door) was believed to sweep out stale or negative energy. Sweeping in circles could gather and contain energy. Some practitioners swept in spirals, spiraling inward to gather protection, or outward to disperse blessings.

Creating a Ritual Broom

To Create a Ritual Broom Blessing:

1. Obtain or Make a Broom: A traditional besom (bound twigs and straw) is ideal, but any broom can be consecrated.

2. Cleanse It: Hold it under running water or pass it through smoke. Speak: "I cleanse this broom of all that came before. It is now a tool of sacred work."

3. Bind It with Red Thread: Tie red thread around the handle in three places (top, middle, bottom) while speaking intentions for each binding:

   - Top: "For clarity of purpose"

   - Middle: "For protection and strength"

- Bottom: "For grounding and action"

4. Sprinkle with Saltwater or Herb Infusion: Use mugwort or rosemary infusion. Say: "By salt and smoke, by sweep and flame, I bless this broom in Brigid's name."

5. Store It Respectfully: Keep your ritual broom separate from mundane cleaning tools, if possible. Some families hung their broom above the hearth or near the front door.

Sweeping Rituals for Different Purposes

Protective Sweeping (Weekly):

Sweep from the back of the home to the front door, symbolically clearing stale energy. As you sweep, speak or think: "I clear this space of heaviness. I invite clarity, safety, and peace."

Cleansing Sweeping (After Illness or Conflict):

Sweep in spirals, beginning at the center of your home and spiraling outward room by room. Speak: "I sweep away sorrow, tension, and pain. I restore this home to wholeness."

Blessing Sweeping (Before a Gathering):

Sweep in clockwise circles, moving through each room. Speak: "I prepare this space for gathering. May all who enter feel welcomed and safe."

Release Sweeping (At Season's Turn):

On the morning of each cross-quarter day, sweep with particular attention. Speak: "I release what no longer serves. I prepare for the turning season."

Seasonal Sweeping:

- Samhain: Sweep to release the year's accumulated heaviness

- Imbolc: Sweep to clear and prepare for new growth

- Bealtaine: Sweep to invigorate and refresh

- Lughnasadh: Sweep to clear and prepare for the harvest's intensity

---

Section 4: Knot Magic and Cord Work

Knotwork is a traditional and subtle form of magic. In Irish folk custom, knots were used to bind blessings, intentions, or protections into garments, cords, and charms. These charms were often portable and discreet, yet powerful. The act of knotting while praying or chanting imbues the object with focus and intention.

Knots serve multiple purposes in folk magic:

- Binding: To tie energy to a specific purpose

- Sealing: To lock blessings or protections in place

- Carrying: To keep magic portable and accessible

- Releasing: To unknot and release what was bound when the work is complete

Basic Knot Magic Practice

Three-Cord Braid with Blessings:

1. Gather three cords: white, red, and green (or colors of your choosing)

2. Begin braiding, whispering or speaking a line of blessing with each cross:

- First cross: "Health in hand"

- Second cross: "Peace in mind"

- Third cross: "Joy in heart"

3. Continue braiding, repeating the pattern or adding new blessings

4. Tie the end with a final knot while speaking the complete blessing: "Health, peace, and joy are woven here. This braid is blessed and sealed."

5. Wear it, gift it, or place it on your altar until the work is complete

Nine-Knot Cord for Protection:

1. Take a length of red or white thread (cord or yarn works too)

2. Tie nine knots, one at a time, spacing them evenly along the cord

3. With each knot, speak a specific protection:

- Knot 1: "Health"

- Knot 2: "Safety"

- Knot 3: "Peace"

- Knot 4: "Clarity"

- Knot 5: "Strength"

- Knot 6: "Joy"

- Knot 7: "Wisdom"

- Knot 8: "Love"

- Knot 9: "Wholeness"

4. Hang it above a child's bed, wear it, or place it on your altar

5. When the protection is no longer needed, unknot it ceremonially while thanking the work

6. Burn or bury the cord to release the magic

Seasonal Knot Cords

Create a cord for each season and place it on your altar for the duration:

Samhain Cord (Dark, Release):

Black and deep purple thread tied in nine knots while releasing what is complete. Unknot and burn at Samhain's close.

Imbolc Cord (White, Inspiration):

White and green thread tied while invoking healing and inspiration. Keep through February.

Bealtaine Cord (Red, Vitality):

Red and gold thread tied in passionate energy. Keep through May.

Lughnasadh Cord (Gold, Gratitude):

Gold and amber thread tied in gratitude for labor and harvest. Keep through August.

Charm Bags and Cord Work

Create a small charm bag using knotted cords:

1. Gather materials: A small cloth pouch, dried herbs, a stone, and cord

2. Place items in the pouch with intention

3. Tie the pouch closed with a knotted cord

4. Tie seven knots (sacred number) while speaking: "This bag holds [protection/love/clarity]. It is sealed and blessed."

5. Carry it, hang it, or place it on your altar

Section 5: Hearthcraft Recipes with Magical Purpose

Each season held dishes that were both nourishing and enchanted. These were meals of memory and intention. Irish cooking, though humble, often carried symbolic ingredients: milk for nurturing, oats for endurance, berries for sweetness and renewal. Preparing these dishes while in a prayerful or mindful state transforms them into spells.

Seasonal Protection Oils

Create a protective oil for each season to anoint doorways, thresholds, or your own body:

Samhain Protection Oil:

- 1/4 cup carrier oil (olive or jojoba)

- 3-4 dried mugwort leaves

- 3 sprigs dried rosemary

- 1 pinch frankincense resin

- 1 black tourmaline stone (optional)

Steep all ingredients in the oil for one lunar cycle (dark moon to dark moon). Strain and bottle. Use to anoint doorways while speaking: "This threshold is protected. Ancestors are honored. Harm cannot enter."

Imbolc Protection Oil:

- 1/4 cup carrier oil

- 5-6 dried lavender buds

- 3 sprigs fresh or dried thyme

- 1 tbsp dried lemon balm

- 1 clear quartz crystal (optional)

Steep and prepare as above. Anoint while speaking Brigid's name.

Bealtaine Protection Oil:

- 1/4 cup carrier oil

- A few hawthorn petals (if available, or dried rose)

- 3 sprigs fresh or dried basil

- 1 small amount raw honey (mixed in just before use)

- 1 garnet stone (optional)

Use to anoint the wrists or doorways before gatherings or transitions.

Lughnasadh Protection Oil:

- 1/4 cup carrier oil

- 1 dried calendula flower head

- 3-4 dried St. John's Wort flowers

- 1 small piece dried goldenrod

- 1 amber stone or gold thread (optional)

Anoint while speaking gratitude and honoring labor.

Milk Blessings for Each Season

Imbolc Milk Blessing:

Warm milk gently (do not boil). Hold the cup in both hands and speak:

"Brigid of the dairy, Brigid of the well, I honor the milk that flows freely. May this nourish healing and inspire the new. May all who drink be blessed with clarity and care."

Pour a small amount outdoors as offering. Drink the rest slowly, mindfully.

Bealtaine Milk Blessing:

Add honey to warm milk. Hold and speak:

"May this milk, sweet with honey, honor the union of earth and sun. May all who drink feel alive, fertile, and blessed."

Share this with loved ones if possible.

Lughnasadh Milk Blessing:

Simply warm milk and hold. Speak:

"I give thanks for the abundance that flows. For the labor of hands and beasts. For nourishment that sustains. All is blessed."

Butter Charms

Churning or making butter was traditionally a time for magic. Even today, you can infuse intention into shop-bought butter:

Protective Butter Charm:

1. Place a stick of butter on your altar

2. Hold it in both hands

3. Speak into it: "This butter carries protection. Those who eat it are shielded."

4. Use this butter to cook meals with intention

Blessing Butter:

After cooking with butter, before serving, touch the dish and speak:

"This food is blessed. It nourishes body and spirit. All who eat are healed."

Herb Bundles for Hanging

Samhain Bundle:

Bundle dried mugwort, rosemary, and bay leaves with red thread. Hang above the threshold or hearth.

Bealtaine Bundle:

Bundle dried lavender, thyme, and basil with red and white thread. Hang for protection and joy.

Lughnasadh Bundle:

Bundle dried goldenrod, calendula, and a bit of grain with gold thread. Hang in gratitude.

Salt Blends for Doorways

Basic Protective Salt Blend:

- 1 cup sea salt

- 1 tbsp dried rosemary

- 1 tbsp dried thyme

- 1 tsp dried mugwort

- Black tourmaline chips (optional)

Mix together and store in a glass jar. Sprinkle at doorways while speaking: "By salt and herb, this threshold is protected."

Section 6: Divination and Household Omen-Reading

The old ways taught us to listen to the land and skies. In a world without modern forecasting, the people read the clouds, the birds, and the wind. This same wisdom can guide us today if we train ourselves to observe.

Traditional Irish Weather Sayings

"Red sky at morning, shepherd's warning; red sky at night, shepherd's delight."

(Morning red = rain coming; evening red = fair weather ahead)

"If the robin sings before rain, the land is ready to drink."

"When the cows lie down, rain is coming."

"Hawthorn flowers late = late spring = long harvest"

"A warm Samhain foretells a hard winter."

"If Imbolc is mild, the rest of winter will be cruel."

Keeping an Omen Log

Keep a journal of:

- Bird sightings (especially unusual ones)

- Sky patterns and colors

- Weather shifts

- Animal behavior

- Dreams at significant times

Over time, you'll notice patterns. You may discover that certain birds always appear before rain, or that a particular dream precedes important changes. These become your personal omen vocabulary.

Interpreting Animal Visitors

Animals that appear unexpectedly often carry messages:

Crow or Raven: Prophecy, intelligence, messages from the Otherworld. Pay attention to what you were thinking when you saw it.

Hawk or Eagle: Clear sight, perspective, focus. What truth are you being asked to see?

Owl: Wisdom, hidden knowledge, transition. Expect changes.

Butterfly or Bee: Transformation, joy, pollination of ideas. New growth is coming.

Deer: Gentleness, intuition, sacred. Be gentle with yourself now.

Fox: Cunning, adaptability, trickery. Think carefully before trusting.

Rabbit: Abundance, fertility, swift movement. Something is multiplying.

Squirrel: Gathering, preparation, playfulness. Prepare for change, but with joy.

Snake: Shedding, renewal, healing. Release the old.

Record these encounters. Ask: What was I thinking about? What follows this animal's appearance?

Section 7: Household Spirit Tending

Not all spirits are ancestors or gods. Some are the presences that dwell in the home itself, guardians, guides, or simply aware beings who cohabit your space. In Irish tradition, these were sometimes called "the good folk" or "the gentry," though more often they were simply acknowledged as "those who dwell here."

To acknowledge household spirits is to recognize that your home is not solely yours, you share it. This recognition can bring protection, peace, and a sense of being held.

Establish an Offering Place

Choose a corner, shelf, or small space. This becomes the spirit's place. Leave simple offerings here weekly or at significant times.

Offerings That Work:

- Milk (most traditional)

- Honey

- Bread (especially fresh)

- Oats

- Water

- Wildflowers or herbs

- A coin (silver if possible)

Speaking to Household Spirits:

"Those who dwell in this home, I acknowledge your presence. You are welcome here. This offering honors you. May we dwell together in peace."

Seasonal Offerings for House Spirits

Samhain: Leave cream and bread at the threshold. Speak: "Wandering ones, you are remembered. Rest here if you will."

Imbolc: Offer fresh milk. Speak: "New light comes. May you be blessed with renewal."

Bealtaine: Offer honey and flower petals. Speak: "Joy returns. May you celebrate with us."

Lughnasadh: Offer bread and grain. Speak: "We gather the harvest together. This is shared gratitude."

Signs of Household Spirit Presence

- Unexplained sounds or creaks

- Things moving or appearing in unexpected places

- Sudden smells (flowers, baking, incense) with no source

- Feelings of comfort or welcome in certain rooms

- A sense of being "watched over" (not threateningly, but protectively)

- Dreams of familiar, comforting presences

If you notice these signs, the spirits are present and engaged. Deepen your offerings and acknowledgment.

Knowing When Spirits are Unhappy

- Persistent, unexplained cold spots

- Repeated things breaking

- Persistent foul smells

- Nightmares or restlessness

- A heavy feeling in the home

If you sense this, clean thoroughly, refresh your offerings, and speak aloud: "I recognize imbalance. I offer this in rebalancing. What is needed? How can we restore peace?"

Section 8: Daily Folk Practices and Blessings

Not every magical act needs to be elaborate. Folk magic thrives in the daily, the small, the quiet. These practices anchor you in the sacred without requiring special time or space.

Quick Daily Practices

Morning Doorstep Blessing (30 seconds):

As you leave your home, place a hand on the frame and speak: "I step into this day with purpose. May I walk safely and return home renewed."

Evening Threshold Greeting (30 seconds):

Before entering your home in the evening, pause outside. Speak: "I return to this sanctuary. I shed the day's weight here. I enter refreshed."

Candle Lighting Before Meals (1 minute):

Light a candle before eating. Speak: "I give thanks for this nourishment. May it feed body and spirit. All are blessed."

Water Scrying (2-5 minutes):

Pour water into a bowl and hold it. Gaze into the water in soft light. Ask a question silently. Notice images, feelings, or words that arise.

Mirror Magic (2 minutes):

Look into a mirror by candlelight. Speak an affirmation or ask for guidance. The mirror reflects not just your face but your soul, use it to see clearly.

Candle Reading (3-5 minutes):

Light a candle and watch the flame. Notice its height, color, flicker. A steady flame = clarity. A flickering flame = confusion or outside influence. A tall flame = rising energy.

Blessings Tied to Days of the Week

In folk tradition, each day of the week held its own energy:

Monday (Moon Day) - Dreams, Intuition, Feminine Energy

Blessing: "Under the moon's glow, I trust my intuition. Dreams guide me. The feminine wisdom flows through me."

Tuesday (Mars Day) - Strength, Courage, Masculine Energy

Blessing: "I step into my power. Courage flows through me. I face this day with strength."

Wednesday (Mercury Day) - Communication, Travel, Ideas

Blessing: "My words are clear. My path is swift. Ideas flow freely through me."

Thursday (Jupiter Day) - Expansion, Luck, Abundance

Blessing: "Abundance flows toward me. Luck surrounds me. All is expanding and blessed."

Friday (Venus Day) - Love, Beauty, Connection

Blessing: "Love fills my heart. Beauty surrounds me. I am connected to all."

Saturday (Saturn Day) - Grounding, Protection, Endings

Blessing: "I am grounded and protected. Endings serve growth. I stand firm."

Sunday (Sun Day) - Clarity, Energy, Radiance

Blessing: "The sun shines within me. My energy is clear and bright. I radiate with purpose."

Speak these blessings aloud each morning, or post them in your kitchen and return to them throughout the day.

Closing Reflection

Folk magic does not require robes or temples. It thrives in homes lit by kettle light, carried in aprons, folded in linens, and baked into loaves. It is the old song returned to your hands. By practicing hearthcraft, you become both the fire and the one who tends it.

This is not performance, it is participation. You are not pretending to be an Irish cunning person of old; you are answering the call that echoes through the stones of your ancestry and the grain of your table. When you bless a loaf of bread, you restore the sacred to the act of feeding. When you sweep with prayer, you become a priest or priestess of clarity.

You return the sacred to its rightful place, beneath the roof, beside the bread, and within the breath of daily life. In this way, the gods are welcomed daily, not just seasonally. The ancestors are fed more than offerings, they are fed through memory.

Let this year be woven with intention. Let your home become a temple of blessing. And may each season find you with hands full, a heart open, and your hearth ever tended.

Remember: it is not the number of rituals that sustains you, but the sincerity with which you hold them. One whispered prayer, offered with heart, turns the entire year sacred.

You are not alone in this practice. Every breath you take with reverence is a leaf added to the forest of the faithful. Let your footsteps echo in the land and time you call home.

Let your hearth burn brightly, and let it burn true.

Chapter 19: Your Own Sacred Wheel

The Wheel you have been reading about—the one marked by fire festivals and solar moments, populated by deities both fierce and tender—is not something distant or theoretical. It is not a map drawn by someone else that you must follow step by step. It is a living structure that invites you to step inside it, to claim it, and to shape it according to your own spirit, your own land, and your own needs.

This chapter is where we shift from learning to living. Everything before this point has been preparation—history, mythology, ritual structure, deity relationships, seasonal practices. Now comes the moment when you take all of that knowledge and ask: What does my Wheel look like?

The answer will be uniquely yours.

Finding Your Entry Point

You do not need to begin at Samhain just because it is the traditional "new year" of the Irish calendar. You do not need to observe all eight festivals. You do not need to honor every deity mentioned in this book. What you need is to find the place where the Wheel touches your life right now, today, and begin there.

Ask yourself:

- Which season am I in right now, literally and metaphorically?

- Which deity has been calling to me through these pages?

- What does my spirit need most—fire, water, earth, or air?

- Where do I feel the most resistance? (That may be where the work begins.)

Some practitioners are drawn immediately to the darkness of Samhain. Others find their footing in the bright expansion of Beltane. Some come to the Wheel through devotion to a single deity—Brigid's flame, the Mórrígan's challenge, Lugh's mastery. There is no wrong door.

Begin where you are called. The rest will unfold.

What "Your Wheel" Means

Your Wheel is not an imitation of someone else's practice. It is not a replica of ancient Irish customs that you must recreate with historical accuracy. It is not a performance for an audience or a checklist to complete.

Your Wheel is the sacred structure you build to hold your relationship with the turning year, the land you live on, and the divine powers you honor. It is shaped by:

Your location: The seasons where you live may not match the Irish climate. Your land has its own spirits, its own rhythms. Your Wheel must reflect the ground beneath your feet.

Your circumstances: A parent with young children will practice differently than a solitary elder. Someone with chronic illness will have different capacities than someone in robust health. Your Wheel must be sustainable for your actual life.

Your devotions: If the Mórrígan has claimed you, your Wheel will look different than someone devoted to Brigid. If you feel no pull toward deities at all but are drawn to land spirits, that shapes your practice. Your Wheel follows your relationships.

Your depth of practice: Some practitioners want daily devotionals, weekly observances, and elaborate festival rituals.

Others need something simpler—seasonal check-ins, monthly offerings, and quiet acknowledgment. Both are valid. Your Wheel must match your capacity and calling.

This is not permission to be lazy or half-hearted. It is permission to be honest. The Wheel asks for sincerity, not perfection.

The Three Foundations of Your Wheel

No matter how you build your practice, three foundations will support it:

1. Seasonal Awareness

You must know what season you are in—not just on the calendar, but in the land around you and within your own life. Notice when the first buds appear. Mark when the darkness overtakes the light. Track the migrations of birds, the blooming of flowers, the shift in temperature. The Wheel is not abstract. It is the actual turning of the Earth beneath your feet.

Practice: Keep a seasonal journal. Note what you observe each week. Over time, you will learn the rhythm of your own land and how it corresponds (or does not correspond) to the traditional Irish calendar.

2. Relationship with the Divine

Whether you work with deities, ancestors, land spirits, or all three, your practice depends on relationship. You cannot honor what you do not know. You cannot serve what you do not love.

Practice: Choose one deity or spirit to focus on for the next season. Read the myths. Speak to them daily. Make offerings. Listen for their response. Relationship is built through consistent, humble attention.

3. Ritual Action

Belief is not enough. Knowledge is not enough. The Wheel turns through action—through lighting candles, speaking prayers, making offerings, celebrating festivals. Even small rituals matter. Even simple acts count.

Practice: Commit to one regular ritual action. It can be as simple as lighting a candle each morning or leaving water for the land spirits each evening. Let this be the thread that holds your practice together.

Permission to Be Imperfect

You will miss festivals. You will forget offerings. You will start practices and let them lapse. You will feel disconnected, confused, or overwhelmed. This is normal.

The deities of the Irish pantheon are not punitive. They do not demand perfection. What they ask for is honesty, effort, and respect. If you approach the Wheel with sincerity—if you try, fail, and try again—you are doing the work.

There is no spiritual police coming to check your devotional record. There is only you, the Wheel, and the turning year. Show up as you can. Begin again as often as needed.

What This Chapter Is Not

This chapter will not give you a step-by-step prescription for your practice. It will not tell you exactly what to do at each festival or which deity to honor first. That would be dishonest, because your practice must be yours.

What this chapter offers instead is permission—permission to claim the Wheel, to adapt it, to make it fit your life rather than bending your life to fit an idealized version of someone else's practice.

The next chapter (Chapter 20) will give you practical tools—seasonal summaries, ritual templates, planning worksheets. But before you get to the "how," you need to answer the "why" and the "who."

Why are you doing this? What calls you to the Wheel?

Who are you in this practice? Not who you think you should be—who you actually are, right now, with your limitations and your gifts.

Answer those questions honestly, and the rest will follow.

Your Wheel, Your Path

The Irish Wheel of the Year is old, but it is not finished. It continues to turn, and with each revolution, it invites new practitioners to walk it. You are one of them.

You bring something to this Wheel that no one else can—your voice, your perspective, your devotion, your questions, your struggle. The Wheel does not need you to be someone else. It needs you to be exactly who you are.

So take what you have learned in these pages. Take the deities who have called to you. Take the festivals that resonate. Take the practices that feel true. And begin.

The Wheel is turning.

Step onto it.

Make it yours.

Chapter 20: Creating Your Yearly Practice Plan

Overview: Planning Your Sacred Year

The festivals and deities of the Irish Wheel are not abstract concepts to study, but living practices to inhabit. The Wheel offers a sacred rhythm, a communal map that links us to the land, the gods, and our ancestors. But your engagement with the Wheel must be personal, shaped by your circumstances, your devotion, and the particular relationships you build with the divine and the land.

This chapter will guide you through creating a practical, sustainable practice plan for the full year. We will cover:

- Understanding your starting point and what "your wheel" means
- Seasonal summary charts for quick reference
- Building your personal festival calendar
- Ritual templates for all eight festivals
- Customization guidelines for your unique circumstances
- A sample year of observance (month-by-month)
- Practice planning worksheets and tools

Understanding Your Starting Point

Every practitioner of Irish Paganism walks a path that is both ancient and new. Before you can plan your year, you need to understand where you are right now.

What Does "Your Wheel" Mean?

In traditional Ireland, sacred time was local. A festival in Munster might be celebrated slightly differently from one in Ulster.

Hilltops, wells, and groves created their own sacred geography. That same principle applies to your practice.

Creating a personal sacred calendar allows you to:

- Adapt to your region's climate and seasons
- Honor family and ancestral traditions
- Establish spiritual consistency and rhythm
- Deepen your relationship with local land spirits and cycles
- Celebrate what matters most to you in your practice

Seasonal Summary: Your Quick Reference

The following charts provide at-a-glance information for the eight festivals. These summaries draw from the detailed festival chapters (9-16) and serve as quick reference for planning your year.

Samhain

Date: October 31-November 1

Meaning: The Hollow Between Worlds

Key Themes: Death, ancestors, divination, liminal space

Winter Solstice

Date: December 20-23

Meaning: The Sun's Return

Key Themes: Rebirth, light returning, hope, new solar year

Imbolc

Date: February 1-2

Meaning: Brigid's Fire

Key Themes: Purification, first light of spring, inspiration, healing

Spring Equinox

Date: March 19-22

Meaning: Balance Beneath the Blossoms

Key Themes: Balance, fertility, sowing, emergence

Beltane

Date: May 1

Meaning: Fire at the Threshold

Key Themes: Fertility, passion, sovereignty, summer begins

Summer Solstice

Date: June 19-23

Meaning: The Sun at Full Power

Key Themes: Maximum light, abundance, strength, celebration

Lughnasadh

Date: August 1

Meaning: The First Harvest

Key Themes: Grain harvest, sacrifice, skills, first fruits

Autumn Equinox

Date: September 20-23

Meaning: The Second Harvest

Key Themes: Balance, preservation, gratitude, preparation

Building Your Personal Festival Calendar

Now that you understand the eight festivals, it's time to decide how you will observe them. Not everyone needs to celebrate all eight festivals with equal intensity. Your practice should be sustainable, meaningful, and aligned with your life circumstances.

Three Approaches to Festival Practice

Approach 1: All Eight Festivals

Observe all eight points of the Wheel with rituals, offerings, and seasonal awareness. This creates maximum alignment with natural rhythms but requires significant time commitment. Best for: Those with flexible schedules, dedicated practitioners, people who thrive on ritual.

Approach 2: The Four Fire Festivals

Focus on the four traditional Irish festivals: Samhain, Imbolc, Beltane, and Lughnasadh. These are the original cross-quarter celebrations with the deepest Irish roots. Acknowledge the solstices and equinoxes but don't perform major rituals. Best for: Those seeking authentic Irish practice, people with limited time, those drawn specifically to Irish tradition.

Approach 3: Personalized Selection

Choose 2-4 festivals that most resonate with you and celebrate those deeply. Acknowledge others with simple awareness (lighting a candle, making an offering). Best for: Beginners, very busy people, those building practice gradually.

Ritual Templates and Customization

Each festival chapter (9-16) contains a complete ritual specific to that celebration. However, all Irish Pagan rituals follow similar structures. Understanding this template allows you to create your own rituals or adapt existing ones.

Basic Irish Ritual Structure

Preparation (5-10 minutes)

Physically clean the space. Spiritually cleanse using smoke (rosemary, juniper, mugwort), sound (bell, chanting), or visualization. Arrange altar. Gather offerings.

Grounding and Centering (2-5 minutes)

Stand comfortably. Take deep breaths. Visualize roots growing from your body into the earth. Feel stable, present, and calm. This connects you to the land.

Opening (3-5 minutes)

Light candles. Speak your intention for the ritual. State why you have gathered. Acknowledge the season, the festival, and the threshold you are marking.

Creating Sacred Space (Optional, 3-5 minutes)

Walk your space clockwise (deosil) with candle, wand, or hand extended. Speak words of boundary and protection. Note: Formal circle casting is Wiccan; Irish practice can be simpler.

Invocations (5-10 minutes)

Call upon relevant deities, ancestors, or land spirits. Speak respectfully. Offer welcome but not command. Example: "Brigid, keeper of the flame, I honor you this Imbolc. If you wish, be present here."

Main Working (15-30 minutes)

This is the heart of your ritual. Might include: meditation, divination, offerings, speaking intentions, symbolic actions, prayers, songs, or silence. Tailor to the festival and your purpose.

Offerings (5 minutes)

Give food, drink, or symbolic items to the deities, ancestors, or spirits you have honored. Speak gratitude. Place offerings on the altar or outdoors (food in earth, drink poured out).

Closing (3-5 minutes)

Thank all beings you invited. Release them with respect: "Spirits who have gathered, I thank you. Go if you must, stay if you will, with my blessing." If you cast a circle, close it by walking counter-clockwise.

Grounding and Integration (5-10 minutes)

Eat bread or drink tea. Touch the earth or a stone. Feel your body and breath. Write in your journal. Let the ritual settle into you. Don't rush back into mundane activity.

Customization Guidelines

Use the basic structure above, but adapt based on:

- Available time: Full ritual (60-90 min) vs. brief observance (15-20 min)
- Space: Indoor altar vs. outdoor ritual vs. no dedicated space
- Privacy: Solo practice vs. family-friendly vs. public circle
- Personal style: Formal ceremonial vs. casual devotional vs. meditative
- Physical ability: Standing/walking rituals vs. seated vs. fully accessible
- Seasonal energy: High-energy summer celebrations vs. quiet winter introspection

A Sample Year of Observance: Month by Month

This section provides a month-by-month guide showing how the Wheel might be lived throughout a full year. This is ONE example—

your year will look different based on your climate, schedule, and devotional focus.

October

Preparation for Samhain. The veil begins to thin. Notice darkness increasing. Begin ancestral reflection. Clean and prepare altar for the dark half of the year. Plan Samhain ritual.

Suggested Practices:

- Research ancestors you want to honor
- Gather black candles, seasonal items (apples, nuts, autumn leaves)
- Practice divination methods (tarot, scrying)
- Begin dream journaling

November

Dark half of the year begins. Samhain (Oct 31-Nov 1) marks the threshold. Ancestors are honored. Winter preparation begins. Introspection deepens.

Suggested Practices:

- Perform Samhain ritual
- Set up winter altar (dark colors, evergreens, ancestor photos)
- Begin winter rest cycle—increase sleep
- Start a hearth fire practice (candle as hearth substitute if needed)

December

Deepest darkness. Winter Solstice (Dec 20-23) celebrates the sun's return. Despite cold, light begins growing. Hope and endurance are themes.

Suggested Practices:

- Perform Winter Solstice ritual at sunrise if possible
- Light candles in windows
- Make warming foods (soups, stews, baked goods)
- Practice gratitude for fire and warmth

January

Deep winter. Rest and restoration. The land sleeps. This is a time for inner work, planning, dreaming. Physical slowness is natural and should be honored.

Suggested Practices:

- Maintain winter altar
- Daily candle lighting practice
- Journaling and reflection
- Seed planning for spring garden (even if just pots)

February

Imbolc (Feb 1-2) marks the first stirring of spring. Brigid's festival. Light is noticeably returning. Energy begins to shift from deep rest toward preparation.

Suggested Practices:

- Perform Imbolc ritual honoring Brigid
- Make Brigid's cross
- Spring cleaning begins—clear stagnant energy
- Plant first seeds indoors if gardening
- Light is growing—notice and celebrate this

March

Spring Equinox (Mar 19-22). Day and night are equal. Balance. The land is waking. Planting season begins in many climates. Emergence and potential.

Suggested Practices:

- Perform Spring Equinox ritual
- Transition altar to spring (pale colors, fresh flowers, seeds)
- Begin outdoor planting if climate allows
- Spend time outside observing growth

April

Spring fully arrives. Energy increases noticeably. Growth is visible everywhere. This is a time of action, beginning, newness. The body naturally wants to move more.

Suggested Practices:

- Daily outdoor time
- Tend garden or plant pots
- Begin spring recipes (fresh greens, light foods)
- Energy work and movement (walking, yoga, dance)

May

Beltane (May 1). The light half of the year begins. Summer's threshold. Fertility, passion, and growth at their peak. Fire festivals celebrated.

Suggested Practices:

- Perform Beltane ritual
- Set up summer altar (bright colors, flowers, symbols of fertility)

- Celebrate outdoors if possible
- Honor sexuality, creativity, abundance

June

Summer Solstice (June 19-23). Longest day. Peak of solar power. Maximum light and energy. Celebration, activity, brightness.

Suggested Practices:

- Perform Summer Solstice ritual at noon or sunset
- Gather at height of day
- Make solar offerings
- Fully engage with life—this is the time of maximum activity

July

Height of summer. Warmth, abundance, growth continues. The year's work is showing results. Gardens producing. Energy remains high though beginning subtle shift toward harvest.

Suggested Practices:

- Maintain summer practices
- Harvest herbs at peak potency
- Preserve summer abundance (dry herbs, freeze berries)
- Celebrate life fully—summer won't last

August

Lughnasadh (Aug 1). First harvest. Grain gathered. Skills honored. Sacrifice acknowledged—what was planted must now be cut. Beginning of the turn toward autumn.

Suggested Practices:

- Perform Lughnasadh ritual
- Bake bread as offering
- Harvest garden (or shop at farmers market)
- Acknowledge summer's peak passing
- Gratitude for abundance

September

Autumn Equinox (Sept 20-23). Day and night equal again. Second harvest. Balance before the descent into darkness. Preservation, preparation, letting go.

Suggested Practices:

- Perform Autumn Equinox ritual
- Transition altar to autumn (orange, brown, harvest symbols)
- Preserve food (canning, freezing, drying)
- Begin letting go—release what no longer serves
- Prepare for darker months ahead

Moving Forward with Your Plan

You now have the tools to create a sustainable, meaningful year-long practice. Remember:

- Start small. Better to do less consistently than everything sporadically.
- Your plan will evolve. Revisit and revise quarterly.
- Life will interrupt. This is normal. Return when you can.
- The Wheel turns whether you mark it or not. Your practice joins a rhythm already present.
- Perfection is not the goal. Presence and relationship are the goal.

The detailed festival rituals in Chapters 9-16 provide specific guidance for each celebration. The practical application chapters that follow (Chapters 21-24) offer additional support for integrating the Wheel into daily life, family practice, and long-term sustainability.

Chapter 21: Daily Living with the Wheel

The Wheel Is Not Just for Festivals

You do not need to wait for ritual time to practice the Wheel. The Wheel is not something you do once a week or on festival dates. The Wheel is something you live. It is a way of paying attention. It is a lens through which you see the world.

Most people's lives are organized by work calendars and school schedules, not by seasons. But you can create a seasonal rhythm that honors the Wheel while you live your ordinary life. This chapter explores how to weave the Wheel into your daily routine, whatever your circumstances.

Creating a Seasonal Rhythm Within Your Existing Life

The foundation of living the Wheel is creating consistent seasonal awareness. This is simpler than you might think, and it does not require overhauling your life. Instead, it requires working with the life you already have.

Monthly Check-In: The Foundation

Begin with a monthly practice. Once a month—choose a day that feels natural to you, perhaps the new moon, the full moon, or the first Sunday of each month—pause and ask three questions:

1. Where am I in the Wheel? What season are we actually in? Not what the calendar says, but what is actually happening in nature around you. Are the leaves turning? Is snow falling? Are flowers blooming?

2. What is happening in nature around me? Take time to notice. What birds are you seeing? What plants are growing or dying? What is the quality of light? What is the temperature? What animals are active?

3. What is happening inside me? How is your energy? How is your body? How is your emotional state? Are you feeling social or introspective? Energetic or tired? Creative or practical? Your inner state often mirrors the season.

Write this down. This simple practice, five minutes a month, keeps you connected to seasonal rhythms. Over time, you will see patterns. You will begin to recognize that in certain seasons, your energy rises or falls naturally, that your body craves different things, that your moods shift.

Seasonal Projects: Anchoring Yourself in Time

The second practice is to choose one project for each season—something tangible that connects you to that season's energy. These do not need to be large or complicated. The goal is to have something concrete that marks the season for you.

Spring:

Choose a garden project. Plant seeds—herbs in pots, vegetables in raised beds, flowers in a window box, or even just microgreens on a kitchen counter. If you have no outdoor space, plant something indoors. Watching seeds germinate and grow teaches the Wheel more powerfully than any book. The act of planting connects you to spring's energy of beginning and potential.

Summer:

Choose something that requires visibility and energy. Start a creative project. Write something. Paint something. Learn something new. Teach something to someone else. Host a gathering. Summer's energy is outward, bright, active. Your project should reflect that. Make something. Share something. Celebrate something.

Fall:

Choose something about harvest and gathering. Preserve food if possible—make jam, dry herbs, ferment vegetables, or freeze berries. If you do not have fresh food to preserve, gather supplies for winter: stack wood, organize your pantry, prepare your home. Fall's energy is about securing resources and preparing for scarcity.

Winter:

Choose something introspective. This might be a journal project, a creative writing project, a meditation practice, or a study practice. Winter is the season of inner work, rest, and reflection. Your project should honor withdrawal and depth. Read a challenging book. Learn something theoretical. Work on your inner landscape.

Over years, these seasonal projects become anchors. You will find yourself anticipating them. Your body will begin to expect spring gardening, summer creation, fall preservation, winter introspection. This is how you internalize the Wheel—through repeated, concrete, seasonal actions.

Seasonal Eating: Nourishment and Connection

Let your meals shift with the seasons. This is one of the most powerful and accessible ways to live the Wheel. Your body knows seasons. It craves different foods at different times. In spring and summer, you naturally want lighter, fresher foods. In fall and winter, you want heavier, warming foods. This is wisdom, not preference.

Spring:

Fresh greens, sprouts, herbs, light vegetables. Your body is waking up and wants lightness. Salads, fresh herbs, young vegetables. Spring is about emergence—eat foods that just emerged.

Summer:

Fresh fruits at their peak, abundant vegetables, lighter preparations, raw foods. Your digestion is strongest in summer. You can handle raw, cold, fresh foods easily. Celebrate summer's abundance by eating what is ripe right now.

Fall:

Root vegetables, squash, apples, grains, heartier preparations. Begin cooking more. Your body wants warmth and substance as temperatures drop. Roasted vegetables, baked goods, preserved foods.

Winter:

Soups, stews, root vegetables, warming spices, heavier grains, fermented foods. Your body needs warmth and nourishment. Long-cooked foods. Bone broths. Hearty meals. Winter eating is about sustenance and comfort.

You do not need to be rigid about this. You do not need to only eat seasonal foods. But when you CAN choose seasonal foods, do. Shop at farmers markets if available. Notice what is fresh at your grocery store. Let the seasons guide your cooking. This simple practice connects you to the Wheel three times a day.

Folk and Hearthcraft Year-Round

The Wheel of the Year is not made solely of fire festivals and great rites. Between the thresholds and holy days, there is the quiet rhythm of daily life, morning and evening, light and dark, breath and heartbeat. The folk practices and hearthcraft traditions of Ireland maintained sacred connection through everyday acts.

Daily Threshold Practices

Morning and evening are natural thresholds. Mark them simply:

- Morning: Light a candle. Take three deep breaths. Speak gratitude for the day. Notice the quality of light outside your window.

- Evening: Light a candle. Take three deep breaths. Release the day. Speak thanks for what was. Notice darkness falling.

- At the hearth (stove): When you cook, remember that food is sacred. Bless your meals. Thank the plants and animals that gave their lives. Cooking is ritual when done with awareness.

- At the threshold (doorway): Pause when you enter or leave your home. Notice the transition. Cross the threshold with intention. Your home is sacred space.

Weekly Practices

- Tend your altar (even 5 minutes): Refresh water. Replace wilted flowers or dried herbs. Light a candle. Speak to your gods or ancestors.

- Cleanse your space: Use smoke, sound, or visualization to clear stagnant energy. Open windows. Let fresh air in.

- Spend time in nature: Even 15 minutes. Stand on earth if possible. Touch a tree. Notice the weather. Breathe outdoor air.

- Cook one meal with full attention: No phone. No distractions. Just cooking. Feel the textures. Smell the scents. Honor the food.

Monthly Practices

- Deep clean one area of your home with intention: Not just physical cleaning but spiritual. Clear clutter. Clear energy. Make space.

- Make an offering to land spirits: Leave biodegradable offerings outside. Water. Grain. Herbs. Speak thanks to the spirits of place.

- Check in with your deities: If you have a devotional relationship with specific gods, dedicate time monthly. Offer. Pray. Listen.

- Review your practice: What worked this month? What didn't? What do you want to continue? What should change?

Adapting the Wheel to Your Actual Life

Not everyone's life looks the same. Some are raising young children. Some are working demanding jobs. Some are dealing with health challenges or disabilities. Some are retired. Some are caregivers. Your practice must adapt to your actual circumstances, not an idealized version of life.

Practicing as a Parent

Parenting is one of the most challenging life circumstances. Time is limited. Energy is stretched. Money is often tight. But the Wheel is perfectly suited to family life because it works with actual rhythms your family already experiences.

- You do not need to do everything. Choose 2-3 festivals to celebrate fully. Acknowledge the rest simply.
- Involve children in your practice. Children naturally understand seasons. A garden teaches them more than any explanation.
- Make it simple. You do not need elaborate rituals. Cook seasonally with your children. Light a candle on festival nights. Tell stories.
- Use existing rhythms. Most families already have seasonal rhythms. School starts and ends. Holidays come. Layer your practice into existing family patterns.
- Teach through life. Do not lecture about the Wheel. Live it visibly. Let your children see you paying attention to seasons.

Practicing While Chronically Ill or Disabled

Physical limitations require adaptation, not abandonment of practice. The Wheel can be practiced from bed, from a chair, without movement, without going outside.

- Altar at bedside: Create sacred space within arm's reach. Small altar on nightstand with candle, seasonal item, deity image.

- Window observations: If you cannot go outside, observe nature through your window. Track the changing light, weather, birds.

- Visualization practice: Travel to sacred sites, outdoor spaces, or seasonal landscapes in meditation when physical travel isn't possible.

- Minimal-energy rituals: Light a candle. Speak a prayer. Make a small offering. Full ritual isn't always possible—simple acts still count.

- Ask for help: If you need someone to set up your altar, gather seasonal items, or facilitate practice, ask. Accepting help is part of the practice.

Practicing with Demanding Work Schedules

Long hours, irregular schedules, and demanding careers make consistent practice difficult. The key is integration, not addition.

- Micro-practices: 2-minute morning candle lighting. 30-second evening gratitude. These maintain connection without requiring time you don't have.

- Seasonal eating at work: Pack seasonal lunches. Drink seasonal teas. Use your lunch break for seasonal awareness.

- Commute·practice: If you drive/ride to work, use that time for seasonal observation, prayer, or meditation.

- Weekend intensives: If weekdays are impossible, dedicate weekend time to practice. One focused hour weekly can sustain you.

- Seasonal sabbaticals: If possible, take time off around festivals that matter most to you. Prioritize your spiritual needs.

Practicing in Life Transitions

Moving, job changes, relationship changes, health crises—major transitions disrupt practice. This is normal. The Wheel continues turning whether you formally mark it or not.

- Minimum viable practice: What is the absolute minimum you can do to maintain connection? Maybe just monthly check-ins. Maybe just seasonal eating. That's enough for now.

- Temporary simplification: It's okay to reduce practice during crisis. You're not abandoning the path—you're surviving. The Wheel will be here when you can return.

- Gentle return: When stability returns, restart slowly. Don't try to make up for lost time. Begin where you are now.

- The Wheel as anchor: Sometimes spiritual practice is the one stable thing during chaos. If the Wheel grounds you, prioritize it.

The Practice Lives in the Living

The Wheel is not separate from your life. It is not something you add to an already-full schedule. The Wheel IS your life, when you pay attention. Every meal can be a ritual. Every threshold can be marked. Every season can be honored. The elaborate festivals and formal rituals are beautiful, but the heart of the practice lives in daily awareness, in small acts repeated with intention, in the choice to see the sacred in the ordinary.

You do not need to be perfect. You do not need to practice every day. You do not need elaborate altars or extensive knowledge. You need only to notice the seasons turning, to eat food that nourishes you, to mark time's passage in some way that feels meaningful. That is enough. That is the Wheel, lived.

Chapter 22: Altars, Self-Care, and Seasonal Wellness

Part 1: Seasonal Self-Care and Wellness

The seasons ask different things of your body and spirit. This is not metaphorical. Your body actually undergoes physiological changes with the seasons. Your circadian rhythms shift. Your melatonin production changes. Your immune system responds to temperature and light. Your appetite, energy, and mood all fluctuate naturally with the year.

Most modern people try to maintain the same level of activity, the same sleep schedule, the same diet, and the same emotional expectations year-round. This works against your body's wisdom and creates unnecessary struggle. The Wheel teaches us to work WITH our biology, not against it.

Winter Wellness: Rest, Restoration, and Inner Work

Winter is the season of going inward. This is not depression. This is not seasonal affective disorder (though those are real conditions that may need professional support). This is your body's natural inclination toward rest, restoration, and conservation of energy.

Sleep—The Primary Winter Medicine

Your body wants to sleep more in winter. Let it. Go to bed earlier. Sleep in if you can. This is not laziness—this is alignment with natural rhythms. Create conditions that support sleep: darkness, quiet, coolness (65-68°F), comfortable bedding. Turn off screens at least one hour before bed. Your body produces more melatonin in winter for a reason.

Warming Practices

Keep your body warm. Dress in layers. Take warm baths. Use warm blankets. Drink warming teas (ginger, cinnamon, turmeric, cayenne). These aren't just comforting—they're medicine. They increase circulation and support your immune system.

Gentle Movement

Winter is not a time for intense exercise. Your body wants to conserve energy. Instead, practice gentle movement: gentle yoga, tai chi, walks, stretching. Move enough to keep from stagnating, but not so much that you exhaust yourself.

Rich, Nourishing Foods

Soups, stews, root vegetables, bone broths, fermented foods, whole grains. Your body needs warmth and substance. Long-cooked foods are easier to digest in winter when your digestive fire is lower. Eat warm, eat cooked, eat nourishing.

Inner Work and Reflection

Winter's gifts are not physical—they're psychological and spiritual. This is the season for journaling, therapy, meditation, deep reading, creative introspection. Do the inner work you avoid in summer's brightness.

Spring Wellness: Awakening, Cleansing, and Emergence

Spring is about awakening. Your body naturally begins to produce less melatonin and more serotonin. Your energy rises. Your digestion strengthens. You crave movement and freshness.

Lighter, Fresher Foods

Your body wants lightness after winter's heaviness. Fresh greens, sprouts, herbs, light vegetables. Salads, steamed vegetables, fresh preparations. Spring is the natural time for cleansing diets if that calls to you.

Increased Movement

Your body wants to move more. Walk. Dance. Garden. Stretch. Your energy is rising—use it. This is the season to start new movement practices or increase intensity.

Spring Cleaning—Physical and Energetic

Clean your home. Clear clutter. Open windows. Let fresh air in. Cleanse your space with smoke or sound. Release what accumulated during winter. Make physical and spiritual space for new growth.

Earlier Rising

As days lengthen, wake earlier. Let yourself naturally adjust to increased daylight. Morning sunlight helps regulate circadian rhythms. Get outside early if possible.

Creative Projects

Spring energy is creative and initiating. Start projects. Begin things. Plant seeds—literal and metaphorical. Spring supports new beginnings.

Summer Wellness: Energy, Activity, and Celebration

Summer is the season of maximum energy, longest days, and strongest digestion. Your body can handle more activity, more social engagement, and more intensity. Use this energy—it won't last.

Fresh, Raw, Abundant Foods

Fruits and vegetables at their peak. Your digestion is strongest in summer—you can handle raw, cold, fresh foods easily. Salads, fresh fruit, grilled vegetables. Celebrate abundance.

Maximum Activity

This is the season for intense movement if that's your practice. Hiking, swimming, running, cycling. Your body has the energy. Use it. Be active. Be outside. Be engaged.

Social Connection

Summer's energy is outward. Gather with people. Host gatherings. Attend festivals. Be social. Community energy is easier to access in summer.

Adequate Hydration

Drink more water. You need it. Add electrolytes if you're very active or sweating heavily. Herbal iced teas. Fresh fruit. Keep hydrated.

Rest When Needed

Even in summer, honor your need for rest. Siesta cultures understand this—afternoon rest during heat makes sense. Don't push past exhaustion just because it's summer.

Fall Wellness: Harvest, Preservation, and Preparation

Fall is about gathering resources and preparing for scarcity. Your body knows winter is coming. Your appetite increases. You crave heartier foods. You begin to slow down.

Heartier, Warming Foods

Root vegetables, squashes, apples, grains. Begin cooking more. Roasted vegetables, baked goods, preserved foods. Your body is preparing for winter—nourish it.

Gradual Decrease in Activity

Don't try to maintain summer's intensity. Let yourself naturally slow. Shorter walks. Gentler movement. Your body is beginning its descent toward rest.

Immune Support

Fall is when colds and flu begin. Support your immune system: adequate sleep, nourishing food, stress management, immune-supporting herbs (elderberry, echinacea, astragalus)

Preservation Activities

Can, freeze, ferment, dry. Preserve the abundance while it's available. This activity is both practical and spiritually satisfying—you're participating in fall's essential work.

Reflection and Gratitude

Fall invites taking stock. What did you harvest this year—literally and metaphorically? What are you grateful for? What will you carry into winter?

Part 2: Creating and Maintaining Seasonal Altars

An altar is a sacred space where you mark time and honor what matters. Seasonal altars change with each season, keeping your practice fresh and alive. They serve multiple functions: they mark the turning year, provide focal points for prayer and meditation, honor deities and ancestors, and create beauty in your living space.

What Is an Altar?

An altar is simply a place where you gather meaningful objects and create sacred space. It is not complicated. It can be: a shelf, a small table, the top of a dresser, a windowsill, a tray that can be put away when not in use, or even a cleared corner of your desk.

Your altar can be public or private. If you live with people who do not understand or support your practice, your altar might be very simple and look like decoration. A vase of seasonal flowers and a candle can be an altar that doesn't announce itself as such.

Seasonal Altars Through the Year

Winter Altar (Samhain through Imbolc)

Colors: Black, dark blue, deep purple, white

Elements: Candles (black or dark colors), evergreen branches (pine, fir, spruce), holly or ivy, photos of ancestors, stones, bones (respectfully sourced), dark fabrics, representations of winter deities (Cailleach, Donn)

Energy: When you look at this altar, it reminds you to go inward, to rest, to reflect, to honor ancestors, to trust that light will return.

Spring Altar (Imbolc through Beltane)

Colors: White, pale green, pale pink, pale yellow, light blue

Elements: Fresh flowers (snowdrops, crocuses, daffodils), seeds for planting, new green branches, Brigid's cross, white candles, images of Brigid, fresh water in a bowl, symbols of new beginnings

Energy: When you look at this altar, it reminds you that light is returning, that new things can grow, that you are capable of renewal and fresh starts.

Summer Altar (Beltane through Lughnasadh)

Colors: Gold, red, orange, yellow, bright green

Elements: Bright flowers at peak bloom, fruits, sun symbols, gold or brass items, representations of solar deities (Lugh), fire-safe bowl for small fires or charcoal, vibrant fabrics

Energy: When you look at this altar, it reminds you of abundance, energy, brightness, celebration, and the peak of life's fullness.

Autumn Altar (Lughnasadh through Samhain)

Colors: Orange, brown, deep red, gold, deep green

Elements: Harvest items (grain, corn, gourds, squashes), apples, nuts, dried leaves, wheat sheaves, symbols of abundance and preservation, representations of harvest deities (Lugh, Tailtiu)

Energy: When you look at this altar, it reminds you to give thanks for abundance, to prepare for scarcity, to acknowledge sacrifice and completion.

Altar Maintenance and Transition

- Change your altar with each season or at each festival—whatever rhythm works for you.
- Refresh offerings regularly. Don't let food rot or water stagnate. This is disrespectful.
- Clean your altar monthly at minimum. Dust the items. Refresh the cloth. Clear old energy.
- When transitioning seasons, thank the previous season before dismantling. Speak gratitude for what that season taught you.
- Dispose of natural offerings respectfully—return to earth, compost, or burn if appropriate.
- If an item on your altar breaks, this is not bad luck. It may have absorbed negative energy. Thank it and release it.
- Not all items need to change seasonally. Some—like deity statues or family heirlooms—may remain year-round with seasonal items rotating around them.

Altars in Small Spaces

- Windowsill altar: One candle, one seasonal item, one deity image. Simple and beautiful.
- Portable altar: Small tray or box that can be set up when needed and put away when not. Perfect for shared spaces.
- Wall altar: Shelf mounted on wall at eye level. Saves floor space.
- Nature altar: If indoor space is impossible, create a small altar outside—under a tree, in a garden corner, on a balcony.

- Digital altar: If physical altars are impossible, create a digital sacred space—desktop wallpaper that changes seasonally, a private Pinterest board, a folder of sacred images you view daily.

Body and Spirit, Season and Space

Your body is a sacred vessel moving through seasonal time. Your altar is a sacred space marking that movement. Both require tending. Both require awareness. Both change with the turning year.

When you care for your body seasonally—sleeping when you need to sleep, eating what your body craves, moving when you need to move—you honor the Wheel through your physical form. When you tend your altar—refreshing it with seasonal beauty, offering to the divine, creating sacred space in your home—you honor the Wheel through ritual and symbol.

These practices support each other. A well-tended altar reminds you to care for your body. A body that feels good makes spiritual practice easier. Together, they create a life that moves in rhythm with the seasons, honoring both the physical and spiritual dimensions of existence.

Chapter 23: Community, Family, and Shared Practice

Practicing with Family

The Wheel does not need to be a solitary practice. If you have family, friends, or community, you can practice together. Practicing together creates deeper bonds, makes the practice more sustainable, and teaches the next generation.

Family provides natural structure for Wheel practice. Families already have rhythms, routines, and gatherings. You can layer Wheel consciousness into these existing structures without requiring anyone to adopt new beliefs or practices.

Family-Friendly Approaches

Seasonal Meals Together

Change how your family eats with each season. This is not about forcing anyone to eat differently—it's about natural seasonal variety. In fall, make harvest meals (roasted squash, apple desserts). In winter, make warming soups and stews. In spring, fresh greens and light foods. In summer, grilled vegetables and fresh fruit. Talk casually about why: "These greens are so fresh right now" or "Isn't it nice to have warm soup in winter?"

Gardening Together

Growing something from seed to harvest teaches children about cycles, patience, and relationship with the earth. Even a small pot of herbs on a windowsill works. Involve children in all aspects: choosing seeds, planting, watering, harvesting. Let them make mistakes. This teaches more than any lecture.

Marking Festivals Simply

You don't need elaborate rituals with family. On Samhain, light candles and talk about people who have passed. On Imbolc, plant seeds together. On Beltane, make flower crowns and celebrate outside. On Lughnasadh, bake bread. Simple acts create memory and awareness without imposing belief.

Nature Time as Family Time

Regular walks. Seasonal hikes. Visiting the same place through all four seasons and noticing changes. Collecting seasonal items (leaves, seeds, flowers). This teaches seasonal awareness through direct experience.

Seasonal Decorating

Let your home reflect the seasons. Fall decorations (gourds, colored leaves). Winter decorations (evergreens, lights). Spring decorations (flowers, pastels). Summer decorations (bright colors, fruits). Children love this, and it marks seasonal change visibly.

Age-Appropriate Practice

Tailor your approach to children's developmental stages:

Ages 0-5:

Very simple. Seasonal walks. Growing plants. Lighting candles (supervised). Seasonal foods. Stories. Singing. Focus on sensory experience and wonder.

Ages 6-10:

More participation. Let them help set up altars. Teach them about deities as story characters. Garden tasks they can do independently. Simple offerings. Beginning to understand cycles.

Ages 11-15:

Can engage more deeply if interested. Explain the Wheel's structure. Teach correspondences. Let them lead parts of rituals if they want. Respect if they're not interested—forcing creates resistance.

Ages 16+:

Treat as autonomous. Offer information if they're interested. Respect if they choose different paths. Your visible practice is teaching whether or not they seem to pay attention.

Building or Finding Community

Solo practice is valid and complete. But many people crave community—others who understand, celebrate together, and share the path. Finding or building Irish Pagan community requires intention and discernment.

Finding Existing Community

- Online groups: Facebook groups, Discord servers, Reddit communities for Irish Paganism or Celtic Reconstructionism. Vet carefully—some groups are higher quality than others.
- Local Pagan groups: Many cities have general Pagan groups. Not all will be Irish-focused, but some members may be. Attend public rituals. Network.
- Irish cultural organizations: Some Irish-American cultural groups welcome Pagans. Not all—some are Catholic-focused. But Irish language classes, cultural festivals, and heritage organizations can connect you with others interested in Irish spirituality.
- Conferences and festivals: Pagan Pride, Pantheacon, and regional gatherings sometimes have Irish Pagan tracks. These are opportunities to meet others.

- Author and teacher events: If Irish Pagan authors or teachers offer workshops, attend. You'll meet like-minded practitioners.

Building Your Own Community

If no community exists where you are, you can create one. Start small. Find even one or two others.

- Post in local Pagan groups or general alternative spirituality spaces expressing interest in Irish Paganism.
- Start a book club or study group focused on Irish mythology, culture, or Pagan practice.
- Host simple seasonal gatherings—potlucks on festival dates, nature walks, craft nights making seasonal items.
- Create online connection if no one is local—start a Discord server or Facebook group for your region.
- Be patient. Building community takes time. Start with whoever shows up, even if it's just one person.
- Set clear boundaries and expectations. Is this a learning group? A ritual circle? A social gathering? Clarity prevents conflict.

Red Flags in Communities

Avoid groups or individuals who:

- Claim you need expensive tools, specific training, or their personal teaching to practice "correctly"
- Mix Irish practice with closed Indigenous traditions without acknowledgment or permission
- Use Irish spirituality to justify bigotry, racism, or exclusion
- Demand absolute authority or discourage questioning
- Create financial dependence or pressure members to give money
- Exhibit cult-like behavior: love-bombing, isolation from outside relationships, us-vs-them mentality

- Make grandiose claims about lineage, initiations, or secret knowledge
- Romanticize or fantasize Ireland without engaging with real Irish history and culture

Practicing the Wheel Across Oceans: Diaspora Challenges

Many practitioners of Irish Paganism live far from Ireland—in America, Canada, Australia, and beyond. This creates unique challenges: different seasons, different plants, different landscapes, and the sense of being disconnected from the tradition's homeland.

Seasonal Inversion (Southern Hemisphere)

If you live in the Southern Hemisphere, your seasons are opposite to Ireland's. Do you celebrate the Wheel according to Irish dates (counter to your local seasons) or according to your actual seasonal experience?

There is no single right answer, but here are two valid approaches:

Approach 1: Follow Irish Dates

Celebrate Samhain on October 31 even though it's spring where you are. This maintains connection to tradition and to practitioners in the Northern Hemisphere. However, it disconnects you from your local land and seasons.

Approach 2: Follow Local Seasons

Celebrate Samhain in April/May when it's actually autumn where you are. This aligns you with your local land and seasonal reality. However, you're out of sync with most other practitioners and traditional dates.

Both are valid. Choose based on what matters most to you: connection to tradition/community or connection to local land.

Some practitioners do both—acknowledge Irish dates with simple observance and celebrate fully when their local season aligns.

Different Plants and Landscapes

Ireland's plants don't grow everywhere. Its landscapes—green hills, ancient sites, specific trees—aren't universal. How do you practice Irish Paganism when your land looks and feels nothing like Ireland?

- Learn your local plants and find functional equivalents. If hawthorn doesn't grow where you are, what tree serves similar purposes—protection, boundary-marking, connection to spirits?
- Honor your local land spirits using Irish frameworks. The practice is Irish; the spirits are local.
- Grow Irish plants in pots if possible. Some herbs adapt. This maintains physical connection to Irish plant allies.
- Visit Irish sites virtually or in person when possible. Connection to the actual land matters, even if you can't live there.
- Remember that Irish people themselves have emigrated everywhere, bringing their practices. You're continuing that tradition of adaptation.
- The gods and spirits are not limited by geography. An Mórrígan can be honored in Australia. Brigid's flame burns anywhere.

Troubleshooting Common Social Challenges

"My Family Thinks This Is Weird"

You do not need anyone's permission to practice. Practice quietly if you need to. Do not push your practice on others. Your practice is not their business unless you make it so.

Over time, your visible relationship with seasons, your seasonal cooking, your garden, your groundedness—these speak louder than explanation. Let your practice demonstrate its value rather than defending it verbally.

If confronted, you can say: "I'm exploring Irish cultural practices and seasonal awareness. It helps me feel connected to nature and ancestry." This is factual and non-threatening. You don't owe anyone elaborate explanations.

"I Have No One to Practice With"

Solo practice is not lesser than group practice. Some of the deepest spiritual work happens alone. The land doesn't care if you're alone or in a group. The gods don't require community—they require sincerity.

If you crave community, use the strategies above to find or build it. But don't delay your practice waiting for community. Begin now. Practice fully. Community may come, or it may not. Either way, your relationship with the Wheel is valid and complete.

"I Don't Feel Connected to Irish Culture or Heritage"

This concern is especially common for people with no Irish ancestry, people who didn't grow up with Irish culture, or people who feel like outsiders to Irish tradition.

Irish spirituality is not a closed practice. It is not only for people with Irish blood. The Irish deities and land spirits welcome sincere practitioners regardless of ancestry. What matters is respect, genuine engagement, and avoiding romanticization or appropriation.

- Approach matters. Learn from Irish sources—Irish authors, Irish practitioners, Irish history and culture.
- Don't romanticize or fantasize Ireland. Engage with real Irish history, including its complexities and pain.
- Study Irish history and culture. Understand the context— colonialism, language suppression, cultural survival.
- If you feel disconnected, visit Ireland if possible. Walk the land. Visit sacred sites. Experience the weather and landscape.
- You don't need Irish ancestry any more than you need Italian ancestry to practice Catholicism. Spiritual traditions can be

learned, practiced, and honored across cultural lines when approached respectfully.

- If you are Irish but feel disconnected, explore your family history. Talk to older relatives. Research your specific regional origins. Connection can be rebuilt.

You Are Not Alone

Whether you practice with family, with community, or in solitude, you are part of a living tradition. Across the world, others are lighting candles at the same festivals, honoring the same gods, walking the same seasonal path. Some are in Ireland. Some are not. Some have Irish ancestry. Some do not. What unites us is commitment to the Wheel, respect for the tradition, and sincere relationship with the divine and the land.

The challenges of practicing across distances, in different cultures, with or without support—these are real. But they are not insurmountable. Humans have always carried their spiritual practices to new lands, adapted to new circumstances, and maintained connection across impossible distances. You are continuing that ancient pattern of adaptation and survival.

Find your people if you can. Build community if you must. Practice alone if that's your path. All of it is valid. All of it is sacred. All of it honors the Wheel.

Chapter 24: Living the Wheel Long-Term

You have explored the Wheel through these chapters. You understand the festivals. You have practical tools for daily, weekly, and seasonal practice. You know how to adapt the Wheel to your actual life. Now comes the most important question: How do you sustain this over years? Over decades? How does practice evolve, deepen, and change?

How Practice Evolves Over Time

Your practice in year one will look different from year five. And year ten will be different again. This is not failure. This is natural, healthy evolution. Understanding how practice evolves helps you recognize growth rather than judging yourself for change.

Year One: Learning and Exploration

Everything is new. You are learning. You are exploring. You might do a lot. You might try many things. Some will resonate deeply. Some will not. This exploration is necessary and valuable.

- Reading extensively—books, websites, trying to learn everything
- Experimenting with different practices to see what fits
- Possible enthusiasm that borders on intensity
- Mistakes, confusion, uncertainty—all normal and expected
- Focus on doing things "right" rather than on relationship
- External validation—seeking approval from others or from sources

Do not worry about being perfect in year one. Embrace the learning. Make mistakes. Try things that don't work. This is how you discover what actually calls to you.

Years Two and Three: Settling and Deepening

You have found what works for you. Your practice begins to settle. It becomes more natural. You stop thinking about what to do and simply do it. You have rhythm.

- Certain practices have become habitual—you do them without conscious effort
- You've identified which festivals matter most to you
- Less reading, more doing. Less learning, more experiencing.
- Beginning to notice patterns—how seasons affect you, what the gods are teaching
- Possible plateaus or boredom—the newness has worn off
- Questioning continues but is different—less "am I doing this right?" and more "what does this mean?"

This is when some practitioners give up, mistaking settling for stagnation. But settling is necessary. You're building foundation. The exciting newness becomes sustainable practice. This is not loss—this is maturation.

Years Five and Beyond: Integration and Mastery

Your practice becomes woven into your life. It is not separate from how you live. Seasonal awareness is simply how you move through the world. You do not think about practicing the Wheel anymore than you think about breathing.

- The Wheel is not something you do—it's how you are
- You teach others, formally or informally, through your living example
- Your relationship with the gods has depth, history, complexity

- You understand paradox and complexity that confused you earlier
- Less concern with externals (altar perfection, ritual precision) and more with essence
- Your practice has survived major life changes and adapted repeatedly
- You know your personal patterns through the Wheel intimately
- You serve as an elder, whether formally recognized or not

How Deepening Happens

The longer you practice, the more the Wheel teaches you. Not because you are learning new information from books or teachers, but because you are learning through direct experience. Your body becomes a sacred text. The seasons become your teachers.

After your first winter, you know intellectually that winter is a time of rest. After your fifth winter, your body knows it. Your bones know it. The moment fall turns toward winter, your body begins to slow without your conscious decision.

After your first garden, you know intellectually that seeds take time to grow and that patience is required. After five gardens, you understand patience at a cellular level. You understand trust in a way that cannot be taught—only experienced.

After your first year of cooking seasonally, you know intellectually that spring foods are different from winter foods. After five years, your palate has changed. Your body actually wants different foods at different times. You crave salad in spring not because you should but because you genuinely do.

After your first Samhain, you understand that the veil thins. After ten Samhains, you have felt the thinning so many times that you recognize its subtle signs—the quality of the air, the feeling in your body, the dreams that come.

This deepening is the real work. This is where the Wheel teaches you at a level deeper than the mind. This is learning through the body, through seasons, through years. No book can give you this. Only time and attention can give you this.

When Your Circumstances Change

You have built a practice that works for your life. Then your life changes. You had time for deep practice—now you have young children. You had a solo practice—now you have a partner. You had flexible work—now you work long hours. Your practice must adapt.

Life changes constantly. This is certain. Your practice must adapt. This is not failure. This is the Wheel teaching you flexibility. It is teaching you that the essence of the practice is not the form— it's the awareness, the relationship, the attention.

- When life changes, simplify immediately. Return to the absolute basics. What is the one practice you can maintain? Do that.
- Do not try to maintain pre-change practice levels during transition. You will fail and feel guilty. Instead, acknowledge reality and adapt.
- Trust that the Wheel continues whether you mark it or not. Missing festivals does not erase your relationship with the divine or the land.
- When stability returns, restart slowly. Do not try to make up for lost time. Begin where you are now.
- Each major life change requires renegotiating your practice. This is normal. It does not mean you are a bad practitioner—it means you are a human one.

Common Long-Term Challenges and How to Navigate Them

Spiritual Burnout

After years of consistent practice, you might feel tired. Rituals feel empty. Festivals feel like obligations. You go through motions without meaning. This is spiritual burnout, and it is common.

- Take a break. Intentionally step back for a season or a cycle. The Wheel will be here when you return.

- Simplify radically. Release everything except the one or two practices that still feel alive.

- Change your approach. If you have been very structured, try spontaneity. If very spontaneous, try structure.

- Seek new inspiration. Read new authors. Talk to different practitioners. Learn something new.

- Remember why you started. What drew you to this path originally? Can you reconnect with that initial spark?

- Consider that burnout might be a call to depth rather than breadth. Maybe you need less variety and more consistency.

Doubt and Questions

Long-term practice often brings sophisticated doubt. Not "does this work?" but "what does this mean?" You question things you accepted earlier. This is not loss of faith—this is deepening of faith.

Let yourself question. Wrestling with complexity is part of mature practice. You do not need certainty. You need honest engagement. Doubt that makes you think more deeply is valuable. Doubt that makes you abandon the path entirely might indicate that this path is not yours—which is also valuable information.

Isolation

Long-term solo practitioners can feel isolated, especially if you have no community. You wonder if anyone else understands. You crave validation or companionship in the practice.

- Seek community online even if local community doesn't exist. Virtual connection is real connection.

- Accept that some paths are meant to be walked alone. Solitude is not the same as isolation.

- Write about your practice. Blog, journal, or simply write for yourself. Articulating experience clarifies it.

- Remember that you walk with the gods, the ancestors, and the land spirits. You are never truly alone.

- Consider teaching or sharing in some way. Even informal sharing helps you feel connected to the larger tradition.

Becoming an Elder: Teaching and Serving the Tradition

After years of practice, you become an elder whether you intend to or not. You have knowledge. You have experience. You have perspective that newer practitioners lack. This creates responsibility.

What Does It Mean to Be an Elder?

- An elder has walked the path long enough to have perspective. You have seen patterns. You have survived challenges. You know that what feels devastating in year one is navigable in year five.

- An elder serves the tradition and the community, not their own ego. You share what you know freely. You support newer practitioners. You preserve and pass forward.

- An elder acknowledges what they do not know. Years of practice teach humility. The more you learn, the more you realize how much you do not know.

- An elder continues learning. Being experienced does not mean being finished. You remain a student even as you teach.

- An elder makes space for different approaches. You do not insist that your way is the only way. You honor diversity of practice.

How to Teach Without Harming

- Never claim more knowledge or authority than you actually have. Be honest about your experience level.

- Do not charge money for basic teaching. Irish spiritual knowledge is not commodity. (Charging for books, intensive workshops, or professional time is different than charging for basic knowledge.)

- Admit when you do not know something. "I don't know" is a complete and acceptable answer.

- Encourage students to verify information. Do not require belief—encourage investigation.

- Create independence, not dependence. Your goal is students who can practice without you.

- Be aware of power dynamics. Even if you do not claim authority, students may grant you authority. Use it carefully.

- Do not mix Irish practice with closed traditions unless you are authorized to teach those traditions.

- Acknowledge your sources. Do not present others' work as your own.

- Be willing to be challenged. Students should question. Encourage critical thinking.

Your Legacy in the Tradition

What will you leave behind? Not in terms of fame or recognition, but in terms of real impact. How does your practice serve something larger than yourself?

- You teach, formally or informally, passing knowledge forward
- You write, sharing your insights and experiences for future practitioners
- You create community, building spaces where others can gather and practice
- You restore land, tending sacred spaces or your own land with awareness
- You live the practice so visibly that others are inspired by example
- You support the tradition financially, helping authors, teachers, or organizations that preserve and share knowledge
- You raise children or mentor young people who understand seasonal awareness
- You simply practice with dedication, adding your energy to the great current of practitioners across time

Your legacy does not need to be grand. Every sincere practitioner who walks the Wheel with awareness strengthens the tradition. Every person who honors the gods, respects the land, and marks the seasons adds to the collective current. You do not need to be famous or influential. You need only to be faithful to the path.

As the Wheel Turns: A Final Blessing

You have come to the end of this book, but not to the end of the path. The Wheel turns. The seasons change. The gods call. The land speaks. This continues whether you have a book in your hands or not.

What you have learned here is foundation. But the real teaching comes from living it—from watching your first snow fall, planting your first garden, celebrating your first Samhain, feeling your body change with the seasons, building relationship with the gods over years, watching your practice deepen from something you do into something you are.

There will be years when your practice flourishes—when you feel aligned, connected, alive to the sacred. There will be years when practice feels dry, when you struggle, when you doubt. Both are part of the path. The Wheel turns through seasons of flourishing and seasons of drought. Your practice will mirror that. This is natural.

You will make mistakes. You will forget festivals. You will let your altar gather dust. You will go months without meaningful practice. You will return, again and again, because something in you knows this matters. Return is sacred. Return is the practice.

The Mórrígan, who has walked with me for three decades and to whom this book is dedicated, teaches this above all: transformation is not comfortable. Growth requires death of what was. The Wheel turns not gently but inevitably. You cannot stop it. You can only choose whether to turn with it or resist.

Turn with it. Let the seasons teach you. Let the land hold you. Let the gods challenge you. Let the years deepen you. Walk this path with honesty, with courage, with reverence, and with joy.

May the road rise to meet you. May the wind be always at your back. May the sun warm your face and the rain fall soft upon your fields. And until we meet again, may the gods hold you in the palm of their hand.

You are not alone in this practice. Every breath you take with reverence is a leaf added to the forest of the faithful. Let your footsteps echo in the land and time you call home.

The Wheel turns. Turn with it.

In service to the old ways and the new practitioners who walk them,

In honor of the land, the gods, and the turning year,

With gratitude for those who taught me and hope for those I may teach,

Blessed be your journey.

Appendix A: Quick Reference Tables

These tables provide at-a-glance reference for planning your seasonal celebrations and deepening your practice throughout the year. Use them to prepare altars, choose appropriate offerings, and align your work with the turning of the Wheel.

Festival Dates & Core Themes

Festival	Date	Season/Meaning	Core Themes	Type
Samhain	Oct 31-Nov 1	Celtic New Year; Beginning of winter	Death, ancestors, divination, thinning veil	Fire Festival
Winter Solstice	Dec 21	Longest night; rebirth of sun	Hope, rebirth, return of light, endurance	Solar Festival
Imbolc	Feb 1-2	First spring; lambing season	Purification, healing, inspiration, Brigid's fire	Fire Festival
Spring Equinox	Mar 21	Light & dark balance; awakening	Balance, growth, planting, fertility, renewal	Solar Festival
Bealtaine	May 1	Beginning of summer; peak fertility	Fire, fertility, passion, protection, fairy activity	Fire Festival
Summer Solstice	Jun 21	Longest day; peak solar power	Abundance, celebration, gratitude, fullness, joy	Solar Festival
Lughnasadh	Aug 1	First harvest; beginning of autumn	Harvest, sacrifice, skill, competition, first fruits	Fire Festival

Festival	Date	Season/Meaning	Core Themes	Type
Autumn Equinox	Sept 21	Light & dark balance; final harvest	Balance, completion, preparation, reflection	Solar Festival

Primary Deity Associations by Festival

Festival	Primary Deities	Associations
Samhain	An Mórrígan, An Cailleach, Ancestors	Death, prophecy, sovereignty, winter's beginning
Winter Solstice	An Dagda, Aengus, Boann	Rebirth, protection, Newgrange alignment
Imbolc	Brigid	Fire, healing, poetry, smithcraft, inspiration
Spring Equinox	Danu, Aengus, Ériu	Fertility, growth, balance, land sovereignty
Bealtaine	Aos Sí, An Dagda, An Mórrígan	Fairy folk, fertility, fire, passion, protection
Summer Solstice	Lugh, Ériu, Manannán	Solar power, abundance, sovereignty, sea
Lughnasadh	Lugh, Tailtiu, An Mórrígan	Harvest, sacrifice, skill, kingship, death
Autumn Equinox	An Mórrígan, Land Spirits	Balance, judgment, preparation for darkness

Altar Colors & Key Symbols

Festival	Colors	Candles	Key Symbols
Samhain	Black, deep purple, dark red, orange	Black, orange, white (ancestors)	Apples, nuts, photos of ancestors, crow feathers, dark stones
Winter Solstice	Deep blue, white, gold, silver	Gold (sun), white (snow), red (holly)	Evergreens, holly, ivy, pine cones, sun wheels, crystals
Imbolc	White, pale green, light blue	White (purity), red (Brigid's fire)	Brigid's cross, milk, snowdrops, white flowers, forge tools
Spring Equinox	Green, yellow, light pastels	Green (growth), yellow (sun), white	Eggs, spring flowers, seeds, feathers, nests
Bealtaine	Red, green, gold, white	Red (passion), white (purity), green	Hawthorn, flowers, ribbons, May crown, fire bowls
Summer Solstice	Gold, yellow, orange, green	Gold (sun), yellow, orange	Sun wheels, summer flowers, honey, mead, oak leaves
Lughnasadh	Gold, brown, rust, orange	Gold (grain), brown (earth), orange	Bread, grain, corn, wheat sheaves, berries
Autumn Equinox	Deep red, rust, gold, dark green	Black & white (balance), brown, red	Apples, gourds, hazelnuts, preserved foods, autumn leaves

Note: These tables provide traditional correspondences drawn from Irish sources and modern practice. Trust your intuition and local availability when selecting materials. The sincerity of your practice matters more than having every 'correct' item.

Appendix B: Quick Reference Guide

This appendix provides the most essential tools for building and maintaining your Irish Pagan practice. For detailed festival information, correspondences, and historical context, refer to the relevant chapters in the main text.

Beginner's First Year Checklist

This checklist provides a realistic progression for someone completely new to Irish Pagan practice. Not everything is required—these are suggestions for building sustainable practice over time.

Month 1 (Start Anytime)

- ☐ Set up basic altar (small table, candle, seasonal item)
- ☐ Begin 5-minute daily practice (light candle, three breaths, gratitude)
- ☐ Read Chapters 1-4 (foundational understanding)
- ☐ Spend 10+ minutes outdoors daily

Month 2

- ☐ Celebrate your first festival (whatever comes next)
- ☐ Add journaling to daily practice
- ☐ Read festival chapter for upcoming celebration
- ☐ Begin noticing seasonal changes

Month 3

- ☐ Choose one deity to learn about (Chapter 7)
- ☐ Begin simple deity devotion if it calls to you
- ☐ Start seasonal eating practice
- ☐ Celebrate second festival

Months 4-6

- ☐ Establish consistent daily practice (even 5 minutes)
- ☐ Celebrate 3-4 festivals
- ☐ Begin seasonal projects (garden in spring, etc.)
- ☐ Deepen relationship with chosen deity

Months 7-9

- ☐ Practice is becoming habitual
- ☐ Celebrate 5-6 festivals
- ☐ Notice seasonal patterns in your energy/mood
- ☐ Begin teaching or sharing with others (if called)

Months 10-12

- ☐ Complete first full turn of the Wheel
- ☐ Reflect on what worked and what didn't
- ☐ Plan Year Two with more confidence
- ☐ Trust your intuition more than books

Remember: This is a suggested progression, not a requirement. Go slower or faster based on your life circumstances. The goal is sustainable practice, not perfect practice.

Basic Ritual Structure

This template provides a simple structure for any Irish Pagan ritual. Adapt as needed for your practice style, time constraints, and specific festival. For detailed festival rituals, see Chapters 9-16.

Nine-Phase Ritual Structure

1. Preparation (5-10 minutes)

Gather ritual items, cleanse your space, and center yourself. This can be done hours before the actual ritual. Take time to be intentional about what you're bringing to the space.

2. Opening (2-3 minutes)

Light candles, ring a bell, or speak words that announce your intent to begin. This marks the boundary between ordinary time and sacred time.

3. Grounding (1-2 minutes)

Take three deep breaths and connect to the land beneath you. Feel your feet on the earth. This is an essential foundation for all that follows.

4. Calling Directions (3-5 minutes, optional)

Honor the four directions if this speaks to you. This is not required in Irish practice—many practitioners skip this step entirely and focus on invoking deities and spirits instead.

5. Invocation (3-5 minutes)

Call upon the deities, ancestors, or spirits relevant to your work. Be specific about who you're calling and why. Speak with respect and clarity.

6. Main Working (10-30 minutes)

This is the heart of your ritual—the core activity, whether that's celebration, magic, devotion, or meditation. The length varies based on your purpose.

7. Offerings (2-3 minutes)

Give food, drink, or items to the spirits and deities you've called. Never skip this step—reciprocity is essential in Irish practice.

8. Gratitude & Release (2-3 minutes)

Thank the beings you've invoked and bid them farewell. Close the connections you've opened with respect and clarity.

9. Closing (2-3 minutes)

Extinguish candles, ground any excess energy back into the earth, and close the ritual space. Mark the return to ordinary time.

Quick Ritual Variations

- **15-Minute Express Ritual:** Opening (2 min) → Invocation (3 min) → Main working (5 min) → Offering & closing (5 min)
- **5-Minute Observance:** Light candle → Speak one prayer/intention → Make small offering → Close
- **Full Ceremonial:** Follow all 9 phases at leisurely pace (60-90 minutes total)

Essential Irish Terms & Pronunciation

These are the most commonly used Irish terms in this book. Pronunciation is given in simplified phonetics. For a complete pronunciation guide, see Appendix B.

Festivals

- **Samhain** (SOW-in) — November 1, festival of ancestors and the new year
- **Imbolc** (IM-bolk) — February 1, festival of Brigid and purification

- **Bealtaine** (BYOWL-tin-uh) — May 1, festival of fertility and fire
- **Lughnasadh** (LOO-nah-sah) — August 1, first harvest festival

Major Deities

- **An Mórrígan** (ahn MOR-ree-gahn) — The Phantom Queen, goddess of sovereignty, war, and fate
- **An Dagda** (ahn DOG-dah) — The Good God, deity of abundance and protection
- **Brigid** (BREED) — Goddess of healing, poetry, and smithcraft
- **Lugh** (LOO) — God of skills, light, and the harvest
- **Manannán mac Lir** (man-ah-NAWN mock LEER) — God of the sea and Otherworld

Key Terms

- **Tuatha Dé Danann** (TOO-ah-hah day DAN-an) — The People of the Goddess Danu, the Irish gods
- **Aos sí** (EES SHEE) — The fairy folk, spirits of the land
- **Sí** (SHEE) — A fairy mound or dwelling place of the aos sí
- **An Cailleach** (ahn KAL-yukh) — The Hag, divine feminine of winter and mountains
- **Sláinte** (SLAWN-chuh) — Health, used as a toast (like 'cheers')

How to Use This Quick Reference

This appendix is designed for quick lookup when you need immediate guidance. Here are suggested uses:

- **Building Your Practice:** Use the Beginner's Checklist for realistic, sustainable progression through your first year.
- **Planning Rituals:** Reference the Basic Ritual Structure when designing celebrations or devotional work.
- **Learning Pronunciation:** Use the Essential Terms list for the most commonly encountered Irish words, or see Appendix B for complete pronunciation guidance.

This appendix provides quick reference only. For detailed festival correspondences, historical context, complete rituals, herb safety information, and deity profiles, always refer to the relevant chapters in the main text. The Wheel of the Year is a living practice—this appendix is a tool to support your journey, not replace genuine engagement with the tradition.

Appendix C: Glossary

This glossary provides definitions and pronunciations for Irish Gaelic terms, mythological names, and Pagan terminology used throughout this book. Irish pronunciation can be challenging for English speakers; phonetic guides are provided to help you speak these sacred names with confidence. For audio pronunciation guides, seek out native Irish speakers online.

A

Aengus (Aonghus, Óengus)

Pronunciation: ANG-gus

Irish god of love, youth, and poetic inspiration. Son of the Dagda and Boann. Associated with Newgrange (Brú na Bóinne) and the festival of Imbolc. Often depicted with birds circling his head, representing kisses or loving words.

An Cailleach

Pronunciation: ahn KAL-yukh or KAL-yakh

The Hag or Veiled One. Ancient divine feminine figure representing winter, sovereignty, and the transformative power of aging. Associated with the formation of mountains and landscape features. Rules from Samhain through Imbolc, when she transforms or yields to Brigid.

An Dagda

Pronunciation: ahn DOG-dah

The Good God or All-Father. Chief deity of the Tuatha Dé Danann, associated with abundance, protection, fertility, and druidic wisdom. Possesses a magical club that can kill or restore life, and an inexhaustible cauldron. Father of Brigid and Aengus.

An Mórrígan (Mórrígan, Morrígan)

Pronunciation: ahn MOR-ree-gahn or MOR-ee-gahn

The Great Queen or Phantom Queen. Sovereign goddess of war, fate, prophecy, and the land itself. Often appears as a triple goddess (with Badb and Macha/Nemain) or as a shapeshifter, particularly as a crow or raven. Associated with Samhain and Lughnasadh. Guardian of thresholds between life and death.

Aos Sí

Pronunciation: EES SHEE

The fairy folk or people of the mounds. Supernatural beings in Irish mythology, often identified with the Tuatha Dé Danann after they retreated into the hollow hills. Neither wholly benevolent nor malevolent, they are powerful, unpredictable, and demand respect. Particularly active at liminal times, especially Samhain and Bealtaine.

B

Badb

Pronunciation: BIVE or BAYV

Crow or Scald-Crow. War goddess and aspect of the Mórrígan, associated with battle frenzy and prophetic visions. Often appears as a hooded crow on the battlefield, inciting warriors or feasting on the slain.

Bealtaine

Pronunciation: BYOWL-tin-uh or BEL-tayn

May Day, the spring fire festival celebrated on May 1st (or at the astronomical cross-quarter). Marks the beginning of summer in the Irish calendar. Sacred to fertility, protection, and the aos sí. Celebrated with bonfires, May poles, flowers, and driving cattle between two fires for blessing and purification.

Brehon Laws

Pronunciation: BREH-un

Ancient legal system of Ireland, governing social relationships, property rights, and obligations from pre-Christian times through the medieval period. Remarkably sophisticated and

egalitarian for its time, granting women significant rights.
Administered by specialized judges called Brehons.

Brigid (Bríg, Brighid)

Pronunciation: BREED or BREE-jid

Goddess of fire, poetry, smithcraft, and healing. Daughter of
the Dagda. Associated with Imbolc, sacred wells, eternal
flames, and the transition from winter to spring. Her cult was
so strong that Christianity absorbed her as St. Brigid of Kildare,
making her one of Ireland's patron saints.

Brú na Bóinne

Pronunciation: BROO nah BOY-nyuh

Palace or Mansion of the Boyne. Neolithic complex in County
Meath including the passage tombs of Newgrange, Knowth,
and Dowth. Newgrange is aligned with the winter solstice
sunrise. In mythology, the dwelling place of Aengus and once
belonging to the Dagda. One of Ireland's most sacred sites.

C

Cross-Quarter Day

The four fire festivals that fall midway between solstices and
equinoxes: Samhain, Imbolc, Bealtaine, and Lughnasadh. These
mark major turning points in the Irish agricultural and pastoral
year and are considered more spiritually significant in Irish
tradition than the solar festivals.

D

Danu (Anu, Dôn)

Pronunciation: DAH-noo

Mother goddess of the Tuatha Dé Danann, whose name means
'the people of the goddess Danu.' Associated with the land,
rivers, abundance, and sovereignty. Sometimes conflated with
Anu. The Paps of Anu (Dá Chích Anann) in County Kerry are
named for her.

Dindshenchas (Dinnsheanchas)

Pronunciation: JEEN-hen-ah-khas

Lore of places. Medieval Irish texts preserving ancient mythological and historical associations with Irish place names, hills, rivers, and landmarks. Essential for understanding the sacred geography of Ireland and the stories embedded in the landscape.

Druid (Druí)

Pronunciation: DREE

Priest, scholar, judge, and ritual specialist in ancient Celtic society. Druids were the intellectual class, responsible for religious ceremonies, legal judgments, education, and preserving oral tradition. Modern Druidry seeks to revive these practices and spiritual connections.

E

Equinox

Astronomical event occurring twice yearly (around March 21 and September 21) when day and night are of equal length. The spring equinox marks the astronomical beginning of spring; the autumn equinox marks the beginning of autumn. While not traditional Irish fire festivals, they are often incorporated into modern Wheel of the Year observances.

Ériu

Pronunciation: AIR-yoo

Sovereignty goddess who gives her name to Ireland (Éire). One of three sisters (with Banba and Fódla) who each represent Ireland. Met the Milesians upon their arrival and asked that the island be named for her. Embodies the personified spirit of the land itself.

F

Feis

Pronunciation: FESH

Assembly, gathering, or festival. Historically, a royal inauguration ceremony involving the symbolic marriage of the king to the sovereignty goddess, ensuring the fertility and prosperity of the land. Also used for regional assemblies and celebrations. Modern Irish uses the term for cultural festivals.

Fili (plural: Filidh)

Pronunciation: FILL-ee

Poet-seers of ancient Ireland who were trained in verse, history, genealogy, and law. Held high status in society, sometimes rivaling druids. The highest rank, ollam, required decades of training. Poets were believed to possess supernatural power through their words, including the ability to curse (satire) or bless.

Fionn mac Cumhaill

Pronunciation: FIN mock COOL

Legendary warrior and leader of the Fianna, the elite warrior band of Irish mythology. Hero of the Fenian Cycle. Gained wisdom and prophetic knowledge by tasting the Salmon of Knowledge. His stories embody the warrior code, wilderness spirituality, and connection to the land.

G

Gaeilge

Pronunciation: GWAYL-guh

The Irish language, a Celtic language belonging to the Goidelic branch. One of the oldest written languages in Europe. Essential for understanding Irish mythology, place names, and spiritual concepts in their original context. Experiencing revival efforts in modern Ireland.

Geis (plural: Geasa)

Pronunciation: GESH (singular), GASH-ah (plural)

Sacred taboo, prohibition, or obligation placed upon a person, often a hero or ruler. Breaking a geis results in dishonor, loss of power, or death. Geasa often create dramatic tension in Irish myths when circumstances force heroes into impossible choices between conflicting prohibitions.

Goibniu

Pronunciation: GUV-nyoo

Divine smith of the Tuatha Dé Danann. Forges magical weapons that never miss their mark and creates the Feast of Goibniu, where his ale grants immortality. Represents the sacred craft of metalworking and the transformative power of fire.

I

Imbolc

Pronunciation: IM-bolk or IM-molg

Festival marking the beginning of spring, celebrated February 1st (or at the astronomical cross-quarter). Sacred to the goddess Brigid. Name derives from 'oimelc' (ewe's milk), as this is the lambing season. Celebrated with fires, Brigid's crosses, well blessings, and rituals of purification and new beginnings.

K

Kingship, Sacred

In Irish tradition, kingship was not merely political but sacred. The king married the sovereignty goddess in ritual, ensuring the land's fertility. A rightful king brought prosperity; an unjust king brought blight. This concept connects directly to the sovereignty goddesses (Ériu, Mórrígan) and the ancient understanding of land-as-divine.

L

Liminal

From Latin 'limen' (threshold). Refers to transitional, in-between spaces and times when the boundaries between worlds are thin. Examples include dawn and dusk, crossroads, shorelines, doorways, and the festival times of Samhain and Bealtaine. Places and times of power, transformation, and heightened spiritual presence.

Lugh

Pronunciation: LOO

The Shining One or Many-Skilled. Solar deity associated with kingship, oaths, crafts, and the harvest. Master of all arts and skills. Foster son of Tailtiu, in whose honor he established the festival of Lughnasadh. One of the most important deities of the Irish pantheon.

Lughnasadh

Pronunciation: LOO-nah-sah

First harvest festival celebrated August 1st (or at the astronomical cross-quarter). Established by Lugh to honor his foster mother Tailtiu, who died clearing the plains of Ireland for agriculture. Celebrated with athletic competitions, handfastings, harvest fairs, and the reaping of first grain. Marks the beginning of autumn in the Irish calendar.

M

Macha

Pronunciation: MOKH-ah

Sovereignty and war goddess, one of the triple aspects of the Mórrígan. Associated with horses, kingship, and the cursing of Ulster. Emain Macha (Navan Fort) is named for her. Appears in multiple forms across Irish mythology, embodying different aspects of sovereignty and battle.

Manannán mac Lir

Pronunciation: man-ah-NAWN mock LEER

God of the sea and the Otherworld. Son of Lir (the sea). Guardian of the blessed isles and psychopomp who guides souls to the afterlife. Associated with magic, shape-shifting, and the mist that conceals the Otherworld from mortal sight. Possesses a magical cloak, boat, and sword.

N

Nemeton

Pronunciation: NEM-eh-ton

Sacred grove or outdoor sanctuary in Celtic tradition. Natural spaces set apart for worship and ritual, often among ancient trees. Nemetons were sacred to the druids and served as gathering places for ceremony, teaching, and connection with the divine in nature.

Nuada

Pronunciation: NOO-ah-dah

Nuada of the Silver Hand. First king of the Tuatha Dé Danann in Ireland. Lost his hand in the First Battle of Mag Tuired and was fitted with a silver prosthetic by the physician-god Dian Cécht. Later healed fully and regained kingship. Wielder of one of the four treasures of the Tuatha Dé Danann, the Sword of Nuada.

O

Ogham

Pronunciation: OH-am or OG-am

Ancient Irish alphabet consisting of twenty characters represented by lines or notches cut into stone or wood. Each letter is associated with a tree or plant. Used from the 4th to 9th centuries CE for inscriptions, boundary markers, and memorial stones. Carries mystical significance in modern Irish Paganism and divination.

Otherworld

The realm of the gods, spirits, and the dead in Irish mythology. Not a distant heaven but parallel to our world, accessible through fairy mounds, caves, lakes, and at certain times (especially Samhain). A place of eternal youth, beauty, and plenty, but also dangerous and alien to mortals. Irish: 'Tír na nÓg' (Land of Youth), 'Mag Mell' (Plain of Honey).

Q

Quarter Days

The two solstices (summer and winter) and two equinoxes (spring and autumn) that divide the solar year into quarters. While important in modern Pagan practice, these solar markers were less emphasized in ancient Irish tradition than the cross-quarter fire festivals. Modern Irish Paganism often incorporates all eight points of the Wheel.

R

Rath

Pronunciation: RAWTH

Ring fort, a circular earthwork enclosure that served as a farmstead or dwelling in Iron Age and early medieval Ireland. Often associated with the aos sí in folklore. Fairy raths were believed to be entrances to the Otherworld and disturbing them was considered extremely dangerous. Thousands still dot the Irish landscape.

S

Samhain

Pronunciation: SOW-in or SAH-win (not sam-HAYN)

The Celtic New Year, celebrated October 31st to November 1st (or at the astronomical cross-quarter). The most important of the fire festivals, marking the end of harvest and the beginning of winter/the dark half of the year. The veil between worlds is thinnest; ancestors are honored, and the aos sí walk freely. Celebrated with bonfires, divination, ancestor veneration, and feasting.

Sí (Sidhe)

Pronunciation: SHEE

Fairy mound or hollow hill. Entrance to the Otherworld. Also refers to the fairy folk themselves (aos sí, or people of the mounds). Major síd include Newgrange (Brú na Bóinne) and the Hill of Tara. These are places of power where the boundary between worlds is especially thin.

Sláinte

Pronunciation: SLAWN-chuh

Health or cheers. Traditional Irish toast meaning 'good health.' Often used in ritual to honor the gods, ancestors, and spirits. Full phrase 'Sláinte mhaith' (slawn-chuh wah) means 'good health.'

Solstice

Astronomical event occurring twice yearly when the sun reaches its highest (summer solstice, around June 21) or lowest (winter solstice, around December 21) point. The longest and shortest days of the year. Marked by many ancient Irish monuments including Newgrange (winter solstice) and celebrations of light and dark.

Sovereignty

Central concept in Irish kingship and mythology. The sovereignty of the land is embodied by goddesses (Ériu, Mórrígan, Macha) who grant or withhold kingship through sacred marriage. A just king brings prosperity; an unjust king brings blight and famine. The land itself chooses its ruler. This concept extends beyond political rule to personal sovereignty and right relationship with place.

T

Tailtiu

Pronunciation: TAHL-tyoo or TAHL-choo

Earth goddess and foster mother of Lugh. Died from exhaustion clearing the plains of Ireland for agriculture. Lugh established the festival of Lughnasadh in her honor, featuring funeral games and harvest celebrations. Represents the sacrifice inherent in cultivation and the relationship between humanity and the land.

Teamhair (Tara)

Pronunciation: TYOW-ar

Hill of Tara in County Meath. Ancient seat of the High Kings of Ireland and one of the most sacred sites in the country. Contains numerous prehistoric monuments and was the site of inaugural ceremonies, assemblies (feis), and connections to sovereignty goddesses. Central to Irish mythology and national identity.

Thin Places

Locations where the boundary between the physical world and the Otherworld is particularly thin or permeable. Can be natural features (wells, caves, certain hills) or built sites (fairy forts, passage tombs). Also refers to liminal times when the veil thins, particularly Samhain and Bealtaine.

Threshold

Liminal space between two states or places. Doorways, gateways, borders, and crossroads. In Irish spirituality, thresholds are places of power and danger, where offerings are made and where one must be especially mindful. The Mórrígan is particularly associated with thresholds and the space between life and death.

Tuatha Dé Danann

Pronunciation: TOO-ah-hah day DAN-an

The People of the Goddess Danu. The Irish gods, a magical race who invaded Ireland in mythological times, defeated the

Fir Bolg and the Fomorians, and were later defeated by the Milesians (mortal Irish). Rather than leave Ireland, they retreated into the hollow hills (síd) and became the aos sí. The pantheon includes the Dagda, Brigid, Lugh, the Mórrígan, and others.

U

Uisneach

Pronunciation: ISH-nakh

The Hill of Uisneach in County Westmeath, considered the sacred center of Ireland. Site of the Stone of Divisions (Aill na Mireann), where the five ancient provinces met. Location of Bealtaine fires and gatherings. One of the most important ritual sites in ancient Ireland, representing the axis mundi (world center).

W

Wheel of the Year

The annual cycle of eight seasonal festivals celebrated in modern Paganism. In Irish tradition, the four cross-quarter fire festivals (Samhain, Imbolc, Bealtaine, Lughnasadh) are indigenous and ancient, while the solstices and equinoxes are more recent additions, influenced by modern reconstructionist and neo-Pagan movements. The Wheel represents the eternal cycle of life, death, and rebirth.

This glossary provides foundational understanding of Irish Pagan terminology. For deeper exploration of individual deities, myths, and practices, refer to the relevant chapters throughout this book and the sources listed in the Bibliography.

Appendix D: Troubleshooting Common Challenges

Irish Pagan practice is meant to be lived, not perfected. Every practitioner faces obstacles—from practical limitations to spiritual uncertainties. This appendix addresses the most common challenges with honest, workable solutions drawn from real experience. Remember: adaptation is not failure. The gods care about sincerity, not pristine execution.

Timing & Scheduling Challenges

What if I can't celebrate on the exact festival date?

Festival energy builds for days before and lingers for days after. Celebrate within 3 days either side of the date—the spirits understand mortal schedules. If even that's impossible, honor the festival on the nearest weekend or evening you have free. A ritual done with full presence three days late beats a rushed, resentful one done 'on time.' Mark your calendar when you do celebrate so you track your personal Wheel.

The astronomical dates don't match my local seasons—what do I do?

You have two solid options: (1) Celebrate by fixed calendar dates (Samhain on Nov 1, Imbolc on Feb 1, etc.) and accept that Irish seasons won't perfectly align with yours. Focus on the mythic and spiritual themes rather than agricultural timing. (2) Shift festivals to match your bioregion's actual seasons—if your spring arrives in March instead of February, celebrate your 'Imbolc' when the land truly awakens. Many Southern Hemisphere practitioners reverse the entire Wheel. Either approach is valid; choose based on whether mythic continuity or land-connection matters more to you.

I work nights/weekends/odd hours—how do I maintain practice?

Shift your sacred time to your waking hours. If you work nights, dawn is your dusk—light your morning candle and call it your evening devotion. The gods don't wear watches. For festivals, many practitioners hold personal observances at non-traditional times: Samhain celebrated at 2 PM on a Tuesday is no less sacred if that's your available window. Consider: a three-minute devotion done consistently in your real schedule beats an hour-long ritual you never have time for.

Space & Location Challenges

I live in an apartment with no outdoor space—can I still practice?

Absolutely. Place your altar by a window to connect with sky, weather, and seasonal light. Use a small potted plant to represent the land. Visit local parks regularly—even 10 minutes sitting under a tree builds relationship with place. For fire festivals, use candles instead of bonfires. For offerings, create a small offering bowl and later pour contents into the earth at a park, or bury them in a potted plant. Urban practice is valid practice—the spirits dwell in cities too.

My living situation doesn't allow visible altars or openly Pagan practice.

Safety first, always. Create a 'portable altar' in a small box or drawer you can set up and pack away. Use a shelf of 'decorative seasonal items' that only you know are sacred. Light 'aromatherapy candles.' Your practice can be entirely internal—devotional prayer, meditation, seasonal awareness—none of which require visible tools. When you travel to safe spaces, practice fully there. Many practitioners living with unsupportive family members keep practice minimal and private until circumstances change. The gods see your heart; the gods can wait.

I want to practice outdoors but have no private land or sacred sites nearby.

Public parks at dawn or dusk offer relative privacy. Scout locations in advance—find a large tree, a pond edge, a quiet corner. Be discreet, be brief, leave no trace. A ten-minute devotion in a park is valid. Can't get to parks? Practice on your balcony, porch, or by an open window. Stand barefoot on any patch of earth you can access. Water your offerings into street trees. The land is everywhere, even under concrete—you can reach it.

Offerings & Practical Concerns

My outdoor offerings attract pests/animals—what should I do?

This is a feature, not a bug. Animals eating offerings is part of the cycle—the spirits receive the essence, the animals take the physical form. If it's truly a problem (rats, dangerous wildlife), shift to biodegradable offerings you can bury immediately, liquid offerings poured directly into earth, or offerings left only briefly then retrieved. Whiskey, mead, milk, and water work well. For indoor altars, use symbolic offerings (stones, written words, art) that don't decay, and give food offerings by eating them yourself mindfully as a shared meal with the spirits.

I can't afford special altar items, ritual tools, or expensive ingredients.

Good. Expensive tools don't make better practitioners. Use a candle from the grocery store, a bowl from your kitchen, a cloth from a thrift store. Gather stones, feathers, and sticks from nature. Your offerings can be water, a piece of bread, or birdseed. Irish practice is fundamentally simple: fire, water, stone, and sincere words. If money is tight, give time instead—clean up a park, tend a neglected piece of land, help an elder. The gods value your effort and attention, not your credit card.

I can't find traditional Irish herbs—can I substitute?

Yes, with thought. Use what grows where you live—the land beneath you has its own sacred plants. Research which local herbs have similar properties to Irish ones. Mugwort grows across North America and Europe. Oak exists on multiple continents. Can't get rowan? Use the protective tree of your region. The principle matters more than the exact species. That said, some herbs (meadowsweet, hawthorn, blackthorn) are deeply woven into Irish mythology—if you want to honor that specificity, many can be ordered online. Balance authenticity with accessibility based on your practice goals.

Working with Irish Deities

What if I call on a deity and nothing happens?

Most divine contact is subtle, not cinematic. You might feel a slight temperature shift, a sense of presence, a particular thought or image. Often you won't know they answered until later—through dreams, synchronicities, or shifts in your life. If you genuinely feel nothing, they may be busy, testing your persistence, or not interested in a relationship with you right now. Try again later. Try a different deity. Some relationships take months or years to develop. Keep showing up. Make offerings without demanding response. Let the connection build naturally.

I'm drawn to a deity known for being difficult or dangerous—should I work with them?

'Difficult' deities often choose people they know can handle the work. If you're called to the Mórrígan, Badb, or An Cailleach, trust that—but proceed with respect and healthy boundaries. Research thoroughly. Start slowly. Make regular offerings before asking for anything. Understand what they demand: honesty, courage, transformation. These relationships are not safe or comfortable; they are real and demanding. If you're genuinely called, begin. If you're romanticizing danger, walk away. Know the difference.

I work with Irish deities but I'm not Irish—is this wrong?

The gods call whom they call, regardless of bloodline. What matters is approaching with respect, not entitlement. Learn the culture. Pronounce names correctly. Don't cherry-pick only the 'fun' aspects. Don't mix Irish practice thoughtlessly with other traditions. Don't claim Irish identity you don't have. Study the history, understand the context, build genuine relationship. Many non-Irish practitioners serve Irish deities with integrity—the difference is in how you approach. If your practice is rooted in sincere devotion, ongoing learning, and cultural respect, you're on solid ground.

Physical Limitations & Accessibility

I have chronic illness/disability and can't do physically demanding rituals.

You don't need to stand for an hour, dance around a fire, or hike to hilltops to honor the gods. Adapt everything. Sit for rituals. Use battery-operated candles if you can't manage flames safely. Speak prayers instead of elaborate gestures. Visualize offerings if you can't physically make them. The spirits honor presence and intention, not physical performance. Many practitioners with chronic conditions maintain deep, powerful practices—sometimes deeper than able-bodied practitioners precisely because they've stripped practice to its essential core.

Smoke from incense or candles triggers my asthma/allergies.

Skip them entirely. Use essential oils in a diffuser. Use potpourri. Simply open a window to let in fresh air as your cleansing. Place herbs on your altar without burning them. Incense isn't required—it's one option among many for engaging the sense of smell. Your health comes first. The gods would rather you breathe easily than struggle through smoke.

I can't kneel, stand for long periods, or perform physical gestures.

Then don't. Create an altar at a height you can reach comfortably while seated. Perform all rituals from a chair. Replace physical gestures with spoken words or simple hand movements that work for your body. Visualization is powerful—if you can't raise your arms, visualize raising them. The gods see your intention and effort, not your range of motion. Wheelchair users, people with chronic pain, and those with limited mobility have rich devotional practices. Yours can too.

Social & Family Challenges

My family/friends are hostile to Paganism—how do I handle this?

Prioritize your safety and well-being. If you're financially dependent or in a situation where being open would cause genuine harm, practice privately and wait. There's no spiritual merit in martyrdom. If the situation is merely uncomfortable rather than dangerous, you have choices: stay quietly private, educate those willing to listen, or be matter-of-fact about your path without forcing discussions. You don't owe anyone explanations, but you also don't need to hide essential parts of yourself from safe people. Assess each relationship individually.

I want to raise my children in Irish Paganism but my partner doesn't.

This requires honest negotiation and compromise. Some solutions: teach your children about many spiritual paths including yours; share seasonal celebrations as 'cultural traditions' without religious framing; agree that children can choose their own path when older; practice your path personally while partner practices theirs, exposing children to both. What doesn't work: forcing practice on reluctant children, undermining your partner's beliefs, or creating religious conflict as family background noise. Kids can grow up religiously bilingual. Focus on values you share—connection to nature, gratitude, community—and build from there.

I'm isolated—there are no other Irish Pagans near me.

Solitary practice is completely valid and often deeply rewarding. Many practitioners never join a group. That said, community exists online: forums, Discord servers, Facebook groups for Irish Paganism. Attend Pagan Pride events in your region even if they're not Irish-focused—you'll find fellow polytheists. Start a local meetup yourself. Write letters to the author or other practitioners. Join online rituals at festivals. Read books and blogs to feel connected to the broader community. Remember: the ancestors and spirits are always with you. You're never truly alone on this path.

Practice & Doubt

I feel like I'm doing everything wrong—am I?

Probably not. This feeling is so common it's almost a rite of passage. Irish Paganism is a reconstructed practice—there's no unbroken lineage handing down 'the right way.' We're all making educated guesses based on historical sources, folklore, and personal gnosis. If you're approaching with sincerity, researching your practice, making regular offerings, and showing up to the Wheel, you're doing fine. Perfectionism is the enemy of practice. The gods want relationship, not flawless performance.

I feel disconnected during rituals—like I'm just going through motions.

Sometimes ritual is work, not ecstasy. You show up, do the thing, and that's enough. Consistent practice builds relationship even when you don't feel dramatic results. That said, if every ritual feels dead, examine: Are you using someone else's words instead of your own? Rushing through without presence? Practicing out of obligation rather than desire? Try stripping ritual to bare bones—just you, a candle, and honest words. Rebuild from there. Sometimes we need to destroy our practice and start over.

What if I'm making it all up—what if the gods aren't real?

This doubt visits every practitioner. Here's what's true: you cannot prove the gods empirically. You can only experience relationship or not. If your practice brings meaning, connection, and positive change to your life, it's working—whether the gods are independent entities or powerful archetypes or something stranger doesn't change that. Many practitioners hold space for uncertainty while still showing up to practice. Faith isn't absence of doubt; it's continuing to show up despite doubt. Keep making offerings. Keep celebrating the festivals. See what happens.

I keep abandoning my practice and coming back—how do I stay consistent?

Start smaller. Most people quit because they set impossible standards. Don't aim for hour-long daily rituals—aim for two minutes. Light a candle and speak one sentence of gratitude. Track your practice where you'll see it. Connect practice to existing habits: morning coffee becomes offering time. When you fall off (you will), return without self-flagellation. The gods don't judge you for being human. Begin again, and again, and again. That's the practice.

Festival & Celebration Challenges

The eight festivals feel overwhelming—do I have to celebrate all of them?

No. Start with the four Irish fire festivals: Samhain, Imbolc, Bealtaine, Lughnasadh. These are the ancient core. Add the solstices and equinoxes later if they call to you, or never if they don't. Some practitioners celebrate only Samhain and Bealtaine. Others focus on festivals aligned with their deity relationships. Choose festivals that resonate with your life circumstances and spiritual needs. Quality over quantity.

I work in retail/hospitality and major holidays are my busiest times.

Then celebrate on your days off near the festival dates. Your Samhain can be November 3rd. Your winter solstice can be December 18th or 23rd. The festival energy extends beyond a single day—choose the nearest time when you actually have space to be present. Consider: a five-minute acknowledgment on the actual day ('Today is Samhain, I honor the ancestors') plus a full ritual when you're free honors both the calendar and your reality.

I don't know how to write my own rituals—can I just use ones from books?

Use book rituals while you're learning, but personalize them. Change deity names to ones you work with. Add local place names. Adjust offerings to what you have. Eventually, you'll notice which parts feel meaningful and which feel hollow. Start modifying. Substitute your words for the author's. Then one day you'll realize you're writing your own rituals—not from scratch, but from lived experience. This is how everyone learns. Books are training wheels, not permanent fixtures.

Remember: Every practitioner faces these challenges. Working through them is part of the practice itself. The gods value persistence, honesty, and adaptation. Your imperfect, adapted, uniquely-yours practice is more valuable than a 'perfect' practice you can't actually sustain. Show up as you are, where you are, with what you have. That is enough.

Resources & Websites

Connect with the Author

Donald Quill — donaldquill.com

The author's website featuring updates on new books, blog posts on Irish Paganism, and resources for practitioners.

Forgotten Rites Publishing — forgottenritespublishing.com

Publisher of this book and other works on Pagan practice, mythology, and spiritual exploration.

Irish Pagan Organizations

Pagan Federation Ireland — paganfed.ie

Ireland's largest Pagan organization, offering community support, events, and resources for practitioners of all traditions.

Irish Pagan School — irishpaganschool.com

Educational organization offering courses on Irish Paganism, mythology, and spiritual practice taught by knowledgeable practitioners.

The Order of Bards, Ovates and Druids — druidry.org

International Druidic order with strong connections to Celtic traditions, offering correspondence courses and community gatherings.

Podcasts & Video Content

The Irish Pagan Podcast

Discussions on Irish mythology, Pagan practice, and interviews with practitioners. Available on major podcast platforms.

Lora O'Brien YouTube Channel

Videos on Irish spirituality, mythology, and sacred sites from an Irish practitioner living in Ireland. Authentic and informative.

Morgan Daimler YouTube Channel

Educational content on Irish Paganism, fairy faith, and reconstructionist practice.

The Druid Cast

Podcast exploring Druidry and Celtic spirituality with a focus on seasonal observances and practical wisdom.

Ritual Supplies & Herbs

Moonlight Mysteries

Specializes in magical herbs for spells and rituals, with a focus on potency and energy. moonlightmysteries.com

Art Of The Root

Pagan and Hoodoo shop offering a wide variety of ritual supplies, altar tools, and traditional ingredients. artoftheroot.com

Green Witch Creations

Features altar and ritual supplies including spell kits, tools, and seasonal items. greenwitchcreations.com

Original Botanica

Provides a variety of botanicals, religious, and spiritual supplies with focus on traditional practices. originalbotanica.com

13 Moons

Offers magickal herbs, spell supplies, and apothecary essentials for the practicing witch or Pagan. 13moons.com

Bibliography & Further Reading

The following sources have informed this work and are recommended for readers seeking to deepen their study of Irish Paganism, Celtic mythology, and the Wheel of the Year.

Primary Sources & Irish Mythology

Cross, Tom Peete, and Clark Harris Slover. *Ancient Irish Tales*. Barnes & Noble, 1996.

    A comprehensive collection of medieval Irish tales, including the Ulster Cycle, Fenian Cycle, and mythological cycles. Essential for understanding the stories that shape Irish Pagan practice.

Gantz, Jeffrey (translator). *Early Irish Myths and Sagas*. Penguin Classics, 1982.

    Accessible translations of key Irish myths including Táin Bó Cúailnge and tales of the Tuatha Dé Danann. An excellent starting point for modern readers.

Kinsella, Thomas (translator). *The Táin: From the Irish Epic Táin Bó Cúailnge*. Oxford University Press, 2002.

    A poetic and powerful translation of Ireland's greatest epic. Indispensable for understanding the Mórrígan and Ulster Cycle mythology.

Koch, John T., and John Carey (editors). *The Celtic Heroic Age: Literary Sources for Ancient Celtic Europe and Early Ireland and Wales*. Celtic Studies Publications, 2003.

Scholarly anthology of primary sources with excellent historical context. For serious students of Celtic traditions.

Modern Irish Pagan Practice

Daimler, Morgan. *Pagan Portals: Irish Paganism: Reconstructing Irish Polytheism*. Moon Books, 2015.

Clear, accessible introduction to reconstructionist Irish Paganism. Daimler's work is grounded in both scholarship and practice, making it ideal for modern practitioners.

Daimler, Morgan. *Gods and Goddesses of Ireland: A Guide to Irish Deities*. Moon Books, 2016.

Thorough exploration of Irish deities with historical context and modern devotional suggestions. Essential reference.

Daimler, Morgan. *Fairy Witchcraft: A Neopagan's Guide to the Celtic Fairy Faith*. Moon Books, 2014.

Explores the relationship between Irish Paganism and fairy faith, bridging folklore and modern practice.

O'Brien, Lora. *Irish Witchcraft from an Irish Witch*. Wolfpack Publishers, 2004.

Written by an Irish practitioner living in Ireland, this book offers authentic perspective on Irish folk magic and modern practice rooted in native tradition.

O'Brien, Lora. *A Practical Guide to Irish Spirituality: Slí Aon Dhraoi*. Wolfpack Publishers, 2018.

Practical guide to living Irish spirituality in the modern world, with emphasis on ethics, relationship with spirits, and honoring the land.

Academic & Historical Sources

Green, Miranda. *Celtic Myths*. University of Texas Press, 1993.

Scholarly overview of Celtic mythology from an archaeological and historical perspective. Excellent for understanding the broader Celtic context.

MacKillop, James. *Dictionary of Celtic Mythology*. Oxford University Press, 2004.

Comprehensive reference work covering gods, heroes, places, and concepts in Celtic mythology. Indispensable desk reference.

Ó Catháin, Séamas, and Patrick O'Flanagan. *The Living Landscape: Kilgalligan, Erris, County Mayo*. Royal Irish Academy, 1975.

Documents Irish folk practices, seasonal customs, and relationship with land. Valuable for understanding traditional observances.

Rees, Alwyn, and Brinley Rees. *Celtic Heritage: Ancient Tradition in Ireland and Wales.* Thames & Hudson, 1961.

Classic scholarly work examining Celtic cosmology, sacred time, and the relationship between mythology and landscape.

The Wheel of the Year

Hutton, Ronald. *The Stations of the Sun: A History of the Ritual Year in Britain.* Oxford University Press, 1996.

Comprehensive historical study of seasonal festivals in Britain and Ireland. Essential for understanding how modern Pagan celebrations evolved.

McNeill, F. Marian. *The Silver Bough: Scottish Folk-Lore and Folk-Belief (4 volumes).* William MacLellan, 1957-1968.

Documents Gaelic folk customs and seasonal observances. While focused on Scotland, many practices overlap with Irish tradition.

Greer, John Michael. *The Druidry Handbook: Spiritual Practice Rooted in the Living Earth.* Weiser Books, 2006.

Practical guide to modern Druidic practice with emphasis on seasonal celebrations and connection to nature.

INDEX

A

B

D

G

I

L

M

N

O

U

W

Acknowledgments

This book would not exist without the support, wisdom, and encouragement of many people.

To my grandmother, Rita Allen, whose inspiration sparked my love of writing and storytelling—this work carries your spirit forward. You taught me that words have power, and I have tried to wield them with care.

To my wife, Carri Adams-Quill, my first reader, my anchor, and my beloved—thank you for your patience, insight, and unwavering belief in this project. You read every draft, offered honest feedback, and held space for me to do this work. I am grateful beyond words.

To my mother, Edwarda Ashby, for your love, your strength, and for raising me to honor my heritage and follow my own path. Thank you for always supporting my spiritual journey, even when it led to unexpected places.

To my beta readers, whose careful eyes and thoughtful questions made this book better—thank you for your time, your care, and your willingness to engage deeply with this material.

I am indebted to the scholars, practitioners, and authors whose work has shaped my understanding of Irish Paganism: Morgan Daimler, Lora O'Brien, and John Michael Greer. Your dedication to preserving and sharing these traditions has been a guiding light.

To the communities and organizations working to keep Irish Pagan traditions alive and accessible—including Pagan Federation Ireland, the Irish Pagan School, and The Order of Bards, Ovates and Druids—thank you for your tireless work and for creating spaces where seekers can learn, connect, and grow.

To the ancestors, the spirits of the land, and the gods who have walked with me on this path—thank you for your presence, your patience, and your lessons. May this work honor you.

And to you, the reader—thank you for picking up this book, for showing up to the Wheel, and for doing the sacred work of remembering. May you find what you seek within these pages.

About the Author

Donald Quill is a practitioner and priest of Irish Paganism with roots that stretch back over three decades. Since 1993, he has walked the path of the Irish spiritual traditions, dedicating his practice to the Mórrígan and the ancient ways of his ancestors.

Of Irish heritage, Donald has spent years deepening his understanding of Celtic mythology, seasonal observances, and the sacred relationship between land and spirit. His practice is grounded in both historical scholarship and lived experience, bridging the wisdom of the past with the realities of modern life.

After decades as a Priest of the Mórrígan, Donald was inspired to write a fantasy series centered around the Great Queen herself. This creative work opened new doors of understanding and ultimately led him to write *Living the Irish Wheel of the Year*, a guide born from personal devotion, scholarly study, and a desire to share these traditions with seekers across the world.

In addition to his non-fiction work on Irish Paganism, Donald is also the author of fiction books that explore themes of mythology, magic, and the liminal spaces where the mortal and divine intersect.

Donald lives in Delaware, USA, where he continues his practice, writes, and serves his community. He can be found online at donaldquill.com.

Also by Donald Quill

 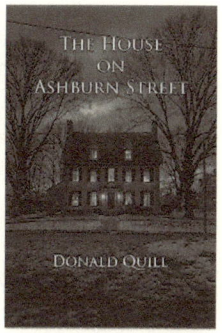

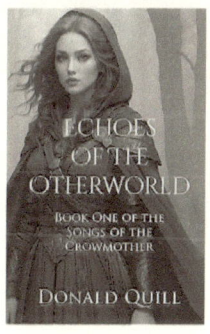 

www.ingramcontent.com/pod-product-compliance
Lightning Source LLC
Chambersburg PA
CBHW021211130626
46554CB00004B/1174